CROSSROADS

CHRISTINE MCCLYMONT
LINDA COO

Gage Editorial Team
Joe Banel
David Friend
Diane Robitaille
Sheree Haughian

gage EDUCATIONAL PUBLISHING COMPANY
A DIVISION OF CANADA PUBLISHING CORPORATION
Vancouver·Calgary·Toronto·London·Halifax

© 2000 Gage Educational Publishing Company
A Division of Canada Publishing Corporation

Managing Editor: Darleen Rotozinski
Contributing Writer: Chelsea Donaldson
Permissions Editor: Elizabeth Long
Photo Researcher: Mary Rose MacLachlan
Researcher: Catherine Rondina, Monika Croyden, Jennifer Sweeney
Bias Reviewer: Margaret Hoogeveen
Cover Illustration: Robert James Potvin
**Design, Art Direction
& Electronic Assembly:** Wycliffe Smith Design

Canadian Cataloguing in Publication Data

Main entry under title:

Gage crossroads 7

ISBN 0-7715-1320-8

1. Readers (Elementary). I. McClymont, Christine
II. Title: Gage crossroads seven. III. Title: Crossroads 7.

PE1121.G2544 2000   428.6   C99-932485-3

We acknowledge the financial support of the Government of Canada through the Book Publishing Industry Development Program for our publishing activities.

ISBN 0-7715-**1320-8**
  3 4 5 BP 04 03 02 01 00
Printed and bound in Canada

We invite you to visit the Gage Web site at <www.gagelearning.com>.

Lines for a Bookmark

by Gael Turnbull

You who read...
May you seek
As you look;
May you keep
What you need;
May you care
What you choose;
And know here
In this book
Something strange,
Something sure,
That will change
You and be yours.

TABLE OF CONTENTS

PERSONAL FOCUS

"Climb high
Climb far
Your goal the sky
Your aim the star

—Anonymous

FIND THE COURAGE

Cooks Brook

Poem by Al Pittman

At the pool where we used to swim
in Cooks Brook
not everyone had guts enough
to dive from the top ledge

not that it would have been
a difficult dive
except for the shelf of rock
that lay two feet below the surface
and reached quarter of the way out
into the width of the pool

one by one the brave few of us
would climb the cliff to the ledge
and stand poised
ready to plunge headfirst
into the dark water below
and always there was that moment
of terror
when you'd doubt that you could
clear the shelf
knowing full well
it would be better to die
skull smashed open in the water
than it would be to climb
backwards down to the beach

GOALS AT A GLANCE

- Respond critically to a poem.
- Describe an experience.

so always there was that moment
when you prayed for wings
then sailed arms outspread into the buoyant air
what you feel is something
impossible to describe
as the water parts like a wound
to engulf you
then closes just as quickly
in a white scar where you entered

and you are surprised always
to find yourself alive
following the streaks of sunlight
that lead you gasping to the surface
where you make your way
leisurely to shore
as though there had been nothing to it
as though it was every day of the week
you daringly defied the demons
who lived so terribly
in the haunted hours of your sleep

- -

RESPONDING TO THE POEM

a. Find the words and phrases that suggest how the speaker feels
about diving into the pool. Do you think they are effective? Explain.

b. Why does the speaker feel that "it would be better to die/skull
smashed open in the water/than it would be to climb/backwards
down to the beach"? Have you ever felt like this? What were the
circumstances?

c. What do you think is the main idea or theme of the poem?

d. Those who dive are considered "the brave few of us." Do you agree
that they are brave? Explain.

Speed skater Gaetan Boucher thrilled
Canada by collecting four medals
in two Olympic Games. What kind
of courage do you think that takes?

An Olympic Moment

Profile by Bud Greenspan

It was perhaps fitting that Canada's twenty-nine-year-old Gaetan Boucher should skate in his last Olympic race before a home crowd at the 1988 Calgary Olympic Games. He was already a Canadian national hero, the finest speed skater the country had ever produced. With his whole nation watching, he would be attempting to defend the 1500-metre championship that he'd won four years before in Sarajevo.

◆◆◆

At seventeen, Boucher had begun his Olympic career at the 1976 Innsbruck Games, where he failed to win any medals. Four years later, in Lake Placid, the luck of the draw in the 1000-metre race paired him with America's Eric Heiden. Heiden would make Olympic history by winning five gold medals in five individual events.

"Heiden was the hero of the Games," said Boucher. "I had little chance to beat him. But I decided I would do my best and maybe something good would happen."

- Write a profile.
- Punctuate dialogue correctly.

Something good did happen. Heiden defeated Boucher by 1 1/2 seconds, but their heat was so fast that Boucher ended up with a silver medal after all the pairs had raced.

With Heiden retiring after the 1980 Lake Placid Games, Boucher was given a good chance to stand on the top step of the awards podium in Sarajevo. Even before the Games began, he was given the honour of carrying the Canadian flag into the stadium during the Opening Ceremonies.

"People were saying that at the last two Olympics, the person who carried the flag on opening day didn't do very well," said Boucher with a smile. "But I had a lot of confidence in 1984, and I wanted to prove that carrying the flag doesn't mean you can't win."

Boucher finished third in the 500-metre race and now had a bronze to go with his silver of four years before. Four days later in the 1000-metre event, he was superb. He defeated his nearest competitor by almost a second to win the gold medal. He immediately called his parents.

"The first words he said to me on the phone were, 'I got you your gold medal,'" Cyrenus Boucher, Gaetan's father, said with a laugh. "We had a joke within the family. I told Gaetan that the first gold medal he won would be mine. The next one would be his."

Two days later, Gaetan Boucher made Canadian Olympic history by winning the 1500-metre race. He became the first Canadian Winter Olympian to win two gold medals. His total of four medals was also the largest number ever won by a Canadian athlete.

◆◆◆

At 6 p.m. on February 20, 1988, at the Calgary speed-skating oval, twenty-nine-year-old Boucher made final preparations for his start in the 1500-metre event, his last race in a career that spanned four Olympic Games.

Forty of the fastest skaters in the world would compete in pairs—two men against each other and against the clock. For the first time in Olympic history, the speed-skating championships would be held indoors. The new 400-metre Calgary oval was the fastest in the world, and records were expected to fall in nearly every event.

Boucher drew the fifteenth of twenty pairs. This fact had particular significance—all of the other favourites in the race drew earlier pairs. Boucher would know in advance how fast a time he would have to skate to win.

The strength of the opposition became clear when the very first pair skated, for Eric Flaim of the United States shattered the world record. This new record lasted less than eight minutes. In the third pair, Andre Hoffmann of East Germany broke Flaim's record by 6/100 of a second.

Hoffmann's world record time held up as pair after pair competed. Finally, it was time for the fifteenth pair—and for Gaetan Boucher's final Olympic appearance.

Boucher went after the world record from the start. After 300 metres, his time was fastest of all. Nearing the halfway mark, he was still in the lead, but he was struggling. The home crowd urged him on, but Boucher could not respond. He was slowing down considerably. As Boucher struggled valiantly in the last lap before the finish, his father shouted from the stands, "Go Gaetan!" As Gaetan moved toward the finish line. Cyrenus Boucher looked at the clock. He stopped cheering and slowly sat down, tears streaming down his face.

After he crossed the finish line, Gaetan Boucher slowly circled the track. His time placed him ninth, but the thousands of fans stood to give him an ovation usually reserved for the winner. They knew that Gaetan Boucher had done his best, honouring the age-old philosophy that has sent Olympians into the arena for centuries: "Ask not alone for victory. Ask for courage. For if you can endure, you bring honour to yourself. Even more, you bring honour to us all."

----

1. RESPONDING TO THE PROFILE

a. Gaetan Boucher is portrayed as an optimistic person who believes in himself. Reread the profile, identifying examples of his positive thinking.

b. Reread the last paragraph. In your own words, explain how the quote at the end of that paragraph applies to Gaetan: "Ask not alone for victory. Ask for courage. For if you can endure, you bring honour to yourself. Even more, you bring honour to us all."

c. In a small group, discuss what courage means to you. Give an example of something you or someone else has done that you feel was courageous.

2. ORAL COMMUNICATION PERFORM A SKIT

All of us at some time have dealt with the negative thoughts of others. In groups of three or four, prepare a skit that shows how someone might respond to negative thinking. For example, you could create a scene in which one of the characters is being discouraged from trying something new or difficult. Remember, your skit can show good or bad ways of handling negativity.

3. WRITING CREATE A PROFILE

Choose a person who interests you. It could be a famous person or simply someone in your life whom you admire. Make a list of questions you would like to ask that person, and then do some research to find the answers to your questions. If possible, interview the person. Next, write a biographical profile about the person, using "An Olympic Moment" or "Courage in Orbit" as a model. Include

- an introduction to the person (name, age, other background information)
- the reasons why you were interested in the person
- a story that reveals the person's admirable qualities
- the answers to the questions you researched

SELF-ASSESSMENT: Reread your profile. Have you presented the information in a logical order? Does your writing make your subject seem like an interesting or remarkable person? Will your reader be able to tell how you feel about your subject?

4. LANGUAGE CONVENTIONS PUNCTUATE DIALOGUE

Find examples of dialogue in the profile and copy them in your notebook exactly. What do you notice about the punctuation marks and where they are placed? Discuss them with a partner and then as a class. With your partner, create a brief dialogue between two people. Your dialogue should include the following punctuation, placed correctly: commas, periods, question marks, exclamation marks, quotation marks, and quotation marks within quotation marks. Remember to begin a new paragraph each time the speaker changes.

As Soon As I Find Out Who I Am You'll Be the First to Know

Poem by Angela Shelf Medearis

I promise to send you a letter
or call you on the phone
as soon as I find
myself.
I promise you'll be the first to know.
But right now,
I'm having a hard time
even communicating with me.
I just can't seem to find
a language
or the right words to say,
to talk about my feelings
with you.

1. RESPONDING TO THE STORY

a. The poem says, "I just can't seem to find/a language/or the right words to say,/to talk about my feelings/with you." Have you ever felt this way? In your journal, describe what that was like.

b. What do you think the speaker means by "as soon as I find/myself"?

c. Who might be the "you" the speaker is addressing in the poem?

d. What do you think has prompted the speaker to say these words?

e. What kind of courage does it take to talk about your real feelings with someone else?

2. VISUAL COMMUNICATION

COMMUNICATE THROUGH COLOUR

Reread the poem. What do you think is the overall emotion the speaker is feeling? What colours would you choose to represent that emotion? Now think about a time when you have felt a strong emotion. What colour would you use to represent it? Explain your ideas to a partner. Create an illustration, collage, or other piece of visual art that captures the emotion you felt. Your visual does not have to show an event. Instead, concentrate on using colour to suggest how you felt.

3. WRITING POETRY

If you read the poem aloud, you'll hear that it sounds very much like the way real people talk. What makes it a poem is its rhythm and the way the poet has broken up the sentences into lines—and the fact that every word counts.

You can turn your own words into poems. Begin by writing a few sentences that express thoughts or feelings that are important to you. Shape your sentences into a poem by breaking them into lines. Here are some pointers:

- If you want to emphasize a word, place it at the end of a line or give it a line of its own.
- Break a line where you want the reader to pause.
- Place the most important idea at the end of your poem.
- Write your completed poem on a clean sheet of paper.

SELF-ASSESSMENT: Read your poem aloud. Do you like the way it sounds? You might want to replace the words that seem dull with words that vividly express your intended meaning.

Andrea feels shy and awkward about almost everything— except logging on to her favourite Internet chat site.

Some Days *You're the Puppy*

Short Story by Trudy Morgan-Cole

Spike J: Well gotta go get back to Real Life.
Mariana: What's so great about Real Life anyway?

I wait a second, then the message Spike J exits flashes on my screen, and I'm alone in the chat room. I flex my fingers over the keys for a second and try to imagine what Spike J is doing now, whoever and wherever he might be. According to him, he's 13/m—that's a thirteen-year-old male—he lives somewhere in the southern United States, he's tall with red hair and green eyes, and he plays basketball.

The only thing is that with people you meet online, you've got to remember that some or none or all of that might be true. After all, as far as Spike knows, I'm 13/f, short, with blond hair and blue eyes, I sing soprano in my school choir, and I live on the fourteenth floor of an apartment building in Toronto.

GOALS AT A GLANCE

■ Use a time line to increase understanding of character.
■ Write a sequel to express predictions.

19

I log off, roll away from the computer, and hear my mom calling from the kitchen. "Andrea! Are you still online?"

"Just got off, Mom," I shout, running downstairs. She's always bugging me if I spend too much time online, complaining that I'm not living in the real world. She says I should get more involved in school activities. What this usually means is that she wants to get at the computer herself. Mom works at home designing Web pages, and Dad is network administrator for the company he works at, so we're a pretty high-tech bunch. We're usually fighting over who gets to use the good computer.

Right now Mom is down in the kitchen, looking pretty low-tech as she peels potatoes for dinner—a job that will quickly be mine if I'm not careful. I breeze past her out onto the back porch. Our house is about as different from a fourteenth-floor Toronto apartment as you can imagine. It's a two-storey house covered in green clapboard on a steep downtown street in St. John's. From the upstairs windows you can see the harbour. Our house is over a hundred years old, and Mom and Dad have been restoring it since they moved in, the year my sister Sheri was born. Sheri's now married with a baby of her own, and our house still isn't finished, but it's comfortable. And I love our backyard. Even now, in November, when the big maple trees are bare and the garden is all dead brown stalks, it's one of my favourite places.

At the other end of the scale, my least favourite place on earth has to be our school cafeteria, where I'm stranded the next day at lunch. I went to a small elementary school, and when I hit junior high this fall I was kind of overwhelmed by the crowds and the noise—in homeroom, in the halls, but worst of all in the cafeteria. I stand there clutching my tray, looking at the crowded tables, and praying I'll find someone to sit with, when I see Molly waving from a table way at the back.

Weaving my way through the crowds, I wonder what I'd do without Molly. She's really my only friend. I wasn't this pathetic last year. You'd have to call me a shy person—I'm not outgoing or loud like Molly—but I had friends in my old school. Now Molly's the only one of my old friends who's in any of my classes, so I stick close to her. Unlike me, she's having a blast in Grade Seven. She makes a new friend every two minutes.

"Coming to my practice this afternoon?" she asks, biting into a granola bar.

"Yeah, I guess."

If I go straight home I can get in an hour or two online before supper, but then I think that's just so pathetic—I mean, I have a chance to do something with real people instead of hanging out in cyberspace. Besides, I like watching Molly's drama practices. If I had enough nerve, I'd be in drama myself.

"You can sit there and drool over Jared McNeill," Molly promises.

I roll my eyes, as if the thought of drooling over Jared has never occurred to me. "No thanks, I don't need Tessa clawing my eyes out."

"Oh, those two are history," says Molly. "I think he dumped her—out looking for new hearts to break."

"Well, mine won't be one of them."

Of course I'd let Jared McNeill break my heart if he wanted. But I wouldn't stand a chance. He's this totally gorgeous grade eight guy. I have to admit, as I sit and watch Molly and the others practise that afternoon, I do give him a few glances. But only a few.

What they're doing today is called "improv," which is basically acting with no script. You make everything up off the top of your head. Molly is great at it. I'd be so terrified! They're getting ready for an improv competition against all the schools in the city. I've already promised Molly I'll go to the contest and scream my lungs out.

But the only person I really know in drama is Molly. While she gabs with all her friends after the practice, I'm left on the sidelines, feeling out of place. It's kind of a relief when I finally do get home and slide in front of the computer. As I log on to my favourite chat site, I'm relaxed. My everyday self—the boring straight brown hair, the tall skinny frame and bland face, the shyness and awkwardness—just drops away and I can become whoever I want to be.

After you chat on the same site for awhile, you get to know people. The chat room is full today and I recognize most of the names, like Princess, Sweet Thang, and Jody. My nickname is Mariana. I like the sound of that.

> Mariana enters.
> Sweet Thang: So any guys wanna chat with me?
> Princess: Hi Mariana, hows it goin'?
> Jody: Hi Mariana.
> Pepper: Stats Sweet Thang?
> Sweet Thang: 14/f/5'2"/blond/green eyes.
> Pepper: Wanna 1-2-1?
> Princess: I'm in computer class. School is so boring!
> Mariana: I'm home from school already and I'm glad.

If Princess is smart—which she isn't—she'll know that means I live further east than she does. I never tell people on chat where I really live, or put in my real e-mail address. That's just basic safety. People say there's a way to check to see where the person's server is and tell where they're logged on from, but I don't think most people bother to do that. Maybe Jody does though, because he asked me once where in Newfoundland I was from. I said I didn't really live in Newfoundland, that I was just here for a couple of weeks visiting my grandmother. That's when I came up with the apartment-building-in-Toronto story.

I love chatting, but you've just got to accept that almost everybody is lying about a lot of stuff. Some of it is just for protection—like not telling where you live or your real name—and some of it is to impress people, like me supposedly being blond, and blue-eyed, and singing in choir. The reason I say Princess is not too smart is that she doesn't seem to grasp this. Or she didn't. She was having this big-time online relationship with this guy Mad Dog (I think the name should tell you something), who was supposedly sixteen and gorgeous. Well, finally she agreed to meet him because he lived near her, and it turned out he was almost thirty and a real jerk. She didn't get into any serious trouble, but she could have. She had to get her phone number changed because she'd given it to him. I don't know how she could have been so dumb.

After awhile, Spike J comes online and says hi to everyone. Then he says:

Spike J: Hey Mariana want to 1-2-1?
Mariana: Sure Spike.

I click on the button to open a private chat with Spike.

Mariana: So what kind of day are you having?
Spike J: Lousy! My girlfriend broke up with me and she's telling all her friends lies about me. I feel like such an idiot.
Mariana: Sounds like she's the idiot not you.
Spike J: No, because I trusted her.
Mariana: You've got to trust somebody if you care about them.
Spike J: Yeah but what if they don't care about you?
Mariana: I guess you have to take that risk if you want a real relationship.
Spike J: Not me, not any more. I'm never trusting anyone again.
Mariana: You shouldn't say that, just because one girl hurt you. I bet you're a great guy and lots of girls like you.
Spike J: I'm not that great. I made stuff up to impress you–like I'm not really on the basketball team. I play a little but I'm not on a team. I'm really into art and drama and stuff like that.
Mariana: But that's cool.
Spike J: Yeah I know but girls seem to like jocks better.
Mariana: Depends what kind of girl.

I can't believe myself. In school I'm so nervous my tongue ties in a knot if I even try to talk to a guy, and here I am giving Spike all this wise advice about his break-up, and then practically flirting with him. The Internet is truly amazing. I feel so brave when no one can see my face.

> Mariana: I'm into drama myself. In fact I'm on my school's drama team for this competition that's coming up.

Now why did I say that? Talk about making stuff up to impress people! I quickly veer the subject away from drama so I won't have to make up any more details, and we chat a little longer, mostly about his ex-girlfriend. When I have to log off I say:

> Mariana: Hope you have a better day tomorrow! Keep smiling.
> Spike J: Thanks. I guess some days you're the puppy and some days you're the fire hydrant.
> Mariana: LOL! That's so funny.
> Spike J: It's something my brother always says. See ya later.

I often type LOL when I'm not really laughing out loud—it's just the usual way to tell people something's funny—but the puppy/fire hydrant saying really does make me laugh. And the whole conversation lifts my spirits. The confidence I have online spills over into real life, and all evening and the next day I'm in a good mood.

I'm in such a good mood that the next afternoon, when I'm watching Molly's practice again, I do something that surprises even me. One of the guys on the improv team is missing so the drama teacher, Ms. Penney, says, "Andrea, will you fill in? In case we need an even number for some of the games?" And before I even have time to think I answer, "OK, sure."

Already I'm nervous, but I figure I won't have to do much. They're playing a game called "Freeze!" where two people are acting out a scene, and someone in the group calls "Freeze!" The actors freeze in place while the person who yelled steps in and changes the scene. I'm watching it, thinking how cool it is, while Molly and this Grade Nine girl, Melissa, are doing a scene. Molly's there with her arms out-stretched, pretending to carry a huge box when I hear my own voice yell, "Freeze!"

Molly freezes, Melissa drops out, and I run up to Molly, grab her outstretched arms, and start ballroom dancing. She catches on right away, and we pretend we're learning to tango. When someone yells "Freeze" and jumps in, I have no problem going with it. Even when the Freeze game ends I'm still really involved, playing games and doing scenes. I'm nervous, but I'm having a blast. Molly looks at me as if I've been taken over by aliens.

At the end of practice Ms. Penney calls me over and says, "Andrea, you're really good at this. Would you like to be an alternate on the team—in case someone gets sick?"

All in all it's a fantastic day. When I get online later that evening, I find Spike's been looking for me. We quickly switch to a private chat.

> Mariana: So were you the puppy or the fire hydrant today?
> Spike J: LOL! I was the hydrant again but not as bad as yesterday. My ex kept her mouth shut today. But I flunked a math test. What about you?
> Mariana: I was the puppy today! It was so cool!

I consider telling him the whole story, about the Freeze game and everything, but it would take a long time to explain. Besides, I'd have to tell him that I lied yesterday about being on the improv team. But today it's not a lie! I end up just saying that some good stuff happened in drama and I'm proud of myself. Then we talk about other things, till Mom yells at me to get off the computer and do my homework.

After that I start going to practice every day. I know I probably won't be in the actual competition—there are two alternates, although the other one isn't into it that much and doesn't show up regularly—but I think I'd be too nervous for that anyway. It's just fun learning all the activities, practising with the others, feeling like part of a team. Ms. Penney's always saying how everyone has to pull together and trust each other, and I feel like I'm really getting to know the other players. Even Jared McNeill turns out to be a nice guy who's good for a laugh, not the god-among-men I had pictured.

With all the practices, I don't get nearly as much online time as I used to, but I do hang out in chat a few times a week. I meet Spike there about three times over the next month, and each time we have a private conversation. He's getting over the break-up and we have a lot of fun chatting. I don't understand some of my online friends who get so excited over having a virtual boyfriend. You can't see the person or go to a movie with them. It's fun, but it's not real life.

Then, the day before the Improv Games, Melissa O'Dea is not in school. She's the best player on the improv team, and she has the flu.

"She'll be better by tomorrow, I'm sure," Molly assures us at practice.

"But if she's not, you'd better come through for us, Andrea," someone else says.

I'm terrified at the thought of replacing anyone, much less Melissa, who's such a good actor. And even though the other team members are really encouraging, I can tell they're scared to lose Melissa too. I don't know if I can take the pressure.

The next day Melissa's still not in school, but she shows up to our practice at lunchtime. She looks horrible, and her voice is almost gone. "But I'll be there tonight," she croaks. Everyone exchanges worried glances, even Ms. Penney. "You'd better come along with us after school," Ms. Penney tells me.

After school we all pile into Ms. Penney's van to head out to where the games are being held. It's a sunny day, even though it's cold, and we're all excited. We sing very loudly off-key as the van rolls out Columbus Drive, past the Avalon Mall and the Village Mall to Mount Pearl. When we get to Mount Pearl Junior High, we meet the other improv teams, go through some warm-up exercises, and eat supper. There's no sign of Melissa, and I'm torn between being thrilled and terrified. Half an hour before the games begin, Melissa walks in. We give her a round of applause, but I'm disappointed as well as relieved.

She's still sick, but she's going to go through with it. I give everyone a hug for good luck before I go to take my seat in the stands. Soon some other students and a few parents and teachers from our school show up, and we have our own little cheering section.

When our team is announced, they run out to do their opening routine, which is full of hand-stands and cartwheels. The first event is a mystery skit. The emcee asks the audience what the murder weapon should be. "A pear!" someone yells above the roar of suggestions.

As the team huddles for fifteen seconds to plan, I'm trying to figure out how they'll work a pear into the story. I wish I was up there doing it.

Even after the first event—which goes great—I wonder if I might get called in, because every time our team takes a break, Melissa rushes for the bathroom. At intermission Molly tells me that Melissa is throwing up every time she's not acting. But when she's out on stage you'd never guess because she's got so much energy! Our whole team is excellent. I'm especially proud of Molly.

Our team gets lots of laughs and cheers from the audience, but when the scores are tallied up at the end of the evening, we're in third place. Even though we knew we couldn't beat the senior high teams, we had hoped to score best in the junior high division. But we didn't even manage that.

I rush up to our team's bench as the audience leaves. "You were great, guys! You should've got more points for that last event. Molly, you were terrific!"

"You were all terrific!" Ms. Penney says, hugging one team member after another. "I'm so proud of all of you."

All the team members are hugging, and slapping each other on the back. "Remember," Ms. Penney says as parents start to arrive to take people home, "the whole team's invited to my classroom for pizza at lunchtime tomorrow. You too, Andrea," she adds. "You're part of the team."

"Yeah thanks, Andrea," says Melissa. "I nearly couldn't do it—it's a good thing you were here."

"Come on, Andrea, my dad'll give you a ride home," Molly tells me.

Behind me, Jared McNeill is picking up his stuff and talking to his older brother, who's driving him home. "You did great, kid," his brother says.

"Yeah, but we never won."

"Oh well—some days you're the puppy, some days—"

"—you're the fire hydrant," Jared finishes.

When I whip around to look at him, I find him glancing at me. Both of us look as if we're about to ask something, say something. He smiles, then I smile, and his brother says, "Come on, Jared, let's go."

There'll be plenty of time to ask questions later.

1. RESPONDING TO THE STORY

a. Do you think that Andrea's mom is right when she says Andrea is "not living in the real world" when she is online? Explain.

b. How does Andrea feel about being in junior high? Can you relate to how she feels? Why or why not?

c. How is Andrea's personality different when she's talking with someone in the chat room? Can you suggest an explanation for this difference? Find evidence from the story to support your answer.

d. What do you think Andrea gains from her participation in the improv practices?

e. What is the meaning of the title? Do you agree with the idea it expresses? Explain.

STRATEGIES

2. READING UNDERSTAND CHARACTER

Many stories and novels focus on how characters change as a result of their experience. With a partner, create a time line to help you understand how Andrea changes. Look through the whole story for examples of the things Andrea says or does that reveal her self-image. Your time line should present examples in chronological order. What does your completed time line tell you about Andrea?

SELF-IMAGE TIME LINE

"I wasn't this pathetic last year."

"If I had enough nerve I'd be in drama myself."

page 20

page 21

3. ORAL COMMUNICATION CREATE A SCENE

In groups of three or four, take turns telling about a time when you have felt like the "puppy" and then like the "fire hydrant." Choose one of the stories and create a scene to present to the class. You might follow this process:

- Decide on the number of parts and choose roles.
- Appoint a director. The director's role is to help the actors prepare for the scene.
- Draft a script together. The script should show all the lines the characters will speak.
- Rehearse the scene, making revisions if necessary.
- Present your scene.

4. WRITING A SEQUEL

Imagine what might happen next in the story. First, in your notebook, create a brief list of questions that a sequel to the story might answer, for example: Do Andrea and Jared reveal themselves to each other? Does Andrea continue to be involved in drama? Does she spend as much time as she used to in the chat room? Write a sequel to "Some Days You're the Puppy." It should answer at least three of the questions from your list. Share your sequel with another classmate who has completed this activity. How does it compare?

SELF-ASSESSMENT: In your sequel, have you portrayed each character in a way that is true to the original story? If you have changed a character's personality, did you include an event that tells the reader why the personality change occurred?

Auntie Cheryl is in a panic because her niece wants some advice.
Will Cheryl's friends be able to help?

Comic Strip by Barbara Brandon

GOALS AT A GLANCE

■ Express personal understandings.
■ Use non-verbal communication techniques.

1. RESPONDING TO THE COMIC STRIP

a. What makes Auntie Cheryl jump to the conclusion that Brianna needs advice of a serious nature?

b. Why do you think Auntie Cheryl is worried about giving such advice? What does she do to bolster her courage?

c. What kind of advice does Brianna get from Auntie Cheryl's friends?

d. How does Brianna feel about this advice, even though it is not exactly what she was looking for?

e. Does this comic strip have only one punch line? Explain your answer.

2. WRITING IN YOUR OWN WORDS

Work with a partner, writing down each piece of advice Brianna was given and explaining what it means. Rewrite each piece of advice in your own words, using a single sentence for each one.

In your journal, tell about some uplifting advice you have received that is like the advice given in the comic strip. Who gave you the advice? How did it affect you? Would you share the same advice with someone else?

3. ORAL COMMUNICATION FACIAL EXPRESSION/GESTURE

Notice how the facial expressions and hand gestures of the characters in "Where I'm Coming From" help to communicate the comic strip's message. In oral communication, we also use facial expressions and gestures to communicate with our audience. In groups of three or four, create a script for a brief dramatization about a person who is looking for help. You may first wish to brainstorm interesting situations. In your dramatization, communicate through facial expressions and gestures as much as you communicate through words.

SELF-ASSESSMENT: Ask your audience to answer these questions about your performance:

• Which facial expressions were most effective? Why?

• Which facial expressions and gestures were hard to understand?

Based on the comments you received, what would you change to improve your dramatization?

How would you feel if lions were prowling around your campsite?

SOUTH AFRICAN ADVENTURE

REFLECTIONS BY SOUTH AFRICAN KIDS, WITH PAINTINGS BY ROBERT BATEMAN

Since 1957, the Wilderness Leadership School has offered teens the unforgettable experience of exploring the South African bush. The kids stay in rough camps and hike the trails in the Umfolozi Game Reserve, constantly watching for the rhinoceros or lion that might be around the next corner! But it's the solo night watch that takes the most courage—an hour of standing guard over the camp, looking out for any wild animals that might wander too close.

The Umfolozi Game Reserve— 96 000 hectares of wilderness!

There is another special aspect to these outings. The Wilderness Leadership School intentionally brings kids of all races and backgrounds together to learn from nature and from each other. They did this even in the days of apartheid, when blacks and whites were kept apart by government regulation. In the following reflections, written when apartheid was still in force, the kids themselves will tell you how their wilderness experience changed their lives.

GOALS AT A GLANCE

■ Create a video or audio recording.
■ Respond critically to a painting.

When we first set off into the bush, I had a "sick feeling" in the pit of my stomach—it was either fear of never having been in a game reserve, or it was the joy of my first trail in the bush. The only times I had ever seen wild animals were either in a cage at the zoo, or through the windows of a car. To be side by side with them in their territory was a completely new experience, an experience that I can never forget.

Brendan Dalzell

One of the most exciting experiences during the trail was night watch. It certainly is an eerie feeling, and some-times also frightening, to be all alone listening to the strange noises of the bush, seeing the glowing eyes in the dark when you shine the torch [flashlight] on some buck. Groups of lions were around us every night, as close as four hundred metres from our camp.

Ingo von Sabler

Although I was afraid of being in the wilderness for a week, I must say that I really enjoyed being amongst other people from different nations, towns, and colleges. The most exciting part was that I was with whites—something I never thought would happen to me.

Millie Belot

Before coming on the wilderness trail I saw myself as something separate from nature. But being in the wilderness and taking part in the discussions helped me to see that I am just part of the ecosystem—nothing more. I have no right to regard the earth as "mine" and to use it as I like, wasting its resources. I have to respect and care for the earth, carrying out the responsibility of stewardship of the earth that God has given to us all.

Vicky Arnold

Members of the group found themselves making friends quickly. Social, cultural, and racial differences were forgotten, and we discovered a harmony unique in South Africa. This harmony, totally relaxed and natural, showed me that basically people can all relate to each other through nature, no matter what their background.   **Robert Butler**

For me it was a real breakthrough, a once-in-a-lifetime experience, just to be away from science, technology, commerce, and industry, which promise the magical push-a-button dream world of leisure, luxury, and licence. Here I could get back to reality, to true life.

Thabang Mumonyane

The wilderness, at times, made me feel small and insignificant. Everything in nature interacts, and we humans are just on the sidelines! Our clumsy efforts to improve things only manage to disturb the balance nature has created within itself.

Fiona J. Newman

If the days were beautiful, then the nights were doubly so. The dark velvet skies high above me were littered with thousands and millions of little diamonds. It was then, especially during my night watch, that the calm and tranquillity really began to make an impression. As you sit, feeling like an island, you can honestly and truly work out your feelings, ideas, and thoughts on everything. I think it is this that really makes you realize that every man, woman, and child needs some time in his or her life to be alone and to analyse everything that happens in this world.

Louise Lagaay

Robert Bateman is a renowned Canadian artist who has always been fascinated with nature. His lifelong love of African animals began with his first trip to Africa in the late 1950s.

He continues to visit Africa and paint its wildlife. The three paintings featured on the preceding pages are taken from the book *Safari,* published in 1999.

1. RESPONDING TO THE REFLECTIONS

a. The introduction reads, "But it's the solo night watch that takes the most courage..." Why do you think the night watch takes the most courage?

b. What other kinds of courage might the participants have needed? Explain.

c. Summarize some of the ways in which their wilderness experience changed the participants' outlook on life.

d. Several of the participants talk about the relationship between humans and nature. Do you agree with their ideas? Explain.

2. RESEARCHING FIND BACKGROUND INFORMATION

Provide some background to the South African context by investigating one of the following topics:

- the people of South Africa
- the geography of the Umfolozi Game Reserve
- the rise and fall of apartheid
- Nelson Mandela's life story
- the conservation of African wildlife

Using the guidelines for preparing a research report on page 86, research your topic carefully. Select an interesting way to present your findings to your classmates. For example, you could create an electronic document containing images and text downloaded from the Internet. Remember to credit your sources.

3. MEDIA CREATE A VISUAL OR AUDIO RECORD

Connect with nature! Plan a trip in which you will make a visual and/or a sound recording of nature—a field, a ravine, the lakeshore, the woods, a local park, or even a backyard garden. For example, you might present your experience through a series of photographs or with a video created on a camcorder. You could enhance your visual presentation by tape recording the sounds of nature, as well as your responses to what you see and hear. Your presentation could include music that expresses how you feel about the natural world.

4. VISUAL COMMUNICATION ANALYSE A PAINTING

In a small group, look carefully at the paintings by Robert Bateman. Together, select one painting and prepare a brief presentation on why it appeals to you. Consider such things as subject matter, colour, *composition* (the way objects are arranged in the painting), and the use of distance and space. In your presentation, make sure you give reasons for the opinion you express.

SELF-ASSESSMENT: Use a camcorder to record your presentation. View the recording and ask these questions about your presentation.

- Did I state my opinion clearly?
- Did I support my opinion by referring to specific elements of the painting?
- Did I present my ideas in a logical order?

A Mountain Legend

SHORT STORY BY JORDAN WHEELER

The school bus drove into a small summer camp at the base of a towering mountain. Boys and girls between the ages of eight and twelve, who had signed up for the three-day camping trip, poured out of the bus. Following instructions from counsellors, they began hurriedly preparing their camp as the sunset dripped over the rock walls towering above them. For many, it was their first time away from the city, which they could still see far off in the distance. Tents were put up and sleeping bags unrolled before the last of the twilight rays gave way to the darkness of night.

GOALS AT A GLANCE

- Present an oral retelling of a legend.
- Recognize and use strong verbs.

41

Roasting marshmallows around a large campfire, the young campers listened intently to stories told by the counsellors. Behind the eager campers, the caretaker of the camp sat on the ground, himself listening to the stories.

As the night grew old, the younger children wearily found their way to their tents, so that by midnight only the twelve-year-olds remained around the fire with one counsellor and the caretaker. Their supply of stories seemingly exhausted, they sat in silence watching the glowing embers of the once fiery blaze shrink into red-hot ash.

"The moon is rising," announced the caretaker in a low, even voice.

All eyes looked up to the glow surrounding the jagged peaks of the mountain. The blackness of the rock formed an eerie silhouette against the gently lit sky.

The caretaker's name was McNabb. He had lived close to the mountain all his life and knew many of the stories the mountain had seen. He threw his long, black, braided hair over his shoulders, drew the collar of his faded jean jacket up against the crisp mountain air, and spoke.

"There is a legend about this mountain once told by the mountain itself," he said, paused for a moment, then continued. "People claim that long ago it told of a young boy who tried to climb up to an eagle's nest, which rested somewhere among the many cliffs. He was from a small camp about a day's journey from here and when he was twelve years old, he thought he was ready to become a warrior. His father disagreed, saying he was too young and too small. But the boy was stubborn, and one morning before dawn he sneaked out of his family's teepee and set off on foot toward the mountain. There were no horses in North America in his time. They were brought later by the Europeans.

"It took most of the day for him to reach the mountain. The next morning, he set out to find an eagle and seek a vision from the mighty bird, as that was the first step in becoming a warrior. But as he was climbing up the rock cliffs to a nest, he fell to his death, releasing a terrible cry that echoed from the mountain far out across the land. The legend says the boy's spirit still wanders the mountain today."

A coyote howled in the distance and the campers jumped.

"Is it true?" asked one of the boys, with worry and fear in his voice.

"Some people say so, and they also say you can still hear his scream every once in a while."

All around the dying fire, eyes were straining up at the menacing rock peaks. The caretaker McNabb, however, wasn't looking at the mountain, he was watching one of the young campers. He was a Cree boy, smaller than the others. The boy was gazing up at the mountain, his curiosity obviously blended with fear. Turning his head, his eyes met those of McNabb. For a fleeting moment, they locked stares, then McNabb relaxed, a knowing expression spreading over his face, while the boy continued to stare at him, wide-eyed and nervous.

There were small discussions around the fire, debating the story's truth, before the counsellor told them it was time for sleep. Both tired and excited, they retreated to their tents and crawled into their sleeping bags.

The boy Jason lay in a tent he shared with two other boys, who lay talking in the dark. As Jason waited for the heat of his body to warm his sleeping bag, he thought of that long-ago boy. He felt a closeness to him and imagined himself in his place.

"Hey, Jason, why don't you climb up that mountain tomorrow morning and try to catch an eagle?" It was Ralph, who was against the far wall of the tent on the other side of Barry.

"Why?" asked Jason.

"You're Cree aren't you? Don't you want to become a warrior?"

True, Jason was Cree, but he knew nothing of becoming a warrior. He had spent all his life in the city. All he knew of his heritage was what his grandmother told him from time to time, which wasn't much. He had been to three powwows in his life, all at a large hall not far from his house, but he never learned very much. His time was spent eating hot dogs, drinking pop, and watching the older boys play pool in the adjoining rooms. Little as he knew though, he wanted Ralph and Barry to think he knew a lot.

"No. It's not time for me to be a warrior yet," he told them.

"Why not?" Barry asked.

"It just isn't, that's all," Jason said, not knowing a better answer.

"You're chicken, you couldn't climb that mountain if you tried," Ralph charged.

"I'm not chicken! I could climb that mountain, no problem. It just isn't time yet."

"You're chicken," Ralph said again.

"Go to sleep!" boomed a voice across the campground.

Ralph gave out three chicken clucks and rolled over to sleep.

Jason lay there in mild anger. He hated being called a chicken, and if the counsellor hadn't shouted at that moment, he would have given Ralph a swift punch. But Ralph was right, the mountain did scare him.

With his anger subsiding, he drifted into a haunting sleep, filled with dreams. Dreams the wind swept through the camp, gently spreading the mountain spirit's stories throughout. A coyote's piercing howl echoed down the rocky cliffs, making Jason flinch in his sleep.

The following morning, Ralph, Barry, and Jason were the first ones up. As they emerged from the tent into the chilled morning air, their attention was immediately grasped by the huge rock peaks looming high above. Ralph's searching eyes spanned the mountain. A light blanket of mist enveloped its lower reaches.

Pointing up he said, "See that ledge up there?" Jason and Barry followed Ralph's arm to a cliff along one of the rock walls just above the tree line. "I bet you can't get to it," he dared Jason.

"I could so," Jason responded.

"Prove it," Ralph said.

Jason was trapped and he knew it. If he said no, he would be admitting he was scared. And there was another challenge in Ralph's voice, unsaid, but Jason heard it. Ralph was daring him to prove his heritage. Jason had lived his whole life in a city on cement ground and among concrete mountains, where climbing was as easy as walking up stairs or pressing an elevator button. To prove to Ralph and himself that he was Cree, Jason had to climb to that ledge. He knew that mountain climbing could end a life. And there were wild animals he might have to deal with. How was he supposed to react? How would he react? He was afraid. He didn't want to go. But if he didn't?

"What's the matter?" Ralph taunted. "Scared?"

At that point, Jason decided he would face the mountain and he would reach that ledge. "OK," he conceded.

At first, the climbing was easy, but his progress became slow and clumsy as he got higher up. Struggling over uneven ground and through trees, he came across a large, flat rock. In need of a rest, he sat down and looked down at the campground he had left right after breakfast an hour ago. He could see bodies scurrying about. If they hadn't noticed by now that he was missing, he thought, no doubt they would soon.

Looking up, he could just see the ledge above the tree line. It wasn't much further, he thought. He could get to it, wave down at the camp to show he had made it, and be back in time for lunch. Raising himself up, he started to climb again, marching through the trees and up the steep slope, over the rough terrain.

A few moments later he heard a loud howl that seemed to come from somewhere above. At first, he thought it was a coyote, but it sounded more like a human. Nervously, he kept going.

In the camp, Ralph and Barry were getting ready to help prepare lunch. McNabb was starting a fire not far away. They, too, heard the howl.

"I never knew coyotes did that during the day," Ralph said to Barry.

Overhearing them, McNabb responded, "That was no coyote."

Half an hour later, Jason stood just above the tree line. The ledge, his goal, was ten metres above, but what lay ahead was treacherous climbing, nearly straight up the rock wall. He scrutinized the rock face, planned his route, and began to pick his way up the last stretch.

The mountain saw the boy encroaching and whispered a warning to the wind sweeping strongly down its face as it remembered a similar event long ago. Jason felt the wind grow stronger, driving high-pitched sound into his ears. Gripping the rock harder, he pulled himself up a bit at a time. The wind seemed to be pushing him back. But he felt something else, too, something urging him on.

When he was about seven metres up the rock face, with his feet firmly on a small ledge, he chanced a look down between his legs. He could see that if he slipped, he would plummet straight down those seven metres, and after hitting the rocks below, he would tumble a great distance further. He knew it would spell death and, for a split second, he considered going back down. But once again he felt an outside force pushing him to go on. It gave him comfort and courage. His face reddened, his heart pounded, and beads of sweat poured from him as he inched his way higher. Straight above, an eagle flew in great circles, slowly moving closer to Jason and the ledge.

Far down the mountain the search for Jason was well underway, but the counsellors had no way of knowing where he was, as Ralph and Barry hadn't told. McNabb also knew where Jason was, but he, too, remained silent.

An eight-year-old girl in the camp lay quietly in her tent, staring up through the screen window at the sky. The search for Jason had been tiring and she had come back for a rest. She was watching a cloud slowly change shape when a large black bird flew by high above. Out of curiosity, she unzipped the tent door and went outside to get a better look. She watched the bird fly in smaller and smaller circles, getting closer and closer to the mountain. She took her eyes off the bird for a moment to look at the huge rock wall, and there, high above the trees and only a metre or so below a ledge, she saw the boy climbing. Right away she knew the boy was in danger. After hesitating for a moment, she ran to tell a counsellor.

Jason paused from climbing, just about a metre below the ledge. He was exhausted and the insides of his hands were raw, the skin having been scraped off by the rough rock. The ledge was so close. He pulled himself up to it, placing his feet inside a crack in the rock for support. Reaching over the edge, he swept one arm along the ledge, found another spot for his feet, hoisted his body up, rolled onto the ledge, and got to his feet. There, an arm's length away on the ledge, were two young eagles in the large nest. For several minutes he just remained there looking at the baby eagles. He had never seen an eagle's nest before. He was so interested in the two young eagles he didn't notice the mother eagle circling high overhead, nor did he hear her swoop down toward him and her nest. She landed in front of him, spread her wings, and let out a loud screech. Jason was so terrified he instinctively jumped, and in doing so, lost his balance. Both feet stepped out

into air as he grabbed the rock.

His hands clung desperately to the ledge as the sharp rock dug into his skin. He looked down and saw his feet dangling in the air. The wind swung him, making it impossible to get his feet back on the rock where they had been moments earlier. A coyote howled and Jason's terror grew. Again he looked down at the rocks below. Tears began streaming down his face. He didn't want to die. He wished he had never accepted Ralph's dare. He could picture them coming up the mountain, finding his dead body among the rocks, and crying over him. He began crying out loud and heard it echoing off the rock. Or he thought it was an echo. He stopped and listened. There was more crying, but not from him. Again he felt the presence of something or someone else. The wind swirled in and whispered to Jason the mountain's legend.

◆◆◆

Though running swiftly, the boy Muskawashee had paced himself expertly for the day's journey. He would arrive at the base of the mountain far earlier than he had expected, and would have plenty of daylight left to catch his supper and find a spot for a good night's sleep. Though small, and having seen only twelve summers, his young body was strong. He would be able to reach the mountain in only two runs, pausing in between to catch a rabbit for lunch.

As his powerful legs moved him gracefully across the prairie, he thought back to the conversation with his father the day before. He had explained how most of his friends were already in preparation for manhood, and he felt he was ready also. He did not want to wait for the next summer.

When some of his friends came back later that day from a successful buffalo hunt, he decided he would go to the mountain alone and seek a vision from the eagle. He knew he would have to rise before the sun to get out of camp without being seen.

When he reached the base of the mountain, the sun was still well above the horizon. He sat down in a sheltered area for a rest. He decided this was where he would sleep for the night.

After a few minutes, he got up and made himself a trap for a rabbit and planted it. After laying the trap, he wandered off to look for some berries to eat while preparing his mind for the following day when he would climb the mountain. After some time, he returned to his trap and found a rabbit in it. He skinned it with a well-sharpened stone knife he had brought with him, and built a fire to cook his meal. He would keep the fire burning all night to keep away the wild animals while he slept.

Finishing his meal, he thanked the creator for his food and safe journey, and prayed for good fortune in his quest for a vision. Then he lay down in the soft moss and fell asleep to the music of the coyote's howls and the whispering wind.

The next morning, he awoke to the sun's warming shine. The still-smouldering fire added an aroma of burnt wood to the fresh air. He again prayed to the creator for good fortune in his quest for a vision and for a safe journey up the mountain. When he finished, he looked up, high above, and saw eagles flying to and from a rock ledge. This would be his goal.

Half an hour later, he stood where the trees stopped growing and the bare rock began. His powerful body had moved steadily through the trees even though he wasn't used to uphill running. Without resting, he continued his climb, knowing he would have to be careful ahead. The mountain could be dangerous and its spirit could be evil.

As he pulled himself up the face of the rock, he heard the mountain spirit warning him to stay away. Its voice was the whispering wind, which grew stronger and seemed to be trying to push him back. With determination, Muskawashee climbed. High above, the powerful eagle circled its nest.

Just over a metre below the ledge, Muskawashee paused. He was dripping with perspiration from fighting the wind and the mountain. Though scared, he would not let fear overcome him. His desire for manhood was stronger. His hands were hurting and covered in blood from the climb, but he reached out again. After several scrabbling attempts, he was able to grab hold of the ledge and pull himself up onto the narrow, flat edge. Eye to eye with two baby eagles, he stopped. He felt great pride and relief in having reached his goal, and stood there savouring those feelings. He didn't hear the approach of the mother eagle. As she landed on the ledge in front of him, she let out a loud screech and spread her wings wide. Muskawashee was startled, stepped back, and lost his footing. A gust of wind shoved him further, and he could feel his body in the air as he tried to get a foot back on the rock. He grabbed the edge, but his arms were trembling and he could not pull himself back up. His fingers ached and began slipping from the edge. Knowing he would soon fall, he began whimpering. He looked up, into the eyes of the eagle. One day, he thought to himself, he would be back.

His fingers let go and he fell, releasing a loud, terrifying scream that echoed from the mountain, far out across the land, and down through time.

❖ ❖ ❖

McNabb and one of the counsellors left the camp when the eight-year-old girl told them what she had seen. Both experienced hikers and mountain climbers, they were able to cover the distance in a third of the time it took Jason. When they heard the scream, they quickened their pace. Minutes later, they reached the edge of the tree line and looked up at the ledge.

Jason, who had been hanging there for several minutes, also heard the scream and looked down into the eyes of Muskawashee as he fell. Jason felt the tension in his fingers, but sensed there were greater forces keeping him there, perhaps the mountain itself was hanging on to him. Whatever it was, Jason remained high above McNabb and the counsellor, who were watching from the tree line. The wind died down and the eagle stepped back, making room for him on the ledge. Jason hoisted a foot back onto the ledge and tried again to haul himself onto the shelf.

Suddenly, he saw Muskawashee standing on the ledge, extending a hand down to him. Jason grabbed his hand and Muskawashee pulled. The two boys faced one another, looking into each other's eyes. The descendent gaining pride in being Cree, and the ancestor completing the quest he had begun hundreds of years earlier. A powerful swirl of wind swept Muskawashee away, leaving Jason alone before the eagle's nest. Jason reached down and picked up a feather out of the nest.

Below him stood the counsellor and McNabb. They had witnessed Jason's rescue.

"Who was that other kid up there?" asked the counsellor in disbelief.

McNabb smiled and answered, "Muskawashee. He will wander this mountain no more." Then, unravelling a long line of heavy rope he said, "Come on, let's get Jason down." ◆

1. RESPONDING TO THE STORY

a. Would you describe Jason as courageous? Give reasons for your opinion.

b. What **stereotype** does Ralph apply to Jason? Why is it unfair to label a person with a stereotypical remark? Explain.

c. Why does Jason feel he must prove to *himself,* as well as to Ralph, that he has a Cree heritage?

d. What finally makes Jason give in to peer pressure, although it means risking his life? Have you experienced or witnessed something similar? What was the situation?

e. Just before he falls, Muskawashee tells himself that one day he will be back. Was he right? What enables him to return?

f. At the end of the story, when Jason and Muskawashee are together, what is the author suggesting about the connection between "descendants" and "ancestors"?

> A **stereotype** is an oversimplified idea about a group of people. It gives them all the same characteristics instead of considering each person as a unique individual.

2. LANGUAGE CONVENTIONS STRONG VERBS

Strong verbs are the backbone of good adventure stories. Compare these sentences:

> **Weak:** He feared he would <u>fall</u> straight down the cliff.
> **Strong:** He feared he would <u>plummet</u> straight down the cliff.

The second sentence uses the strong verb *plummet* from "A Mountain Legend," on page 47. It creates a more vivid picture than *falls*.

Reread the story and identify verbs that create vivid pictures or convey excitement. Write down each example in context: "the sunset <u>dripped</u> over the rock walls." Next, look through a piece of your own writing and find five examples of verbs you could improve. Ask a classmate for feedback on your revisions.

3. ORAL COMMUNICATION STORYTELLING

In "A Mountain Legend," the counsellors tell stories around the campfire. Now it's your turn to be the storyteller. Find a book of legends and choose one legend to tell to the class. Pick one that is short enough for you to remember easily, or boil it down to its essential details. (Use McNabb's legend, on page 42, as a model.)

Here are some ideas that can help you with your storytelling:

- Pick out the major events in the plot. Too many details may make your story difficult for your listeners to follow.
- When you practise your story, tell it from start to finish as completely as you can. It's not necessary to memorize the legend word for word.
- Vary the tone of your voice as you are speaking, and pause occasionally to create suspense or emphasize something.
- If you use gestures, keep them simple and natural.

SELF-ASSESSMENT: When you told your legend, did you speak clearly and loudly? Did you vary your tone of voice appropriately to keep your audience interested?

4. READING FLASHBACKS

Near the end of "A Mountain Legend," the author interrupts Jason's story with a **flashback** that tells the story of Muskawashee. Notice that the print changes from one type font to another one (that looks like this). What is the purpose of this change in appearance? Reread the flashback. With a partner, discuss why the author might have included the flashback. Do you think the flashback makes the story stronger? List the positive and/or negative aspects you discuss, and then share your ideas with the class.

> A **flashback** is a self-contained scene inserted into a story; the flashback tells about something that happened before the main story began.

HOW TO WRITE A PERSONAL NARRATIVE

Goals at a Glance

● Relate personal experiences. ● Seek feedback and revise writing.

A personal narrative is a true story about yourself. It tells others who you are and what you have experienced in your life. Personal narratives are most interesting when the author *shows* what he or she is like, instead of telling. As Mark Twain wrote, "Don't tell me the old lady screamed. Bring her on and have her scream!"

Gather Information about Yourself

This is enjoyable and easy. After all, you are the expert! Here are some suggestions:

- Gather some objects that remind you of interesting moments in your life: old photos, special gifts, prizes, items you've collected, and so on.
- In a notebook, jot down your memories of funny, exciting, or scary incidents.
- Ask others for tales they remember about trips you have taken or special events you have participated in—any stories they might know in more detail than you do.

- Make a timeline of the important events in your life.

Plan Your Narrative

Before you start writing you must select a specific topic. Which story about yourself would be most interesting for other readers? It may be something that had a great impact on you, or a humorous event, or a learning experience that you will never forget.

Next, you should make an outline of your narrative. Use simple headings for your outline. A four-paragraph narrative about a visit to Vietnam might have an outline like this:

- opening paragraph: "hook" my readers
- first paragraph: describe arrival in Vietnam
- second paragraph: tell about meeting Vietnamese relatives
- third paragraph: describe getting lost in market
- fourth paragraph: tell how I was found
- closing sentence: wrap things up

PROCESS

Write a Draft

The key to interesting storytelling is to provide details about the place, the people, and the events—and your feelings about them. Why? Because your reader needs to understand everything clearly. Here are some other hints:

- Start a new paragraph for each change of topic or event.
- Include conversation, if it suits your story.
- Show, don't tell!

Ask for Feedback

Set up a writing conference with a partner. In a writing conference, you can ask for help with specific problems. Your partner will help by asking questions and making suggestions, for example:

WRITER: I'm not sure how to end my narrative.

READER: Why don't you tell how you felt when you said goodbye to your relatives at the airport?

Revise Your Narrative

After your conference, it's time to revise your work.

- Consider your partner's suggestions and make the appropriate changes.
- When you revise, it helps to read your work aloud or have someone else read it to you. Does the writing truly sound like you? If not, revise it so that it sounds more authentic.
- Pay attention to sentence structure. Starting every sentence with "I" can be boring. You can add variety by beginning with a phrase or clause, for example: "I ran like an Olympic sprinter when I saw that bear," becomes "When I saw that bear, I ran like an Olympic sprinter."

Edit Your Writing

Take care of spelling problems using a dictionary and/or a spell checker, and then look for grammar and punctuation mistakes. Don't hesitate to ask for assistance from your teacher and classmates. When you are satisfied with your story, make a neat final draft.

Publish Your Personal Narrative

You might share your personal narrative

- in a class anthology, illustrated with photos
- in the school newspaper or literary magazine
- by reading it aloud to friends and family
- by submitting it to a contest or a Web site that publishes student writing

Self-Assessment

Use the following checklist to reflect on the process you followed.

- ❑ I thought about possible topics and selected the best one.
- ❑ I created an outline for my narrative.
- ❑ When my draft was complete, I got feedback from a partner.
- ❑ I read my narrative aloud to help me revise it.
- ❑ I edited my writing for spelling and grammar errors before completing the final draft.

PROCESS

To her sister, Roberta Bondar has demonstrated true courage many times. As you read this profile, decide for yourself which experience from Roberta's life shows the most courage.

COURAGE in Orbit

Personal Essay by Barbara Bondar

Mine was always a pretty nifty kid sister. When we played together with the rest of the neighbour-hood kids, she was a reliable teammate, inventive and competitive. When we were on the same team, that team needed only two. Anytime. The two of us against the world, and we always won everything.

In high school we were split up. When our teams met then, it was tough work trying to win a game. That was about the first time I paid attention to the kid's courage. She was a grade behind me when she fell in love with basketball in Grade Nine. She tried out for the junior team and didn't make it. We spent the summer playing basketball. When she tried out in Grade Ten for the junior team, she didn't make it either—because they placed her on the senior team!

Well into her astronaut training, she taught me much more about courage.

Courage is putting your life on hold for eight years to train for a single mission that will take eight days. You never get the time back from those eight years to meet friends you might have met or spend it with family and friends you love. So when your father dies, and then your uncle, and then your grandmother, and then your crewmate, you know they will never be there to see what you've worked so long for. And you stick with it anyway because they knew you'd never let them down.

Courage is training with six big, strong guys who are fighter and helicopter pilots and experienced astronauts. But you made the senior basketball team back in Grade Ten, so you gave them a run for their money every single day.

Courage is learning new things in the sciences you did not study in

university in front of the best scientists in the world and knowing if you fail, you won't get to fly. But you impress them, so they choose you to do their experiments on the space shuttle.

Courage is wrapping your arm tightly around your sister's waist the day before the launch, knowing this could be the last time you are together. The arm is tight to pass your courage through to her and from her to your family. And to keep you both from crying.

Courage is knowing that if something goes wrong, you are strapped to a bomb, and nothing and no one can save you. And you go anyway. Willingly. Because it's your chance to learn and do things that will

"As I look down, across, and above from the flight-deck window, the shining planet curves from left to right. I have never in my life seen anything as big as this."

make life a little better for people on Earth.

Courage is being nauseated in microgravity for many hours and working longer than your shift to get things done with a smile on your face so that your family, watching you on television 250 km below, won't worry about you.

Courage is trying to walk when you land when every part of your body feels like cement and just wants to go to sleep. You keep trying to move. Even when no one is watching, you still do it.

Courage is returning to Earth, working even harder, going with even less sleep for months, answering everyone's questions.

And, finally, courage is never mentioning how much courage it takes to do every one of these things.

Lifeline of an Astronaut

When Roberta Bondar boarded the space shuttle *Discovery* in January 1992, she became Canada's first woman in space and fulfilled a lifelong dream. Her career is a tribute to the value of setting lofty goals, and approaching life with imagination and courage.

1945 — born on December 4 in Sault Ste. Marie, Ontario

1954 — built plastic models of rockets, space stations, and satellites, often gazing up at the stars to imagine how Earth would look from space

1968 — received a Bachelor of Science degree in zoology and agriculture

1971 — obtained a Master of Science degree

1974 — received a doctorate in neurobiology

1977 — became a medical doctor

1981 — graduated as a specialist in neurology

1983 — was one of the six original Canadian astronauts selected for space research

1984 — began astronaut training in the United States

1992 — studied how the human body reacts to weightlessness as Payload Specialist on the *Discovery* mission

1995 — co-wrote *Touching the Earth,* a book containing her reflections on space and Earth.

Today Bondar uses knowledge gained from experiments in space in her ongoing research into the treatment of disease. She enjoys hiking, biking, flying, parachuting, and scuba diving. An accomplished photographer, her current goal is to photograph all of Canada's national parks.

OTHER CANADIANS IN SPACE

WHO	WHEN	WHAT THEY DID
MARC GARNEAU	October 1984	• helped crew deploy Earth Radiation Budget Satellite
	May 1996	• helped deploy two satellites and performed biotechnology experiments
STEVE MACLEAN	October 1992	• conducted Space Vision Systems test using the Canadarm
CHRIS HADFIELD	November 1995	• served on NASA's second mission to rendezvous with Russian Space Station Mir
BOB THIRSK	June 1996	• studied life and materials science
BJARNI TRYGGVASON	August 1997	• explored the behaviour of materials fluids in space
DAVID WILLIAMS	April 1998	• conducted experiments on the effect of microgravity on the brain and nervous system
JULIE PAYETTE	May 1999	• participated in an International Space Station assembly mission

At the end of her mission, reporters asked Julie Payette where she might travel on her summer vacation. Her reply: "Somewhere on Earth!"

1. RESPONDING TO THE ESSAY

a. When did Barbara Bondar first notice her sister Roberta's courageous spirit? What does that story about Roberta tell you about her character?

b. In your notebook, list at least five ways in which Roberta was courageous. Compare your list with a partner's.

c. What are some of the sacrifices Roberta made to become an astronaut? What do you think the hardest sacrifice would have been? Explain.

d. Read the final sentence of the essay. Explain to a partner what you think Barbara means.

2. READING SIDEBARS

In many books and magazines, information is set aside in special boxes, sometimes referred to as *sidebars.* Although this information is separated from the main part of the text, it is often interesting or important. Read the sidebar entitled "Lifeline of an Astronaut." With a partner, discuss the different things you learned about Roberta by reading the sidebar. Did the new information change your ideas about her? Explain.

3. RESEARCHING OBTAIN INFORMATION

Roberta Bondar has done something that very few other people have experienced—she has travelled in space. In "Courage in Orbit," we are told a little about what it takes to become an astronaut. Through research, you can find out more about the training of astronauts, or about Roberta Bondar, or one of the other Canadian astronauts. Select a focus for your research and make a list of the things you would like to know. Next, do some research to find out the answers to your questions. You might want to start by checking out the NASA Web site on the Internet.

   Use your findings to create "Did You Know?" cards for an astronaut display board—for example, "Did you know that astronauts are not allowed to eat broccoli while on the shuttle?"

SELF-ASSESSMENT: Did you use the Internet to conduct your research? If so, what are some of the advantages and disadvantages of using the Internet to gather information?

SELF-ASSESSMENT: WRITING

As you worked on activities in this unit what did you learn about

- writing personal narratives?
- creating biographical profiles?
- crafting a poem?
- writing a sequel?
- using strong verbs?
- punctuating dialogue?
- revising and editing?

Select and reread one draft piece of writing you worked on during this unit. Write notes on your draft, showing how you could improve it.

ORAL COMMUNICATION GIVE A SPEECH

Imagine that you are one of the people or characters you have read about in this unit. (Select whichever one interests you most.) Make notes about what that person might think and feel about being courageous. In your role as that person, write a speech that gives advice about finding courage in difficult situations. Deliver your speech to an audience of your peers.

VISUAL COMMUNICATION CREATE AN IMAGE

Choose one person from your own life who you think is courageous. Tell others about this person's courage in a visual way, for example, through a poster, a collage, an advertisement, or a scrapbook. You can either create the visual(s) yourself, or look for appropriate images—paintings or photos from books or magazines, for instance. Write a caption that tells about the person you chose and explains why the visual is appropriate.

MEDIA CONNECT WITH MOVIES

After reading this unit, how would you define courage? Courage is also a favourite theme in movies. Make a list of five movies that you have seen in which courage, as portrayed in this unit, is important. As a class, create a Top Ten List of movies about courage. Together, discuss the different kinds of courage in these movies. Do you think certain kinds of courage are shown more frequently than others? Discuss some possible reasons.

INNOVATIONS

"Intelligence
consists of
recognizing opportunity."
Chinese Proverb

INNOVATIONS

THINK OUTSIDE THE BOX

To You

Poem by Langston Hughes

To sit and dream, to sit and read,

To sit and learn about the world

Outside our world of here and now—

Our problem world—

To dream of vast horizons of the soul

Through dreams made whole,

Unfettered, free—help me!

All you who are dreamers too,

Help me to make

Our world anew.

I reach out my dreams to you.

RESPONDING TO THE POEM

a. What does the line "To dream of vast horizons of the soul" suggest to you?

b. What is the poem asking you, the reader, to do?

c. What ideas do you think the poet had in mind when he wrote this poem? Discuss your opinion with a classmate.

d. The poet suggests that you not only "sit and dream," but also "sit and read" and "learn about the world/Outside our world of here and now." In what ways do you think that reading and learning can help to change the world?

GOALS AT A GLANCE

■ Respond critically to poetry.
■ Relate literature to personal experience.

When a team with vision gets together, anything is possible. Even creating...

A Spider for the Bones

ARTICLE BY SHEREE HAUGHIAN

Finding a cure for a disease is a task for highly trained research scientists, right? Not always! Four teenaged girls from Vancouver have challenged the belief that only adults make medical breakthroughs. They've created an award-winning idea that may someday improve life for many people.

Patricia Lau, Robin Massel, Olivia Maginley, and Katie Mogan are grade nine students at Point Grey Mini School. Their invention won top place in their division of Toshiba's ExploraVision contest for 1999. This competition asks young inventors to select an area of research that has meaning in their own lives—such as medicine or the environment—then to design an invention. The hope is that the invention could actually be built by the year 2020, as technology advances.

The four teens decided to develop a treatment for osteoporosis, a disease in which a person's bones become brittle and fragile. Osteoporosis is most common among older women, and Robin Massel's grandmother has the condition. Watching someone she loved begin to break bones helped Robin realize how important it was to find a remedy.

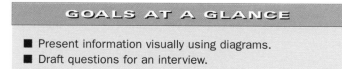

GOALS AT A GLANCE

- Present information visually using diagrams.
- Draft questions for an interview.

"Osteoporosis is a major problem. As females we're at high risk to get it some day," says Patricia Lau. "As well, 1999 was named the Year of the Elderly by the United Nations."

Although they chose to tackle a very difficult problem, the girls insist they had a fantastic time working on the project.

Robin organized the team. Her group had won second place the previous year, and she was determined to make another try for the top prize. In September, 1998, she asked three friends to join her.

Olivia is a talented writer who helped with the research and writing. Katie provided the illustrations for the storyboards they submitted with their entry, and Patricia designed the computer graphics. Robin's previous experience earned her the role of group leader. Recognizing each other's strengths contributed to the team's success.

The would-be inventors haunted libraries, probed the Internet, and even obtained advice from a medical specialist. But some of their greatest support came from closer to home. Robin's mother, Lynn Massel, acted as community sponsor for the group. A science teacher herself, she oversaw their meetings every Friday and helped them direct their research. She suggested the girls break up their project into tasks that could be more easily managed.

The team's science and math teacher, John O'Connor, was also on hand with guidance and support. Point Grey Mini School is home to many innovative projects supervised by Mr. O'Connor. He gives particular praise to this group of students.

"Intellectual ability is not enough," he remarks. "The students who really succeed also have to be self-directed and tolerant of each other. This team had those qualities."

Keeping the project on track wasn't always easy. Finding time to meet presented a challenge. The teens also discovered that inventing involves trial, error, and yet more trial. Sometimes the ideas they came up with just wouldn't work.

"We originally thought of using plastic to harden the bones," says Patricia. "But when we found out plastic would be rejected by the body, we had to come up with something else."

So what did the four girls invent? It's a high-tech solution called WEBS (Woven Engineered Bone System).

Storyboard for the WEBS Video

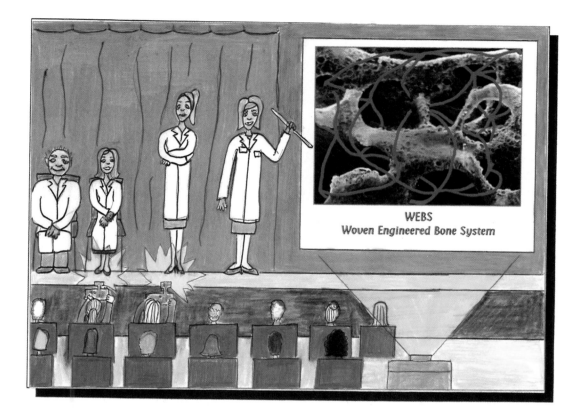

WEBS
Woven Engineered Bone System

"We, the scientists, are very excited to present WEBS to you at this press conference. It took many years of research and collaboration to come up with this technology. We made major breakthroughs to create the WEBS. The titanium alloy Tibond was created to be magnetic, and form very strong bonds once in the correct position. We created Cartigel as the vehicle for Tibond to move to the inside of the porous bone. Our next challenge was the Spider, which photographed the inside of the bone, and then created a force field to line the Tibond in the three-dimensional web position, and finally fixed the WEBS in place. This slide shows the amazing WEBS in the bone."

Here's how their treatment should work—when the medical technology of the future catches up.

First, a substance the girls call "cartigel" is injected into a patient with osteoporosis. Cartigel contains special material to harden bones. The patient then steps into a tubular chamber called a "spider." The spider is hooked up to a computer, which reveals an image of the inside of the patient's bones. An electromagnetic field around the spider puts the cartigel into place. Finally, a low-voltage electrical current transforms the cartigel into a solid, three-dimensional web inside the bones. When the patient exits the spider chamber, he or she has stronger bones.

In spite of the cheering sections at home and school, the process of creating something new took its toll on the girls. They began the project in early October. By winter, their red-hot enthusiasm had cooled. But they persevered and were ready to submit their idea in early February. When they learned it had won the regional level of the competition, excitement spurred them on.

The next step was to create a video about their WEBS invention. They had six weeks to do it. Showing yet more creative flair, they decided to film themselves playing the roles of characters who discover a cure for osteoporosis! Then there was nothing to do but wait —until they found out that they were the winners. In early June, the girls flew to Washington, D.C. with their families and teacher to accept their award. Each girl received $10 000. The money will go toward further education, but the experience they gained has no price tag.

The competition sponsor now owns their idea, which may be used in the future. "We don't think it will happen exactly as we described it in our project. Scientists may actually get it to work another way," Patricia comments.

According to the girls, being young can be an advantage when it comes to inventing. When you're fifteen, or thirteen, or eleven, you believe that anything is still possible. An open mind allows a free flow of new ideas.

"We're naive, and that can be an advantage," says Katie. "If you want to create something, just go for it. It's a lot of fun."

"If you have an idea," echoes Patricia, "don't let anyone stop you from trying it. Follow your dreams."

1. RESPONDING TO THE ARTICLE

a. With a partner, create a list of what you think are the key reasons for the girls' success.

b. What motivated the girls to develop their specific invention? What aspects of the girls' submission do you think would have captured the interest of the contest judges?

c. Do you think that the girls would have achieved as much working individually? Explain. Have you ever been part of an effective team? What made your team work well? What could your team have done better?

2. VISUAL COMMUNICATION CREATE DIAGRAMS

In a small group, make a list of common diseases and disabilities. Together, brainstorm ideas for an invention that would help a person who is coping with one of those diseases or disabilities. (You might want to do some general research about the disease or disability first.) When you have come up with your invention, draw diagrams that illustrate what it might look like and explain how it would work. Label your diagrams carefully and write captions for them. Present your invention to the class, using your visuals to help you communicate your ideas.

SELF-ASSESSMENT: Before you make your presentation, look carefully at your diagrams. Do they clearly show how your invention works? Is there enough detail in each diagram? Are your labels and captions easy to read and understand? If necessary, revise your diagrams to make them more effective.

3. MEDIA DRAFT INTERVIEW QUESTIONS

Imagine that you are a journalist who has been asked to write an in-depth magazine article about the girls' invention. You have arranged to interview the four inventors so you can gather information for your article. What questions would you ask? Reread the article, especially the parts in which the invention is described. Draft the ten questions that would best help you learn about all the different aspects of the invention. Give each question a specific focus so the response will provide the details you need.

*A boy's inventive photographs
are still admired a century
after they were taken.
What makes them so special?*

Photographer *at Play*

Profile by John Cech • Photographs by Jacques-Henri Lartigue

Nearly a hundred years ago, long before Polaroids and Instamatics, a French boy named Jacques-Henri Lartigue began taking photographs for the sheer, pure fun of it. Many of these pictures, made between the time he was seven and seventeen years old, are now among the world's great photographs.

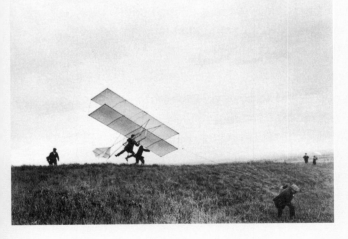

Born in 1894, the youngest son of a well-to-do businessman, Jacques-Henri grew up around the many remarkable new inventions (such as automobiles, airplanes, and cameras) that were filling the roads, the skies, and people's imaginations in the years before World War I. In France, this period of prosperity and luxury was called *La Belle Époque*, "the beautiful time."

In 1904, a few months before his tenth birthday, Lartigue took the only picture of one of the first glider flights in France. Notice that he waited until the glider had completely left the ground before he took his picture.

GOALS AT A GLANCE

- Brainstorm ideas.
- Plan and take photos.

The Lartigues were a large, wealthy, fun-loving family that could easily afford the latest advances in automotive or photographic technology. And they had the leisure time to enjoy them in their Paris home or at one of the country estates where they lived during the summers. The Lartigues, along with their many relatives and friends, seemed always to be on the move and at play. They built go-carts and scooters, launched floating watercraft in their swimming pool, flew hot air balloons and kites, and even made their own airplanes.

Lartigue's father, Henri, was an enthusiastic amateur photographer, and when other kids might have been trying to learn to ride a bike, Jacques-Henri was busy following his father around and learning how to take and develop photographs. For his seventh birthday, his father gave Jacques-Henri the smallest of his cameras. Still, with the tripod needed to hold it steady, it weighed nearly twenty-five kilograms. The pictures were taken on the small glass plates that most cameras used instead of film. The camera was very expensive and the best available at the time.

Jacques-Henri thought photography was a miracle; everything was asking to have its picture taken and, he announced, "I will take them all." He ran through plates (and later film) so fast that his mother joked that he would bankrupt the family. (By the time he died in 1986 at the age of ninety-two, Lartigue had taken several hundred thousand pictures.)

In the next few years he got better cameras that could take faster pictures. This was especially important to him because what Jacques-Henri

To take this self-portrait in 1904, Jacques-Henri floated his camera on a board in the bathtub. After carefully focussing the camera, he lowered himself into the water, waited for the ripples to calm down, then called his mother to come in and snap the shutter.

liked most was to take pictures of things and people in motion, things moving fast.

Innovations

Look carefully at Lartigue's pictures and you will notice how unusual most of them are. Jacques-Henri had learned a lot about photography from his father; he could judge distance and light perfectly, long before cameras did it automatically.

Once Jacques-Henri mastered the basics of photography, he felt free to experiment. And his father encouraged his creative independence. Jacques-Henri followed his own instincts and looked for what interested him in a subject, a camera angle, a kind of light, a mood. Since he was taking these pictures for himself, he could photograph whatever he thought was interesting, funny, or important.

This picture, taken in 1905, is a double exposure (two pictures on the same frame of film) of Zissou, Jacques-Henri's brother. He's lying on a bench in the background, waving at the camera, and also appears in the foreground as a ghost.

A Contrast of Style

Lartigue realized early that a photograph could be quite different from the formal, posed portraits that most photographers were taking at the time. In fact, most of the photographs we take today still follow the traditional look-at-the-camera-hold-still-and-say-cheese approach. But Jacques-Henri brought something unique and fresh to his photographs—drama, humour, and, above all, motion. Lartigue didn't ask people to hold still when he took a photograph. He wanted to show people moving, jumping, and flying. By the time he was nine years old, he had a camera that used film and could take a picture in a hundredth of a second, instead of the three seconds or more it sometimes took for a glass plate to capture an image. These photographic improvements made it possible for Jacques-Henri to take his candid, energetic snapshots.

A stiff, formal photograph of the time.

The shot of his cousin, Bichonnade, soaring gracefully as she turns to smile at the camera, has become one of Lartigue's most famous pictures. It expresses, in one image, the spirit of play that Lartigue brought to all of his work.

Taking a Picture

Careful and skilled as he was, Jacques-Henri soon found out that he could never be completely certain he would get the photograph he wanted. So in his journal he made small drawings of the photos he had taken in case they didn't turn out or develop correctly. Jacques-Henri kept a journal from the time he began to write, and in it he recorded the activities of his busy days, which often began before dawn.

As his artistry matured, Jacques-Henri realized that sometimes it took a number of tries (like drafts for a story or sketches for a painting) to get the perfect shot. Happily, the subjects of his photographs, who were often family and friends, dusted themselves off and obliged the budding artist with another try.◆

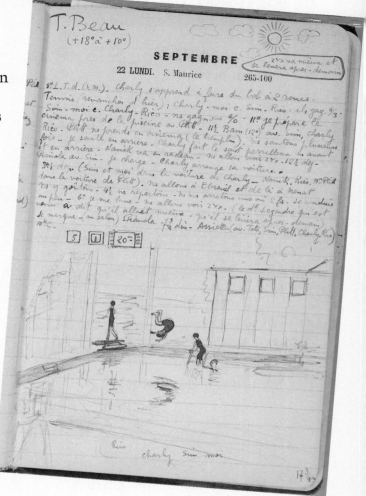

This page from Jacques-Henri's journal describes the day's events, which included tennis and swimming. He also sketched a photograph that he took of a friend jumping into a pool.

People in motion—Lartigue's specialty. The diver looks very similar to the man drawn in the journal.

1. RESPONDING TO THE PROFILE

a. Which of Jacques-Henri Lartigue's photos do you find most innovative? Why?

b. How do his photos compare with most of the photos that are taken by ordinary people today? Explain.

c. What factors in Jacques-Henri's life made it possible for him to pursue his hobby?

2. MEDIA TAKE ACTION PHOTOS

Most of us take snapshots of friends or family standing still in front of an interesting scene. But Jacques-Henri shows us that photos of people in action can be much more interesting. On your own or with a partner, take some innovative photos of people in motion. If you don't own a camera, borrow one from a friend or the school. Alternatively, you can buy a disposable camera. Before you start, try Jacques-Henri's idea of sketching the pictures you would like to capture. Don't be afraid to take many shots in order to get one good one—that's what professionals do! Make a class display of your action photos. Hint: High-speed film (such as 400 ASA) is best for action shots.

SELF-ASSESSMENT: Did your photos turn out as you hoped? If not, how would you change your techniques or subject matter to improve your photos?

3. LANGUAGE CONVENTIONS ADJECTIVES AND ADVERBS

Effective **adjectives** and **adverbs** can make your writing more interesting and exciting, creating a clear picture for the reader.

> **Weak:** *Good* snapshots express emotion *nicely*.
> **Stronger:** *Candid, energetic* snapshots express emotion *perfectly*.

Reread "Photographer at Play" and find several examples of adjectives and adverbs that help to create a vivid picture of what is taking place. Check a piece of your own writing to see whether you have used adjectives and adverbs appropriately and creatively.

> An **adjective** is a word that modifies (or describes) a noun or pronoun. An **adverb** is a word that modifies a verb, an adjective, or another adverb.

4. WRITER'S CRAFT BRAINSTORM IDEAS

How did Jacques-Henri's father encourage his son's creativity? Write your ideas in your notebook, and then make this list the start of a brainstorming session on the topic "How to Be Inventive."

When you brainstorm, you want to bring out all the ideas you have on a subject. Here are some suggestions:

- Doodling, drawing, and free-writing can help you to come up with ideas. To free-write, just write quickly without thinking about grammar or sentences. The goal is to get down as many ideas as possible by letting your mind wander freely.
- Creating a web can help you to organize your ideas. For example:

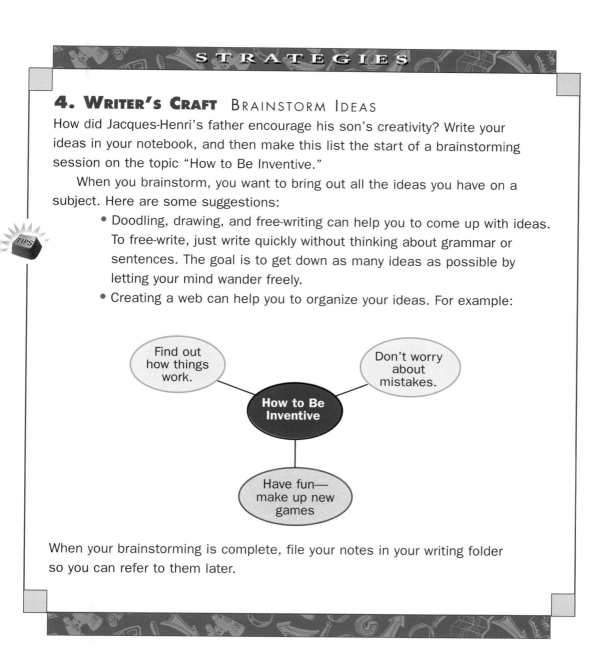

When your brainstorming is complete, file your notes in your writing folder so you can refer to them later.

Who gets the credit for the "crunch" of a McIntosh apple, the "bounce" of a Jolly Jumper, or the "WOW!" of an IMAX movie? Canadians!

Eureka!
We've Done It!

Article by Winston Collins

Quickly now, what do the telephone and the zipper have in common? Yes, they are both things we use daily. And yes, it's hard to imagine life without them. But there's another correct answer as well: both the telephone and the zipper are Canadian inventions. Which of the following items were also invented by Canadians?

- the paint roller
- the snowblower
- the Jolly Jumper
- the baby seat
- five-pin bowling
- the electronic organ
- instant mashed potatoes

As you probably suspected, that was a trick question, because the answer is...all of them are Canadian inventions.

A more difficult challenge would be to identify the names of the men and women who invented these items. While inventions are essential parts of our everyday lives, we seldom consider the fact that someone actually had the creative inspiration and practical ability to bring these things into our lives—such as Norman Breakey of Toronto, who invented the paint roller; Arthur Sicard of rural Quebec, who invented the snowblower; and Olivia Poole of North Vancouver, who invented the Jolly Jumper.

Many Canadian inventions have become as common and indispensable as Alexander Graham Bell's telephone and Gideon Sundback's zipper. The time shown on our clocks is set to an international standard originally conceived by Canadian inventor Sir Sandford Fleming. When we eat McIntosh apples, Pablum, frozen fish, or instant mashed potatoes, we're consuming food products that originated in this country.

Canadian inventors have also provided us with a wide variety of fun and games: basketball, five-pin bowling, table hockey, the Laser sailboat, and Trivial Pursuit.

Inventions make day-to-day living more convenient, comfortable, and enjoyable. We live easier, happier, and altogether better lives because Canadians have created (and continue to create) new and better ways of doing things—whether it's painting walls, clearing snow, listening to the radio, caring for the baby, or communicating over long distances with family and friends. Our health is improved and our lives are prolonged because of breakthroughs by Canadian medical researchers who invent new drugs and treatments for diseases. In short, our lifestyles and the very quality of our lives themselves owe a great deal to our nation's inventors.

The Inventive Drive

Why do people invent? One answer is because we must. It has been said that human inventiveness is a response to the fact that we are physically ill-equipped creatures. While animals have sharp teeth and claws to protect themselves, humans must rely on their brain power to mould the environment to their well-being.

Satisfying human needs is undoubtedly the single greatest motivator for inventors past and present. Natural curiosity and creative desire also help explain why inventors invent. Technical know-how and problem-solving ability are essentials for successful inventors. As the famous inventor Thomas Edison said, "Genius is one percent inspiration and ninety-nine percent perspiration."

Who Are the Inventors Now?

While the human need to create new and better ways of doing things has remained constant, the nature of inventing has gone through a recent change. Until well into the twentieth century, virtually every invention resulted from an individual working alone. Today, however, most inventions come about through teams of specialists working together in corporate, university, or government research laboratories. Nevertheless, the lone inventor is still alive and well in Canada. A federal government study once noted that half the people in this country have the right stuff to be inventors—but only one in a thousand ever attempts to invent anything.

Somewhere in Canada right now there are homemakers, welders, business executives—as well as single parents, high-school students, and retired seniors—at work on some kind of invention. Only a few of them will ultimately introduce the public to new and better ways of doing things. Still, their collective spirit of inventiveness deserves to be encouraged and recognized as the essential social and economic dynamo it is.

Would you really choose to live without a telephone or the zipper? And wouldn't you be pleased to have a better light bulb—or mousetrap—in your home? Thanks to inventors, that too will come to pass.

Quiz

*Check your knowledge of
Canadian inventions.
Record your answers
in your notebook.*

❶ What board game created by Canadians Scott Abbott and Chris Haney became a best-selling mind-teaser around the world in the 1980s?

  a. Scrabble

  b. Vancouver Stock Exchange

  c. Trivial Pursuit

❷ Nearly 200 years ago, a Canadian named John McIntosh hit upon something that would make "McIntosh" a household name at home and abroad. What was it?

  a. A kind of apple

  b. A kind of computer

  c. A kind of raincoat

❸ Canadian medical researchers Charles Best and Frederick Banting discovered what lifesaving therapy for diabetes in the 1920s?

  a. Insulin

  b. Aspirin

  c. Sugar-free chocolate

❹ First Nations cradle boards inspired Olivia Poole to create which invention?

  a. The skateboard

  b. The car seat

  c. The Jolly Jumper

❺ Sir Sandford Fleming, an inventor and engineer who came to Canada from Scotland, is credited with introducing international standard time. In 1851, he designed a now commonplace item that was then the first of its kind in Canada. What was it?

  a. The gas barbecue

  b. The postage stamp

  c. The loonie

❻ Harriet Brooks Pitcher made pioneering discoveries about radioactivity. What was her profession?

  a. Doctor

  b. Chemist

  c. Nuclear physicist

❼ James Naismith, a physical education instructor who hailed from Almonte, Ontario, invented a whole new ball game in 1891. What was it?

  a. Baseball

  b. Basketball

  c. Table tennis

❽ Pablum, the first precooked cereal for babies, was developed in Canada in the 1930s by the three-person team of Frederick Tisdall, Theodore Drake, and Alan Brown. What was their profession?

  a. Doctors at the Hospital for Sick Children, Toronto

  b. Food scientists at the University of Alberta, Edmonton

  c. Chefs at the Ritz Carlton Hotel, Montréal

To check your answers, see page 350.

Time Line

DAME FELICITÉ MARAIS of Montreal was the first woman in Canada to receive a patent. In 1866 she invented a revolutionary cleaning solution, which she called "English Cleansing Fluid."

ELIJAH McCOY was born in Canada, educated in Scotland, and employed in the United States. His most famous invention, developed in 1882, was an automatic lubricator for train engines. In all, he patented fifty ideas. His name became famous for high quality and gave us the phrase "the real McCoy."

HARRIET BROOKS PITCHER, a nuclear physicist, was a pioneer in the area of radioactivity. Between 1901 and 1905 she identified the first step in the process of radioactive decay.

DR. CLUNY McPHERSON of St. John's, Newfoundland and Labrador, invented the gas mask in 1915 to protect Allied soldiers against poison gas in World War I.

ARTHUR SICARD, who grew up on a Québec farm, developed the snowblower in 1925.

DON MUNRO

patented the Table Top Hockey Game in 1932; his small Ontario company became the largest manufacturer of table-top hockey games in the world.

OLIVIA POOLE invented

the Jolly Jumper during the 1950s. Her internationally popular baby seat was inspired by the cradle boards suspended from tree branches that she remembered from growing up on a First Nations reservation.

ROLAND GALARNEAU

of Hull, Québec, invented a computerized method of translating printed text into Braille in 1972. Nearly blind since birth, Galarneau built a special computer in his basement workshop for the six-year project.

The IMAX projector was developed in the 1960s by **WILLIAM CHESTER SHAW** of Ontario. With a screen six storeys high and six-track stereo from eighty-eight speakers, IMAX movies surround the viewer; you are part of the action!

WENDY MURPHY, a medical research technician in Toronto, designed and developed the world's first evacuation stretcher for babies. The Weevac 6 (so named because it can transport six wee babies) has been purchased by hospitals around the world since the first one was produced in 1989.

1. RESPONDING TO THE ARTICLE

a. Were you surprised by the many inventions Canadians have made? Why or why not?

b. Which invention mentioned in the article is the one you think we could not live without? Support your opinion.

c. Why do people invent? Find at least three reasons given in the article. Do you agree that these are the reasons? Explain. Can you think of any other reasons why we invent things? Discuss your ideas with a partner.

d. Why do you think most of today's inventions are developed by "teams of specialists" rather than by lone inventors? Discuss your ideas with a partner.

2. WORD CRAFT USE TERMINOLOGY

The following words and phrases from the article are all closely related to the idea of invention: *creative inspiration, practical ability, indispensable, conceived, breakthroughs,* and *dynamo*. Add five other invention-related words to your list. In your notebook, use each word in its own sentence about inventiveness. Use your dictionary if you need help with meanings.

3. WRITING TIME LINES

Review the time line of Canadian inventions. What are the features of a time line? Why is a time line a good way to present the history of a subject like inventions?

Choose one of the following topics and create your own illustrated time line:
- The Story of My Life
- How I Learned to Swim (Ride a Bike, Speak Another Language...)
- Places I've Been
- Your own idea

Share your time line with your class, discussing the events you've chosen to highlight.

SELF-ASSESSMENT: Look over your time line. Does each entry include an accurate date and a brief description of the event you're recording? Have you arranged the events in chronological order? Are there other important events that you now realize you should add?

4. RESEARCHING LOCATE BIOGRAPHICAL INFORMATION

Find out more about one of the inventors mentioned in "Eureka! We've Done it!" Read "How to Conduct Research" on page 86 for some ideas about finding information on a topic. Focus on collecting key biographical information about the inventor, such as birthdate and place of birth, education, interests, and achievements. You might present your findings in a brief written or oral research report.

STRATEGIES

5. ORAL COMMUNICATION PREPARE A PRESENTATION

Inventors often have to make presentations to convince people that their inventions are worthwhile. Here are some suggestions for preparing an effective presentation:

- Know your subject thoroughly and be ready to answer questions.
- Organize your information carefully so that it is easy to understand.
- Write your information in large print and in point form on cue cards or paper so that the information will be easy for you to read.
- If possible, use graphics software to prepare appealing visuals.
- Mark your notes to remind you where you want to use visuals or props.
- Ensure that any visuals you use, such as drawings, charts, or photos, are attractively displayed and large enough for your audience to see.
- Learn how to use the visual equipment you will need, and make sure it will be available for your presentation.
- Rehearse your presentation to determine how long it is and to ensure it flows smoothly. You might ask a friend to sit at the back of the room and give you feedback about your voice and the visuals.

Use the suggestions above to help you prepare a brief presentation about an invention you admire or think is necessary.

SELF-ASSESSMENT: After your rehearsal, think about the following: Was your presentation clear and smooth? Did you use visuals and props effectively? Would your audience be able to understand and see everything? What else should you do to ensure your presentation is successful?

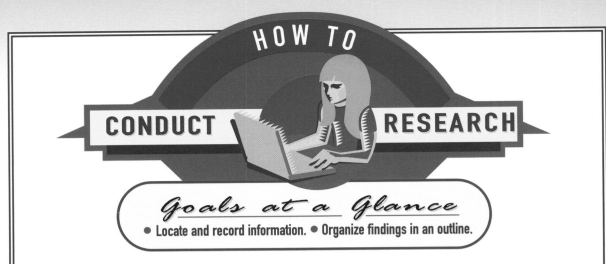

HOW TO

CONDUCT   RESEARCH

Define Your Topic

First, choose a specific topic that interests you. Let's say your teacher has identified the general subject of "Great Inventions." As a fan of aircraft, you decide that "Flying Machines" is the specific topic for you. You are sure that there is a lot of information on this topic, which is important if you want to present a good report.

Plan Your Research

Where are you going to find the information you need? Make a list of the resources you want to explore. Good resources include books, magazines, encyclopedias, the Internet, CD-ROMs, and resource people such as librarians. Make another list of key words that will help you to conduct your research into the history of flight. Key words are especially useful for library computer catalogues and the Internet. Sample key words are *flight*, *inventors*, *transportation*, *air travel*.

Collect Information

As you gather resources, you will need to decide how reliable and relevant the information is. Ask yourself questions like these:

• Is the book/magazine/Web site up to date? Check for copyright dates on printed material and on Web sites.
• Where did the information originate? The most reliable sources include museums, scientific organizations, and well-known publishers and institutions.
• Could the information be biassed? Try to determine whether the information source shows different points of view or only one.
• Does the information fit my topic? Is it easy to understand? Does it provide the right amount of detail?

Record Your Findings

As you search, take notes of the information you think you'll include in your report. It's often useful to prepare some basic questions about

PROCESS

your topic, and then write each question on a separate index card. As you find answers to each question, make point-form notes on the card. Here are some sample questions:

- What was the first successful flying machine?
- Who are some famous inventors in the history of flight?
- What were some interesting flying failures?
- When was the jet plane invented?
- What is the fastest flight ever made?

Here is a sample note card:

What was the first successful flying machine?
—first flight was in biplane called Flyer
—December 17, Kitty Hawk, North Carolina 1903
—Orville Wright lay on wings — brother Wilbur ran alongside
—rose 3m into air, flew 36m before diving into the sand

If you want to quote sentences or paragraphs in your report, write them out word for word. Include the name of the author, the source (book or magazine title, for example), the date the source was published, and the page number or Web site address.

Organize Your Information

Now it's time to arrange your information in some kind of order. You could use chronological order (a history of flying machines from the earliest times to the present), or you could focus on the flying machines that interest you most and give details about them. By sorting and re-sorting your index cards, you can experiment with different ways of organizing.

Now you are ready to make an outline. Begin with headings, spaced several lines apart. To finish your outline, add point-form details after each heading. Here are some sample headings:

A. EARLY ATTEMPTS AT FLIGHT

B. FIRST SUCCESSFUL FLIGHT

C. TWENTIETH CENTURY ADVANCES

D. THE FASTEST FLYING MACHINE EVER

E. OUTLOOK FOR THE FUTURE

If you decide to do a written research report, include these headings in your report. If you are presenting an oral report to the class, your outline will be the basis of your talk. In either case, add photos, charts, maps, diagrams, or other visuals to enhance your final presentation.

Self-Assessment

❏ I selected a specific topic that interested me.
❏ I located a variety of reliable resources.
❏ I recorded relevant information.
❏ I organized my notes and wrote an outline.
❏ I prepared my report, including interesting visuals.

PROCESS

A Different Drummer

Profile by Christine McClymont

Evelyn Glennie plays an amazing array of instruments. On stage, she leaps from instrument to instrument with the grace of a gazelle. For one piece she plays cymbals, marimba, Japanese bells, a pair of bongos, conga drums, a vibraphone, four smaller drums, four wood blocks, and a set of drum-like tubes called "boobams." She's that very rare musician, a solo percussionist. She's also deaf.

Born in Scotland, Evelyn began studying drums and other percussion instruments at the age of twelve. She continued at the Royal Academy of Music in London, England, where she won prize after prize. Now she has an international concert schedule that takes her from Alaska to Brazil, from Norway to New Zealand, from Canada to Japan. Although she is a classically-trained musician, Evelyn also loves pop and world music. Besides playing the Highland bagpipes, she has performed with a gamelan* orchestra in Indonesia and a samba** band in Brazil.

Evelyn has to be an innovator, because very little music has been written for solo percussion. As a result, she works closely with composers who write pieces especially for her. When audiences attend an Evelyn Glennie concert, they know they will hear new sounds put together in new ways. She has musical surprises galore to offer her listeners, as you can hear on CDs such as *Wind in the Bamboo Grove* and *Reflected in Brass*. Recently, she has composed music for TV dramas, travel shows, and commercials.

---

*gamelan: A Balinese or Javanese orchestra made of up of bowed, stringed, and a variety of percussion instruments.
**samba: A Brazilian dance of African origin.

GOALS AT A GLANCE

■ Express and support an opinion.
■ Participate in small group discussion.

To play her instruments, she uses her senses of touch and sight. Performing barefoot heightens her sensitivity to vibrations. As she explains it, "People have the wrong idea about deafness. They think you live in a world of total silence, but that isn't the way it works."

"I don't think in terms of loud and soft," says Evelyn. "Instead I think of sounds as thin or fat, strong or weak. The sounds you can create with just one cymbal are infinite."

Evelyn has created a scholarship to encourage children who are hard of hearing to play musical instruments, and she supports many other organizations for the deaf in Britain. But she would rather be known as a role model for all young musicians, not just young deaf people. Her ability to perform brilliantly in front of a huge symphony orchestra—and to push the boundaries of percussion music—inspires everyone who hears her.

If you would like to know more about Evelyn and her music, she has her own Web site at <http://www.evelyn.co.uk/>.

RESPONDING TO THE PROFILE

a. Do you think a solo percussionist would find it easy or difficult to attract an audience? Why or why not?

b. If you are standing by the side of the road and a large truck goes by, you can feel the vibrations. List other vibrations that you can feel.

c. Evelyn's husband writes, "If the audience is only wondering how a deaf musician can play percussion then Evelyn [feels she] has failed as a musician." With a partner, discuss why Evelyn might feel that way.

Hanging Upside Down

Bananas

Poem by **Donna Wasiczko**

It may be
necessary to hang upside
down from a tree
to get a new
perspective. Then you can
see that grass grows
up. What a dance
to measure lizard
jumps and spider
dangles at eye
level! To hear
birds fly
over your feet—
match shadows to faces,
feathers to wings,
footsteps to eyes.

GOALS AT A GLANCE

■ Respond personally and critically to poetry.
■ Write a poem.

Empty Head

Poem by Malick Fall

Translated from the French by John Reed and Clive Wake

An idea came
Into my head
So slender
So slight
An idea came
Fleetingly
Fearfully
Came to alight
It wheeled about
Stretched itself out
An idea came
That I wanted to stay
But it brushed my hand
And taking its flight
Through my fingers
Slipped away.

---

1. RESPONDING TO THE POEMS

a. Which of the two poems do you like better? Explain why.

b. What do "Bananas" and "Empty Head" tell us about how people think—and lose their thoughts?

2. WRITING POETRY

Imagine that you are hanging upside down—anywhere in the world. How do you feel? What do you see and hear? What thoughts are passing through your head? Write an "upside-down" poem that reveals a new perspective on the world. Read your poem aloud to a classmate.

CYBERSPACE

Sam was teased, mocked, and misunderstood— all because he spent his time surfing the Net. Could Sam last even one day in an unwired environment?

SAM

Short Story by W.D. Valgardson

Solitario Adolphus Muggins surfed the Net, read CD-ROMS, e-mailed, and downloaded more than was good for him. Or so his family thought.

After breakfast one Saturday, his mother asked the family where they were going.

"To the mall to be with my friends," Carol said.

"To the schoolyard to shoot some baskets," his brother, Greg, said. He was home from college for the summer.

"To the garage to get a tire repaired," his father said.

They all turned to look at Solitario Adolphus Muggins, or Sam, as they called him.

"Cyberspace," he replied.

"That kid's got a problem," his brother said, after Sam had disappeared into the Internet.

"It's just a stage," his mother said. "With you it was skateboards."

"He reads the dictionary," his sister complained. "If we don't do something, he'll carry a briefcase and wear one of those plastic things in his shirt pocket when he goes into Grade Nine. I'll be ostracized."

"We need to open a dialogue with him," his father said.

GOALS AT A GLANCE

■ Analyse stereotypes.
■ Use communication strategies in role-playing.

He taught at the local college. "Communication is everything."

At supper, Sam's father suddenly blurted out, "Dinosaurs." Someone at work had told him dinosaurs were very popular.

"A group of extinct reptiles, widely distributed during the Mesozoic period. Anything you want to know, I can find for you on <http://cord.iupui.edu/~nmrosentallabout.html>." To mark the slashes, Sam swung his right hand up and down at an angle.

"What am I going to do?" Carol asked her mother. "His role model is Data. He wants to be an android."

Their mother's basic life philosophy was that everything would come out all right eventually, but even she looked a bit concerned. Sort of the way she'd looked when Carol had got her nose ring.

"I was transplanting baby's breath today and as he went by he said, 'Gypsophila,' just like that."

"You see what I mean?" Carol said. "Weird."

The next morning, Carol, who really loved her brother dearly, stopped beside Sam. "Hit EXIT!" she ordered. When the screen saver came on, she put her hand on his shoulder. "You need to get a life."

"I live everywhere," Sam answered. "I have e-mail from thirty-six countries."

"You're twelve," his sister said. "And I'll bet you don't even know the difference between boys and girls."

"Don't be ridiculous. Of course I do. Girls have two X chromosomes. Boys have an X and a Y."

When Carol told her father about this incident, he agreed that something drastic had to be done.

"All his reality is virtual," Greg said. "We've got to get him in touch with real reality. Here and now."

But what, they all asked each other. What and where and how would there be no computer, no batteries, no disks, no programs, no e-mail, no cyberspace, no Internet, no Web.

"Camping," Sam's father shouted, snapping his fingers.

"Camping," Greg shouted back.

"Camping," Carol agreed with a sigh. She didn't like camping, but she was desperate. When he got to high school, Sam would be a bigger liability than a pair of Nikes among the Doc Martens.

"I can't go," Sam's mother said. "I've got reports to write." She attended meetings for the Social Services ministry. "I'll drop you off and pick you up in two days at the provincial park."

They sang all the way to the starting point. That is, Sam's father and mother and brother and sister sang. Sam played computer games on a pad of paper. He knew the opening situations by heart.

"Look at your brother," his father said when they were setting up camp. "Getting the canoes packed for tomorrow. That's experience working. Practice makes perfect. Look at your sister chopping wood. That's the result of lifting those weights. And watch me whip together supper over an open fire." He took a deep breath. "There's nothing like it. The Great Outdoors. Just like our ancestors."

"In Finland, people have saunas," Sam said. "You heat rocks until they're red-hot, then pour water over them. You get hot as a roasting ham, then run outside and roll around in the snow. That's what

<ago.helsinki.pi> tells me. Personally, I like lukewarm showers and a warm bath towel."

"Wait until tomorrow when we get into our canoes and start down the river. You'll forget all this computer stuff for a couple of days. We'll be *coureurs de bois*." His father tried to sing something in French but he couldn't remember the words, so he sang a couple of verses of "Davy Crockett" with a French accent.

That night Sam lay awake, staring at the stars.

"Beautiful," Carol sighed. "I wonder what their names are?"

"If you'd have let me bring my laptop, I could have told you. I have a star identification program."

"You're hopeless," she snapped. "Go to sleep."

The next morning, they headed out in two canoes. Greg and Carol were in one, and Sam and his father were in the other. They had all their equipment in the centre of the canoes. The river was fast but shallow. In some places, they had to jump out and drag the canoes over the gravel bottom. Sometimes there were pools. They stopped and swam in these and had water fights.

They had lunch on a sandbar. They stopped to do some fishing and caught two fish, which they put in a cooler so they could have them for supper.

"This is reality, see," Greg explained. "Everything's in real time. You've got to grunt and sweat to get somewhere. No make-believe. This is where you learn to deal with life." Greg always wore white socks and played six different sports.

"Here, and in the mall. Social life is real, too. You've got to learn to get along, Sam. Fit in. Manners make the man," Carol added.

"There's manners on the Internet," Sam replied. "You don't follow them, you get flamed."

"If you're going to be weird, keep it in," Greg said. "Deal with reality."

They canoed with the current, guiding the canoes around rocks and trees and sandbars. They saw deer and raccoons and lots of birds.

The current picked up speed. They were coming around a sharp curve when Sam's canoe swung to the side, hit a fallen tree, and tipped sideways with the open part toward the current. Sam jumped clear, but his father fell on his side, and his right leg went under the canoe. The canoe pinned him to the gravel bottom. Then the force of the water pushed him and the canoe under the tree trunk. Sam's father tried to pull free, but the weight of the canoe held him against the bottom.

Greg and Carol jumped out of their canoe. They grabbed the tipped-over canoe and pulled on it with all their might. The force of the water was too great. The canoe kept edging farther under the tree.

With each centimetre, Sam's father was forced down into the water. He had to push himself up to keep his head from going under.

"Grab one end," Greg yelled. All three of them grabbed one end and tried to pivot the canoe. The canoe twisted slightly but pulled their father farther under.

"Pull!" Sam's father yelled. "It'll drag me down."

They pulled and pushed with all their might. The canoe moved under again.

"Help," Carol called, but there wasn't anyone around. There were just some cows in a nearby field watching them curiously.

"Help!" Greg called. Nobody heard him.

The canoe held steady. Then a rock that was blocking it pulled loose, and the canoe scraped forward. Their father's head was nearly pulled underwater.

Sam yelled, "X equals s times r." He let go of the canoe.

"What are you doing?" Greg yelled back.

"X equals s times r," Sam repeated. He scrambled around in the water on his hands and knees.

"Help," Greg and Carol both yelled. They were straining with all their might but the canoe was pulling them forward.

Sam ignored them. He stood up suddenly, holding the axe that had fallen out of the canoe.

"Not my leg," his father yelled. "Don't chop off my leg!"

Sam ran around to the back of the canoe and took a swing. He chopped a hole in the canoe, then another one, and another one. He kept chopping, making more and more holes.

"Are you crazy?" his brother screamed. "What'll we tell the rental people?"

"X equals s times r," Sam shouted back.

He kept chopping until there was a long line of holes. His brother and sister pulled with all their might, and the canoe gradually lifted off the bottom. His father dragged his leg from underneath.

They helped him to shore. They set up the tent, rescued the rest of the equipment, and dragged the two canoes up onto the bank.

"What were you yelling?" his father asked. His leg wasn't broken, but it looked like an overripe banana in places.

"The formula for water pressure against a surface. The force equals the surface times the rate of the current. We needed to create more pressure than that to free the canoe. We couldn't do it. So we had two alternatives. Stop the water. We couldn't do that. Or reduce the size of the surface. I reduced the size of the surface. There's sort of a Web site for physics. We work out problems and stuff."

Greg and Carol looked at each other. Then they stared at Sam but didn't say anything. Their father patted Sam on the head.

"We'll stay here tonight,"he said. "Then you'll have to walk along beside the good canoe and float me down to the park. I'm not going to be walking for a couple of days."

"If I had a cellular," Sam said, "we'd be out of here in no time." ◆

1. RESPONDING TO THE STORY

a. Why does Sam's family tease him so much? Do you agree that Sam has a problem because he spends so much time in cyberspace? Explain your opinion.

b. What is "virtual reality"? How is it different from "real reality"?

c. What is the family's purpose in planning a camping trip and taking Sam along? Do you think they did the right thing? Why?

d. How does Sam prove that he is an innovative person? Were you surprised by what Sam could do? Explain.

2. READING ANALYSE STEREOTYPES

Sam, Greg, and Carol could be described as stereotyped characters. (See page 52 for a definition of *stereotype*.) Copy the chart below in your notebook. Look through the story for the specific details that help to create those stereotypes, adding them to your chart. Do you think the author wants readers to think of Sam as a stereotype? Explain. What details in the story help to break each stereotype?

Character	Stereotype	Evidence
Sam		
Greg		
Carol		

SELF-ASSESSMENT: Did you find several pieces of evidence for each stereotype? With a partner, compare charts to see if you noticed the same details, adding those you missed to your chart.

3. ORAL COMMUNICATION COMMUNICATE EFFECTIVELY

Sam's father wants to communicate better with Sam. Do you think he succeeds? Why or why not? Sam's father might have benefited from the following suggestions about how to communicate effectively:

- Think about what you want to say and express yourself clearly so that the listener will not be confused. Use words the person will understand. If you are going to speak in a formal situation, you may want to rehearse what you want to say.
- Listen—when the other person is speaking, focus all your attention on what the person is saying.
- If you have difficulty understanding, restate what the person has said to check your interpretation. Ask for a further explanation if necessary.
- Be open-minded—true communication occurs when you are open to the other person's ideas.

Working with a partner, and keeping these suggestions in mind, role-play a conversation in which Sam and his father communicate effectively with one another.

4. MEDIA EVALUATE A WEB SITE

Conduct an Internet search to find an excellent Web site on problem-solving skills. Make a list of the key words that will help you search and then use them to locate specific Web sites. After you explore two or three Web sites that seem related to your search, choose the one you think is best. Make notes on what you like about the Web site, and then share your findings with other students. Did different students choose the same sites?

It's tough being an inventor.
Getting the credit you deserve
can be even tougher.

Inventively Female

Essay adapted from *Newscience*

From earliest times women were inventive. Around the world, they created "firsts" in everything from cooking and pottery to weaving, tanning, hut-building and crop-raising. Through the ages, women continued to improve their daily lives with inventions such as:

- the flat-bottomed paper bag by Margaret Knight in 1870
- the sad iron (a flatiron pointed at both ends) by Mary Potts in 1876
- the exact-measurement cookbook by Fannie Farmer in 1896
- the drip coffee pot by Melitta Bentz in 1908
- and the disposable diaper by Marion Donovan in 1951

The contributions of women inventors, for the most part, have gone unnoticed. Why? Before 1800, women had trouble getting recognition as inventors because they weren't allowed to own patents (or property). The first patent issued to an American colonist was in 1715. It went to Thomas Masters for a machine that refined maize into cornmeal—but historical records show that his wife Sybilla actually invented it.

GOALS AT A GLANCE

- Prepare a research report.
- Show how evidence is used to support an opinion.

Even when they could get credit for their inventions, some women were simply not interested. Instead, they would share their inventions with friends and neighbours or freely publish their findings. Such was the case with Polish scientist Marie Curie, the only person ever to win two Nobel Prizes (for physics, in 1903 and 1911). Working in Paris, Curie "discovered" radium, invented a process for extracting radioactive material from uranium ore, and created the prototype for the Geiger counter. But she refused to make money by patenting her inventions.

As more women began to attend university and take jobs outside their homes, the scope of their inventions widened. During World War I, women worked in weapons factories and invented weapons, too: an automatic pistol, a railway torpedo, and a submarine mine, among many others. Around the same time, engineer Kate Gleason invented mass-produced housing—the model for today's suburban homes.

Marie Curie won the Nobel Prize for physics in 1903 and 1911.

More recently, Stephanie Kwolek invented Kevlar, a fibre used in radial tires and bullet-proof vests. Patsy Sherman, working at 3M, co-invented Scotchguard; and Barbara Askins created a way to obtain clearer pictures from old negatives.

Over the years, many female inventors have been denied their places in patent history. *Mothers of Invention*, the first book ever written about women inventors, provides plenty of examples. It points out that Lady Mary Montague introduced smallpox vaccination to Europe in 1717, eighty years before British doctor Edward Jenner was credited with this life-saving procedure.

Similarly, Dr. Lise Meitner discovered and named nuclear fission, the process that led to the atomic bomb and nuclear energy. Yet only her male colleague received the Nobel Prize in 1944.

Even today, only about ten of a thousand patents granted yearly in Canada belong to women. A Canadian venture called the Women Inventors Project is seeking to change this. Founded by two Waterloo, Ontario, women—Shelly Beauchamp and Lisa Avedon—this unique organization is dedicated to helping innovative Canadian women develop their ideas by providing workshops and role models.

Web page from the Women Inventors Project.

Recent inventions patented by Canadian women are increasingly high-tech: Professor Mary Anne White's new class of heat storage chemicals; Carolyn Gelhorn's Trip Trak, which tracks car mileage and collects trip data; and Leslie Dolman's PC A.I.D. device, which allows people with disabilities to use an IBM or compatible computer.

Are you a potential patent-holder? According to the Women Inventors Project, you don't have to be a research scientist. You just have to be someone who identifies a problem and sets out to invent a practical solution. Easier said than done, perhaps. But in the words of inventor Rosalyn Yalow, "The world cannot afford the loss of the talents of half of its people, if we are to solve the many problems which beset us." ◆

Women Inventors Project

Teaching Tools

Order Catalogue

Women Inventors Quiz

Friends of Women Inventors

Canadian Women: Risktakers and Changemakers

Rachel Zimmerman
Inventor
Ontario, Canada

Rachel Zimmerman is the inventor of a computer program which uses Blissymbols. These symbols allow non-speaking people to communicate. The user "talks" by pointing to the various symbols on a page or board.

With traditional Bliss board, the individual can only communicate with a person who is in the same room at the same time, watching the Bliss-user point to a sequence of symbols. With Rachel's "Blissymbol Printer" program, the 'speaker' touches the symbols on a touch-sensitive board, and then computer translates them into written language. This method is fast, lets the user communicate independently, and allows information to be stored or sent over a distance.

This invention is perhaps even more impressive when you realize that Rachel was only twelve when she developed it. The system started out as a project for a school science fair and ended up competing at the World Exhibition of Achievement of Young Inventors, held in Bulgaria. She is also a winner of a YTV Achievement Award for Innovation. Recently, Rachel added French text to the program, and is exploring the possibilities of adding Hebrew text, as well as a modem and voice output to her system.

Document (above) from
the Women Inventors Project Web site.

1. Responding to the Essay

a. Which of the inventors or inventions mentioned in the article would you like to learn more about? Why?

b. Do you think it is it important to take out a patent when you develop a good invention? Why or why not?

c. What is the purpose of the Women Inventors Project? What steps do you think they should take to achieve their purpose?

2. Researching Prepare a Research Report

Research a female Canadian inventor. You may wish to have a look at the Women Inventors Project Web site for possible subjects. Before you begin your research, make a list of some of the questions you would like your research to answer. (See page 86 for other ideas about researching.) Present your findings in the form of a brief written or oral research report.

Self-Assessment: In your research, were you able to find answers to the questions you listed? Did you encounter difficulties in your research? If so, what were they and how did you overcome them?

3. Essay Craft Support an Opinion

The essay is a form of writing in which an author presents an opinion about a topic. In order to persuade the reader, the author must give evidence that supports his or her opinion. *Facts* (statements that can be confirmed as true) are the best kind of evidence.

With a partner, reread "Inventively Female." What are the author's opinions about women inventors? What evidence does the author include to support these opinions? Were you convinced by the author's evidence? Why or why not?

Not all innovators are scientists or engineers—meet sculptor Andy Goldsworthy.

A COLLABORATION WITH NATURE

Book review by Agnieszka Biskup

Sculptures and captions by Andy Goldsworthy

Y ou don't need expensive marble and bronze to make a beautiful sculpture. And a sculpture doesn't need to be displayed on a pedestal in a museum, a gallery, or a public park to be considered art. As British artist Andy Goldsworthy shows, it's possible to create art by using what's around you, and leaving it right where you made it. Goldsworthy makes his sculptures outdoors and uses materials he finds in nature: ice, snow, leaves, petals, earth, branches, thorns, and rocks. He shapes his materials into arches, circles, spirals, and lines, patterns suggesting nature's rhythm, growth, and decay. He constructs most of his sculptures within a day, then photographs them before, or while, they're broken down by the wind, rain, or the sun's warmth. Though he's made his sculptures all over the world—from Australia to the North Pole—a stretch of woods near his home in Dumfriesshire, Scotland, remains at the centre of his work. His photographs have been collected in a series of beautiful books, including *Hand to Earth: Andy Goldsworthy Sculpture 1976-1990, Andy Goldsworthy: A Collaboration with Nature,* and the simply titled *Wood* and *Stone.* The images on these pages are good examples of how Goldsworthy makes you see nature in a completely different way.

GOALS AT A GLANCE

- Analyse art.
- Recognize sentence fragments.

Feathers plucked from
dead heron
cut with sharp stone
stripped down one side
about three-and-a-half feet
overall length
made over three calm days
cold frosty mornings
smell from heron pungent as
each day warmed up

Swindale Beck Wood, Cumbria
February 24–26, 1982

Icicles
thick ends dipped in snow
then water
held until frozen together
occasionally using forked sticks
as support until stuck
a tense moment when taking
them away
breathing on the stick first
to release it

Scaur Water, Dumfriesshire
January 12, 1987

Derwent Water, Cumbria
February 20 &
March 8–9, 1988

Early morning calm
knotweed stalks
pushed into lake bottom
made complete by their own reflections

1. RESPONDING TO THE SCULPTURES

a. In what ways are Andy Goldsworthy's sculptures different from most other sculptures?

b. Which of the pieces shown here do you like best? Why?

c. Do Andy's captions add to your appreciation of the sculptures? Explain.

d. Why do you think that Andy creates art that disappears?

2. VISUAL COMMUNICATION ANALYSE ART

We are told that Andy's work is symbolic of "nature's rhythm, growth, and decay." With a partner, look closely at the pictures. How does each piece of art represent the cycles of nature? What shapes are most prominent in each piece? Which piece is the most inventive? Why do you think so? In your opinion, has the artist been successful in creating art that shows nature's rhythm, growth, and decay? You and your partner should be prepared to explain your conclusions.

3. LANGUAGE CONVENTIONS SENTENCE FRAGMENTS

Andy's captions are made of bits and pieces of sentences, called *sentence fragments*. A sentence fragment is an incomplete sentence, lacking either a *subject* or a *predicate*. The *subject* of a sentence contains the noun or pronoun that tells who or what the sentence is about. The *predicate* contains the verb that tells what the subject did or was.

subject   predicate

The big red plastic cow **fell on its side.**

In your notebook, rewrite one caption in correct sentence form, adding punctuation and additional words as necessary. Do you prefer the original caption or your version? Why might sentence fragments be appropriate in Andy's captions but not in formal writing?

SELF-ASSESSMENT: Search for sentence fragments in your own writing. Add any necessary subjects or predicates, or explain why you think the sentence fragment is effective.

Daedalus and Icarus

"Ah, if only I could fly like the birds!" sighed Daedalus. Would the mythical inventor succeed, or would his dream come crashing to the ground?

GREEK MYTH RETOLD BY JAMES REEVES

Of all the Greeks, Daedalus, an Athenian, was most widely known throughout the ancient world as a cunning craftsperson, artist, and inventor. He perfected the art of sculpture. There had been statues before his time, but none had ever been so lifelike. They were famous not only in Greece, but over the sea in Egypt and other parts of Africa. But he was not simply a sculptor; he was also an inventor and an improver. He built baths in Greece and a great reservoir in sun-baked Sicily. He constructed the masts and yards of ships, while his son Icarus was thought to have been the inventor of sails.

One of the principal crafts invented by Daedalus was carpentry. He was said by ancient writers to have invented glue, the plumb line, the gimlet, the axe, and the saw. But some say it was his pupil Perdix who invented the saw, making the first examples from the backbones of big fish.

PRONUNCIATION GUIDE

Aegean	— ay JEE in
Athene	— a THEE nee
Cnossos	— NOSS us
Crete	— kreet
Daedalus	— DED a lus
Icarus	— ICK a rus
Minos	— MY nus
Minotaur	— MIN a tore
Pasiphae	— puh SIFF ee
Perdix	— PURR dix
Poseidon	— puh SY dun

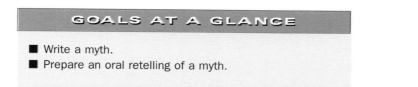

GOALS AT A GLANCE

■ Write a myth.
■ Prepare an oral retelling of a myth.

Daedalus had become very proud of his worldwide reputation as a sculptor and inventor, and he was glad to take as a pupil his sister's son, Perdix. But Perdix became so quick and clever a pupil that people began to say he was better than his master. This made Daedalus jealous. One day, in rage and envy, he took the young man to the top of a high tower he had built, in order, as he said, to show him the wonders of Athens. Then, when Perdix was gazing out toward the sea, Daedalus pushed him from the top of the tower, intending to kill him. But the young man was protected by the goddess Athene, who turned him into a partridge before he hit the ground. So by becoming a bird Perdix narrowly escaped death, and from that time to this the partridge has always flown low.

For this attempted murder Daedalus was condemned to death by the Athenian court of justice. No sooner had he heard his sentence than he fled the city and took refuge in the island of Crete. King Minos had already heard of Daedalus's great skill as an inventor, so he welcomed him into his service and made him construct many ingenious things at his palace of Cnossos.

Now the god Poseidon had sent a beautiful white bull to Crete with orders that it should be sacrificed to him there. But Minos's wife Pasiphae fell in love with the bull, and persuaded her husband not to sacrifice it. In revenge Poseidon caused Pasiphae to give birth to a monster with the head of a bull and the body of a man. This was the famous Minotaur, and it was such a cause of shame to King Minos that he determined to hide it. Accordingly, he sent for Daedalus and made him construct a hiding place in which the monster might live without being seen. Daedalus built a maze or labyrinth, in which a series of cunning passages led to the centre. So intricate was the labyrinth that Daedalus himself could scarcely find his way out to the entrance. Here the Minotaur was able to stamp about and charge angrily back and forth amidst the maze of alleyways, unseen by anyone.

"This is indeed a marvellous construction," said Minos, "and it is easy to see that you are the cleverest designer the world has ever seen."

So Minos kept Daedalus in Crete, making him construct other marvels of ingenuity—baths and fountains, temples and statues, paved floors and splendid flights of stairs.

Then at last Daedalus grew tired of the service of King Minos and longed to return to Athens, where he felt that his crime might have been forgotten or at least forgiven. He had brought with him to Crete his young son Icarus, and the boy too, now grown to manhood, wished to see his native land. But Daedalus could at first think of no way of escape. Crete was an island far distant from Athens, and Daedalus and his son could not build a ship in secrecy and supply it with a crew for the voyage home. But his cunning brain was hard at work. At last he hit on the most daring invention of his life. Many an hour he had spent looking thoughtfully at the sea birds as they wheeled and circled about the rocky coast. "Ah," said he, "if only I could fly like them! But why not? The gods have not given wings to humans, but they have given them a brain and hands to fashion wings for themselves."

So in a secret place, hidden from idle curiosity, he collected together all the feathers of birds he could find, great and small. He sent his son Icarus about the island to bring back as many as he could. Then he laid them out on the ground in order—first the big feathers, then the small. When he decided he had enough, he fastened them together with wax, curving the wings like those of a bird. Icarus watched his father intently. At last the wings were finished, and Daedalus strapped them to his shoulders and went up to a piece of rising ground. Turning into the wind, he ran forward and was delighted to find himself airborne. Day after day he practised on higher and higher slopes until he reckoned the time had come to make the flight to Greece. He constructed a second pair of wings for Icarus, and together the young man and his father mastered the art of flying.

At last the day of departure came. The sun was high in the unclouded heavens, and the wind was favourable. Daedalus and Icarus carried their wings to a lofty cliff looking toward Greece, and prepared for flight. When the wings were strapped firmly on their backs, Daedalus said to his son:

"Follow me. Do as I do. Don't fly too low or your wings will be weighed down with spray from the sea. Don't fly too near the sun either, or its heat will melt the wax that holds the feathers in place.

Either way you will be destroyed. Do as I say, and may the gods go with you. Now let us be off."

So saying, he ran toward the edge of the cliff and launched himself into the air. Borne up by the wind, he journeyed straight toward his native shore.

Icarus did just as his father had done. But he was so happy to find himself aloft in the pure blue sky that he soon forgot the good advice he had been given. He wheeled and dipped like a great sea bird, and then he soared upward till the land and even the sea were almost out of sight. How brilliant the blazing sun appeared! Icarus was fascinated by it and could not withstand the temptation to see how high he could

The Fall of Icarus by Italian seventeenth-century artist Carlo Saraceni.

fly. Hotter and hotter it blazed down upon him. Too late he felt the wax on his wings begin to melt. He could not descend fast enough for the wax to cool. The wings that had borne him aloft now began to break up, and soon the ill-fated young man plunged helplessly into the sea, like a falling star. Icarus was drowned.

Daedalus had crossed the Aegean Sea and was almost home to Athens before he turned to catch sight of his son. Icarus was not to be seen. In alarm Daedalus turned and flew back to the south. It was not long before he saw, as he swooped down toward the blue waves, a pair of damaged wings floating uselessly on the sea. In sorrow Daedalus returned to Athens alone. The sea where his son had met his death was named the Icarian Sea.

----

1. RESPONDING TO THE MYTH

a. The story of Daedalus and Icarus is an old and well-known myth. Why do you think it continues to hold people's interest?

b. What hints does the story of Perdix contain about later events?

c. What is a labyrinth? Why was Daedalus asked to build one? Describe any labyrinths you have encountered in other stories, movies, or games.

d. What motivated Daedalus to create the most daring invention of his life?

e. What made Icarus ignore his father's advice and fly toward the sun? Have you ever been tempted to ignore good advice? What happened?

2. WRITING CREATE A MYTH

List some of the ways in which the story "Daedalus and Icarus" is a **myth**. Now write a myth of your own. Be inventive! Your myth might explain the existence of something (such as volcanoes, rivers, sunshine, snow) or it might tell the story of a great adventure.

A **myth** is an old story that tells about heroes, gods, and supernatural events. Many myths also explain something about the world, such as why there is a sun or how the earth was created.

3. LANGUAGE CONVENTIONS SPECIFIC NOUNS

Writers use specific **nouns** to help readers imagine what is being described. As you can see from the examples below, a specific noun contains more information than a vague noun.

> A **noun** is a word that refers to people, places, qualities, things, actions or ideas.

> **Vague:** Daedalus built a *place* to hold the Minotaur.

> **Specific:** Daedalus built a *maze* to hold the Minotaur.

Reread the myth, making a list of ten specific nouns that helped you clearly imagine what the writer was describing. Are there any that you had difficulty understanding? Make a second list of challenging nouns.
Use a dictionary to find out what they mean, and then write a definition in your own words for each one.

4. ORAL COMMUNICATION RETELL A MYTH

There are many myths from many cultures. Find one myth that interests you and prepare a retelling of it for the class. Refer to the information on storytelling (page 53) for assistance. Focus on using your voice to bring the story to life. Speak clearly, express emotion, and vary how loudly and how quickly you speak to emphasize different parts of the myth.

SELF-ASSESSMENT: Did you feel confident and well prepared when you told your myth? Was your audience quiet and attentive? Ask your classmates whether you used your voice effectively. What could you do to improve your storytelling next time?

SELF-ASSESSMENT: RESEARCHING

As you worked on activities in this unit what did you learn about
- brainstorming ideas?
- finding information?
- using an Internet search engine?
- evaluating a Web site?
- preparing a research report?
- presenting your findings?

Reflect on the research-related tasks you completed throughout the unit. What went well? Did you encounter any problems? Based on your research experiences, create a list of five to ten tips that will serve as useful reminders the next time you have a research assignment.

VISUAL COMMUNICATION DESIGN A POSTER

Imagine that you have been given the task of advertising one of the inventions mentioned in this unit. Create an attention-grabbing poster to advertise the invention. Your poster should include a strong visual element, a catchy slogan, and interesting text that tells something about the invention.

MEDIA PREPARE AN INTERVIEW

You are a reporter and your assignment is to interview one of the inventors presented in this unit. Prepare a list of interesting questions. Have a classmate take the role of the inventor while you conduct the interview.

WRITING CREATE AN INVENTOR'S CODE

Sometimes an invention causes more harm than good; Daedalus's wings are one example. In a group, brainstorm a list of inventions that have had destructive results. Discuss whether inventors should try to imagine the possible harmful effects of their innovations. Together, write an "Inventor's Code" that all responsible inventors should follow, or write a brief argument explaining why inventors should pursue their work no matter what.

SHORT STORIES

"You just jot down ideas
as they occur to you.
The jotting is simplicity itself—
it is the occurring
which is difficult."

—*Stephen Leacock*

SHORT STORIES

A FICTION MIX

Does what you wear really matter?

The Hockey Sweater

Short Story by Roch Carrier

Translated by Sheila Fischman

The winters of my childhood were long, long seasons. We lived in three places—the school, the church, and the skating rink—but our real life was on the skating rink. Real battles were won on the skating rink. Real strength appeared on the skating rink. The real leaders showed themselves on the skating rink. School was a sort of punishment. Parents always want to punish children and school is their most natural way of punishing us. However, school was also a quiet place where we could prepare for the next hockey game, lay out our next strategies. As for church, we found there the tranquillity of God; there we forgot school and dreamed about the next hockey game. Through our daydreams it might happen that we would recite a prayer; we would ask God to help us play as well as Maurice Richard.

We all wore the same uniform as he, the red, white, and blue uniform of the Montreal Canadiens, the best hockey team in the world; we all combed our hair in the same style as Maurice Richard, and to keep it in place we used a sort of glue—a great deal of glue. We laced our skates like Maurice Richard, we taped our sticks like Maurice Richard. We cut all his pictures out of the papers. Truly, we knew everything about him.

GOALS AT A GLANCE

- Identify features of good beginnings and endings.
- Analyse sentence variety.

On the ice, when the referee blew his whistle the two teams would rush at the puck; we were five Maurice Richards taking it away from five other Maurice Richards; we were ten players, all of us wearing, with the same blazing enthusiasm, the uniform of the Montreal Canadiens. On our backs, we all wore the famous number 9.

One day, my Montreal Canadiens sweater had become too small; then it got torn and had holes in it. My mother said, "If you wear that old sweater, people are going to think we're poor!" Then she did what she did whenever we needed new clothes. She started to leaf through the catalogue the Eaton company sent us in the mail every year. My mother was proud. She didn't want to buy our clothes at the general store; the only things that were good enough for us were the latest styles from Eaton's catalogue. My mother didn't like the order forms included with the catalogue; they were written in English and she didn't understand a word of it. To order my hockey sweater, she did as she usually did; she took out her writing paper and wrote in her gentle schoolteacher's hand: "Cher Monsieur Eaton, Would you be kind enough to send me a Canadiens' sweater for my son who is ten years old and a little too tall for his age and Docteur Robitaille thinks he's a little too thin? I'm sending you three dollars and please send me what's left if there's anything left. I hope your wrapping will be better than last time."

Monsieur Eaton was quick to answer my mother's letter. Two weeks later we received the sweater. That day I had one of the greatest disappointments of my life! I would even say that on that day I experienced a very great sorrow. Instead of the red, white, and blue Montreal Canadiens sweater, Monsieur Eaton had sent us a blue and white sweater with a maple leaf on the front—the sweater of the Toronto Maple Leafs. I'd always worn the red, white, and blue Montreal Canadiens sweater; all my friends wore the red, white, and blue sweater; never had anyone in my village ever worn the Toronto sweater, never had we even seen a Toronto Maple Leafs sweater. Besides, the Toronto team was regularly trounced by the triumphant Canadiens. With tears in my eyes, I found the strength to say, "I'll never wear that uniform."

"My boy, first you're going to try it on! If you make up your mind about things before you try, my boy, you won't go very far in this life."

My mother had pulled the blue and white Toronto Maple Leafs sweater over my shoulders and already my arms were inside the sleeves. She pulled the sweater down and carefully smoothed all the creases in the abominable maple leaf on which, right in the middle of my chest, were written the words "Toronto Maple Leafs." I wept.

"I'll never wear it."

"Why not? This sweater fits you...like a glove."

"Maurice Richard would never put it on his back."

"You aren't Maurice Richard. Anyway, it isn't what's on your back that counts, it's what you've got inside your head."

"You'll never put it in my head to wear a Toronto Maple Leafs sweater."

My mother sighed in despair and explained to me.

"If you don't keep this sweater which fits you perfectly I'll have to write to Monsieur Eaton and explain that you don't want to wear the Toronto sweater. Monsieur Eaton's an *Anglais*; he'll be insulted because he likes the Maple Leafs. And if he's insulted do you think he'll be in a hurry to answer us? Spring will be here and you won't

have played a single game, just because you didn't want to wear that perfectly nice blue sweater."

So I was obliged to wear the Maple Leafs sweater. When I arrived on the rink, all the Maurice Richards in red, white, and blue came up, one by one, to take a look. When the referee blew his whistle I went to take my usual position. The captain came and warned me I'd be better to stay on the forward line. A few minutes later the second line was called; I jumped onto the ice. The Maple Leafs sweater weighed on my shoulders like a mountain. The captain came and told me to wait; he'd need me later, on defence. By the third period I still hadn't played; one of the defencemen was hit in the nose with a stick and it was bleeding. I jumped on the ice; my moment had come! The referee blew his whistle; he gave me a penalty. He claimed I'd jumped on the ice when there were already five players. That was too much! It was unfair! It was persecution! It was because of my blue sweater! I struck my stick against the ice so hard it broke. Relieved, I bent down to pick up the debris. As I straightened up I saw the young vicar, on skates, before me. "My child," he said, "just because you're wearing a new Toronto Maple Leafs sweater unlike the others, it doesn't mean you're going to make the laws around here. A proper young man doesn't lose his temper. Now take off your skates and go to the church and ask God to forgive you."

Wearing my Maple Leafs sweater I went to the church, where I prayed to God; I asked him to send, as quickly as possible, moths that would eat up my Toronto Maple Leafs sweater.

---

1. Responding to the Story

a. How does the boy in the story feel about Maurice Richard? Have you ever felt that way about someone? Explain why or why not.

b. How does the boy feel about his new hockey sweater when it arrives? Have you ever had a similar experience? Describe what happened.

c. If you were the boy, would your mother's words have convinced you to wear the hockey sweater? Why or why not? What would you have said in response? With a partner, role-play that conversation.

d. In your opinion, what are the three funniest moments in the story? Why did they amuse you?

2. STORY CRAFT BEGINNINGS AND ENDINGS

In small groups, read the opening paragraph of the story. Do you think Roch Carrier manages to grab his readers' attention? Discuss why the paragraph is or is not an effective opening. Now read the last paragraph of the story and discuss whether it provides a good ending. As a group, talk about some good beginnings and endings you remember from other stories you have read. Together, create a list of ideas about beginnings and endings. Use these headings: "The Qualities of a Good Beginning Are..." and "The Qualities of a Good Ending Are..." Share your list with the class.

3. WRITING MEMORIES FROM LIFE

"The Hockey Sweater" rings true because it seems to be based on a real childhood memory. If you were writing a story based on your own experience, what story would you tell? Think of a vivid memory from your life, funny or not. Make some notes that you could use to develop your memory into a story. First, summarize your memory in a few sentences, and then describe what kind of story you would write (sad, humorous, exciting, and so on). In point form, record some details you could include in your story (for example, personal feelings, sights and sounds, lines of dialogue). Finally, draft a strong beginning that would hook a reader's attention.

SELF-ASSESSMENT: Reread the preparation you have done. Did you select a memory that you would like to write about that a reader would find interesting? In your opening, what techniques did you use to hook the reader?

4. LANGUAGE CONVENTIONS SENTENCE VARIETY

In "The Hockey Sweater," Roch Carrier uses a wide variety of sentences. With a partner, choose one of the longer paragraphs in the story. Together, investigate the ways in which the sentences differ from one another, considering factors such as length and complexity. Jot down any questions you have about the way the author uses punctuation. Present your observations and questions to the class.

"I can't write a poem," Geraldine told the teacher,
and she really meant it.

Geraldine Moore
the Poet

SHORT STORY
BY TONI CADE BAMBARA

Geraldine paused at the corner to pull up her knee socks. The rubber bands she was using to hold them up made her legs itch. She dropped her books on the sidewalk while she gave a good scratch. But when she pulled the socks up again, two fingers poked right through the top of her left one.

"That stupid dog," she muttered to herself, grabbing at her books and crossing against traffic. "First he chews up my gym suit and gets me into trouble, and now my socks."

Geraldine shifted her books to the other hand and kept muttering angrily to herself about Mrs. Watson's dog, which she minded two days a week for a dollar. She passed the hot-dog vendor on the corner and waved. He shrugged as if to say business was very bad.

Must be, she thought to herself. *Three guys before you had to pack up and forget it. Nobody's got hot-dog money around here.*

Geraldine turned down her street, wondering what her sister Anita would have for her lunch. She was glad she didn't have to eat the free lunches in high school any more. She was sick of the funny-looking tomato soup and the dried-out cheese sandwiches and those oranges that were more green than orange.

When Geraldine's mother first took sick and went away, Geraldine had been on her own except when Miss Gladys next door came in on Thursdays and cleaned the apartment and made a meat loaf so Geraldine could have dinner. But in those days Geraldine

---

never quite managed to get breakfast for herself. So she'd sit through social studies class, scraping her feet to cover up the noise of her stomach growling.

Now Anita, Geraldine's older sister, was living at home waiting for her husband to get out of the Army. She usually had something good for lunch—chicken and dumplings if she managed to get up in time, or baked ham from the night before and sweet-potato bread. But even if there was only a hot dog and some baked beans— sometimes just a TV dinner if those soap operas kept Anita glued to the TV set—anything was better than the noisy school lunchroom where monitors kept pushing you into a straight line or rushing you to the tables. Anything was better than that.

Geraldine was almost home when she stopped dead. Right outside her building was a pile of furniture and some boxes. That wasn't anything new. She had seen people get put out in the street before, but this time the ironing board looked familiar. And she recognized the big, ugly sofa standing on its arm, its underbelly showing the hole where Mrs. Watson's dog had gotten to it.

Miss Gladys was sitting on the stoop, and she looked up and took off her glasses. "Well, Gerry," she said slowly, wiping her glasses on the hem of her dress, "looks like you'll be staying with me for a while." She looked at the men carrying out a big box with an old doll sticking up over the edge. "Anita's upstairs. Go on up and get your lunch."

Geraldine stepped past the old woman and almost bumped into the superintendent. He took off his cap to wipe away the sweat.

"Darn shame," he said to no one in particular. "Poor people sure got a hard row to hoe."

"That's the truth," said Miss Gladys, standing up with her hands on her hips to watch the men set things on the sidewalk.

Upstairs, Geraldine went into the apartment and found Anita in the kitchen.

"I dunno, Gerry," Anita said. "I just don't know what we're going to do. But everything's going to be all right soon as Ma gets well." Anita's voice cracked as she sat a bowl of soup before Geraldine.

"What's this?" Geraldine said.

"It's tomato soup, Gerry."

Geraldine was about to say something. But when she looked up at her big sister, she saw how Anita's face was getting all twisted as she began to cry.

That afternoon, Mr. Stern, the geometry teacher, started drawing cubes and cylinders on the board. Geraldine sat at her desk adding up a column of figures in her notebook—the rent, the light and gas bills, a new gym suit, some socks. Maybe they would move somewhere else, and she could have her own room. Geraldine turned the squares and triangles into little houses in the country.

"For your homework," Mr. Stern was saying with his back to the class, "set up your problems this way." He wrote GIVEN: in large letters, and then gave the formula for the first problem. Then he wrote TO FIND: and listed three items they were to include in their answers.

Geraldine started to raise her hand to ask what all these squares and angles had to do with solving real problems, like the one she had. *Better not*, she warned herself, and sat on her hands. *Your big mouth got you in trouble last term.*

In health class, Mrs. Potter kept saying that the body was a wonderful machine. Every time Geraldine looked up from her notebook, she would hear the same thing. "Right now your body is manufacturing all the proteins and tissues and energy you will need to get through tomorrow."

And Geraldine kept wondering, *How? How does my body know what it will need, when I don't even know what I'll need to get through tomorrow?*

As she headed down the hall to her next class, Geraldine remembered that she hadn't done the homework for English. Mrs. Scott had said to write a poem, and Geraldine had meant to do it at lunchtime. After all, there was nothing to it—a flower here, a raindrop there, moon, June, rose, nose. But the men carrying off the furniture had made her forget.

"And now put away your books," Mrs. Scott was saying as Geraldine tried to scribble a poem quickly. "Today we can give King Arthur's knights a rest. Let's talk about poetry."

Mrs. Scott moved up and down the aisles, talking about her favourite poems and reciting a line now and then. She got very excited whenever she passed a desk and could pick up the homework from a student who had remembered to do the assignment.

"A poem is your own special way of saying what you feel and what you see," Mrs. Scott went on, her lips moist. It was her favourite subject.

"Some poets write about the light that...that...makes the world sunny," she said, passing Geraldine's desk. "Sometimes an idea takes the form of a picture—an image."

For almost half an hour, Mrs. Scott stood at the front of the room, reading poems and talking about the lives of the great poets. Geraldine drew more houses, and designs for curtains.

"So for those who haven't done their homework, try it now," Mrs. Scott said. "Try expressing what it is like to be...to be alive in this...this glorious world."

"Oh, brother," Geraldine muttered to herself as Mrs. Scott moved up and down the aisles again, waving her hands and leaning over the students' shoulders and saying, "That's nice," or "Keep trying." Finally she came to Geraldine's desk and stopped, looking down at her.

"I can't write a poem," Geraldine said flatly, before she even realized she was going to speak at all. She said it very loudly, and the whole class looked up.

"And why not?" Mrs. Scott asked, looking hurt.

"I can't write a poem, Mrs. Scott, because nothing lovely's been happening in my life. I haven't seen a flower since Mother's Day, and the sun don't even shine on my side of the street. No robins come sing on my window sill."

Geraldine swallowed hard. She thought about saying that her father doesn't even come to visit any more, but changed her mind. "Just the rain comes," she went on, "and the bills come, and the men to move out our furniture. I'm sorry, but I can't write no pretty poem."

Teddy Johnson leaned over and was about to giggle and crack the whole class up, but Mrs. Scott looked so serious that he changed his mind.

"You have just said the most...the most poetic thing, Geraldine Moore," said Mrs. Scott. Her hands flew up to touch the silk scarf around her neck. "'Nothing lovely's been happening in my life.'" She repeated it so quietly that everyone had to lean forward to hear.

"Class," Mrs. Scott said very sadly, clearing her throat, "you have just heard the best poem you will ever hear." She went to the board and stood there for a long time staring at the chalk in her hand.

"I'd like you to copy it down," she said. She wrote it just as Geraldine had said it, bad grammar and all.

Nothing lovely's been happening in my life.
I haven't seen a flower since Mother's Day,
And the sun don't even shine on my side of the street.
No robins come sing on my window sill.
Just the rain comes, and the bills come,
And the men to move out our furniture.
I'm sorry, but I can't write no pretty poem.

Mrs. Scott stopped writing, but she kept her back to the class for a long time—long after Geraldine had closed her notebook.

And even when the bell rang, and everyone came over to smile at Geraldine or to tap her on the shoulder or to kid her about being the school poet, Geraldine waited for Mrs. Scott to put the chalk down and turn around. Finally Geraldine stacked up her books and started to leave. Then she thought she heard a whimper—the way Mrs. Watson's dog whimpered sometimes—and she saw Mrs. Scott's shoulders shake a little. ◆

1. Responding to the Story

a. How does Geraldine feel when Anita gives her tomato soup for lunch? Why does she decide to say nothing about it?

b. Geraldine wonders what math problems at school have to do with her real problems. Can you understand her attitude? Explain.

c. Why is Geraldine's "poem," according to Mrs. Scott, the best poem the class will ever hear? Do you agree with her?

d. How is Mrs. Scott feeling at the end of the story? How do you know? How do you think Geraldine is feeling?

2. Reading DRAW CONCLUSIONS

The author never tells us directly that Geraldine is poor. Instead she shows significant details about Geraldine's life and lets the readers draw their own conclusions, for example: "The rubber bands she was using to hold them up [her socks] made her legs itch." List other details that show the reader what Geraldine's life is like. With a partner, discuss why an author might want to *show* something important rather than *tell* readers directly.

3. Writing DESCRIBE CHARACTER

After reading the story, you know Geraldine and her feelings quite well. Write a diary entry in which you describe Geraldine as if you had just met her. Your description should tell what Geraldine is like, using details from the story. You can also invent details about her that aren't in the story, but could be true.

4. Editor's Desk CRAFT A POEM

Imagine that you are working on the same assignment that Geraldine was given: "Express what it is like to be alive in this world." Write down a few sentences that express what you feel about being alive right now.

Shape your sentences into a poem that is similar to Geraldine's. You might share your poem with two or three classmates.

Look closely at your poem. Does each sentence help the reader to see, hear, taste, smell, and/or feel something specific? If not, how could you rewrite your sentences to express your message more vividly?

ZOO

Short Story by Edward D. Hoch

The children were always good during the month of August, especially when it began to get near the twenty-third. It was on this day that the great silver spaceship carrying Professor Hugo's Interplanetary Zoo settled down for its annual six-hour visit to the Chicago area.

Before daybreak the crowds would form, long lines of children and adults both, each one clutching his or her dollar, and waiting with wonderment to see what race of strange creatures the Professor had brought this year.

In the past they had sometimes been treated to three-legged creatures from Venus, or tall, thin men from Mars, or even snake-like horrors from somewhere more distant. This year, as the great round ship settled slowly to earth in the huge tri-city parking area just outside of Chicago, they watched with awe as the sides slowly slid up to reveal the familiar barred cages. In them was some wild breed of nightmare— small, horse-like animals that moved with quick, jerking motions and constantly chattered in a high-pitched tongue. The citizens of Earth clustered around as Professor Hugo's crew quickly collected the waiting dollars, and soon the good Professor himself made an appearance, wearing his many-coloured rainbow cape and top hat. "People of Earth," he called into his microphone.

The crowd's noise died down and he continued. "People of Earth, this year you see a real treat for your single dollar—the little-known horse-spider people of Kaan—brought to you across a million kilometres of space at great expense. Gather around, see them, study them, listen to them, tell your friends about them. But hurry! My ship can remain here only six hours!"

And the crowds slowly filed by, at once horrified and fascinated by these strange creatures that looked like horses but ran up the walls of their cages like spiders. "This is certainly worth a dollar," one man remarked, hurrying away. "I'm going home to get my wife."

All day long it went like that, until ten thousand people had filed by the barred cages set into the side of the spaceship. Then, as the six-hour limit ran out, Professor Hugo once more took the microphone in hand. "We must go now, but we will return next year on this date. And if you enjoyed our Zoo this year, telephone your friends in other cities about it. We will land in New York tomorrow, and next week on to London, Paris, Rome, Hong Kong, and Tokyo. Then on to other worlds!"

He waved farewell to them, and as the ship rose from the ground, the Earth people agreed that this had been the very best Zoo yet...

◆ ◆ ◆

Some two months and three planets later, the silver ship of Professor Hugo settled at last onto the familiar jagged rocks of Kaan, and the queer horse-spider creatures filed quickly out of their cages. Professor Hugo was there to say a few parting words, and then they scurried away in a hundred different directions, seeking their homes among the rocks.

In one house, the she-creature was happy to see the return of her mate and offspring. She babbled a greeting in the strange tongue and hurried to embrace them. "It was a long time you were gone. Was it good?"

And the he-creature nodded. "The little one enjoyed it especially. We visited eight worlds and saw many things."

The little one ran up the wall of the cave. "On the place called Earth it was the best. The creatures there wear garments over their skins, and they walk on two legs."

"But isn't it dangerous?" asked the she-creature.

"No," her mate answered. "There are bars to protect us from them. We remain right in the ship. Next time you must come with us. It is well worth the nineteen commocs it costs."

And the little one nodded. "It was the very best Zoo ever..."

----

1. RESPONDING TO THE STORY

a. Were you surprised by the "twist" at the end of this story? If not, when did you guess what was happening?

b. What is amusing about Professor Hugo's claim that the creatures have been brought to Earth "at great expense"?

c. Which creatures do you think are really on display in the Zoo? Explain your answer.

d. Do you think Professor Hugo is a human from Earth, or another sort of being altogether? Why?

2. STORY CRAFT POINT OF VIEW

Did you notice that the author changes the narrative point of view part way through "Zoo"? The first part of the story is seen through human eyes, while the second part is seen through the eyes of the horse-spiders of Kaan. With a partner, discuss possible reasons why the author crafted his story in this way.

Write a very short story told from two different points of view. For example, you could write a story about a hiker who encounters a bear. Tell the story first from the hiker's point of view, and then from the bear's point of view. Try to "get inside the head" of your characters, revealing what each one thinks and feels.

SELF-ASSESSMENT: After you've drafted your story, consider these questions. In your story, did two different characters tell their own version of the same events? Did the two characters see things in very different or even opposite ways?

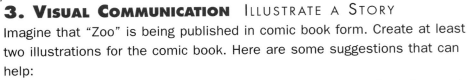

STRATEGIES

3. VISUAL COMMUNICATION ILLUSTRATE A STORY

Imagine that "Zoo" is being published in comic book form. Create at least two illustrations for the comic book. Here are some suggestions that can help:

- Reread the story and identify the most important characters and events.
- When you've decided what to illustrate, read any relevant passages carefully so that your illustration accurately reflects the details mentioned in the story (for example, setting, physical appearance, clothing, and so on).
- Determine the mood of the story (for example, humorous, suspenseful) and try to capture that mood in your work.
- When details are lacking, use your imagination!

Compare your illustrations with those done by others. Did you illustrate the same events? How are your interpretations similar and different?

Home alone in a thunderstorm, babysitting a snake! How could things get any worse?

For Pete's Snake

Short Story by Ellen Conford

The last, tearful words my sister, Petra, said to me as they drove her off to the hospital were, "Please, Will, take care of my Coily!"

It was Saturday evening, on the Fourth of July weekend. My parents didn't know how long they'd have to wait in the emergency room. But they were used to it. This was not the first time Pete had fallen out of a tree. Or off the roof. Or off her skateboard.

Pete is a major klutz. She breaks things. Mostly her bones. Whenever anyone asks my father for a credit card, he says, "Visa, American Express, or County General?"

So there was really nothing new about Pete being carried off to the hospital again.

Except that this time I had promised to babysit a boa constrictor.

Well, I hadn't really promised. But I had nodded. I'm her brother, what else could I do? The kid was in pain, in tears, and in the car. If I'd said no, she might have jumped out of the car and tried to take Coily with her to the hospital. Then my mother and father would probably have argued over who would get to shoot me.

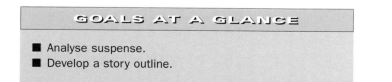

135

And besides, I thought, as I sat down on the front steps, it's a snake, not a baby. It's not as if I'd have to pick him up, or rock him, or burp him, or anything.

As Pete told my mother when she begged to adopt the beast, "They're really no trouble at all. You don't have to walk them, and you only have to feed them every two weeks. And they eat mice."

"We don't have any mice," my mother had pointed out.

"So we'll get some," Pete said.

The sky was beginning to turn a coppery colour, and I could see hard-edged dark clouds on the horizon. The air was heavy and still. I hoped we weren't going to have a thunderstorm.

It's not that I'm really afraid of storms. It's just that when I was five, I wandered away from our tent during a family camping trip. I got lost, and this monster thunderstorm came up—

Well, ever since then I've been a little tense about thunder and lightning.

Except for the occasional sound of a distant firecracker, the neighbourhood was unnaturally quiet. A lot of people were away for the holiday weekend, and the others were at Waterside Park, waiting for the fireworks display.

Which is where we were planning to go before Petra fell out of the tree.

I can go anyway, I realized. After all, it wasn't as if I had to do anything for Coily. Mostly he lay on the flat rock in his tank, or wrapped himself around the tree branch in there, or hid inside the copper water pipe Pete had found for him.

"They like to hide," Pete explained. "Where they can't be seen."

"Great," I'd told her. "The less I see him, the better."

Not that I'm afraid of snakes—but, hey, even Indiana Jones thinks they're repulsive. So I'd just look in on Coily—very briefly—and then go off to see the fireworks. If I could find someone to drive me.

I went into the house, flipping on light switches as I made my way to the kitchen. It was getting pretty dark. The fireworks would probably begin in about an hour.

I phoned my friend Josh, hoping he was home.

"Hey, Will!" he shouted. "Boy, am I glad to hear somebody who doesn't sound like Popeye the Sailor Man."

"Excuse me?"

"There's a six-hour Popeye marathon on cable. We're into the fourth hour here."

"Then you'll be glad to know why I'm calling," I said. "Though it does involve water." I explained about Pete and the hospital, and about how I wanted to go down to the Waterside Park.

"That would be great," he said.

"OK, come over and pick me up and—"

"Except that I have to sit with Steffie." Steffie is Josh's five-year-old sister.

"Bring her along," I said.

"She's got strep throat," Josh said. "I can't take her anywhere."

"It's hot out," I said. "It wouldn't hurt her to just lie on a blanket and watch—"

"She's got a fever of almost thirty-nine degrees," he said. "Hey, I have to go. I think I hear her croaking for something. Enjoy the fireworks."

"How can I—" But he'd already hung up. How can I enjoy the fireworks, I'd been about to ask, with no one to drive me there? The park is seven kilometres away.

Shelly! I thought. My friend Shelly had a brand-new driver's licence and was always looking for an excuse to drive somewhere.

I heard a lot of noise in the background when Mrs. Getz answered the phone. Kid noise. Like a bunch of preteenies squealing and giggling.

"Hi, Mrs. Getz. It's Will. May I speak to Shelly?"

"She's sort of tied up at the moment," said Mrs. Getz. "Can she call you back?"

"What's going on there?" I asked. "Is that Shelly screaming?"

"I think so," Mrs. Getz answered. "She's supposed to be running Carol's birthday party." Carol is Shelly's eleven-year-old sister.

"I forgot about the party," I said glumly. "I guess she'll be tied up for a while then."

"She will until I go untie her," said Mrs. Getz. "I believe they're playing Joan of Arc."

"Boy," I said, thinking of Pete and Steffie, "kids can sure be a pain sometimes."

Mrs. Getz snorted. "Tell me about it," she said, and hung up.

I dropped the phone back on the hook. I peered out the window over the kitchen sink. It was only 7:30, but the darkness was closing in fast.

I called three other friends. Two weren't home. Chip, the third, had to shout over the sound of an electric guitar, and some horrible wailing.

"Family reunion!" he yelled. "That's my cousin Dennis."

"What's he doing?"

"Elvis Presley. Why don't you come over? We're barbecuing."

"Dennis, I hope," I muttered.

"What? I can't hear you."

"I said, great, I'll be right there." It was only a kilometre to Chip's, and even if I'd have to listen to Dennis, it was better than sitting alone in the house with a boa constrictor.

And then I heard a distant rumble.

"Was that thunder?" I asked.

"I can't hear a thing," Chip shouted. "Dennis is doing 'Hound Dog.'"

Another rumble. Closer.

"I think it's starting to rain," Chip said. "It doesn't matter. Come on over."

"Well, maybe not," I said. "I mean, if it's raining."

"That's OK. We'll go inside. Whoo, there goes the lightning."

"I'd better stay here," I said. "My folks might try to call."

"Oh, yeah," Chip said. "You have this thing about thunderstorms."

"I do *not* have a thing about thunderstorms," I said defensively. "I just don't feel like walking a kilometre in a downpour, that's all." With lightning striking all around me.

"Suit yourself," Chip said. "I'd better help Dennis get his amp inside before he's electrocuted."

"Right." I slammed the phone down. OK. Fine. I'll stay home. I'll read. I'll watch TV. I'll listen to music. I'll worry about my sister.

I'll be alone in the house with a boa constrictor.

Big deal. It doesn't scare me. All he ever does is lie on his rock. Or curl up inside his pipe. I won't bother him, he won't bother me. I'm not really afraid of snakes anyway. I just happen to find them repulsive, disgusting, and evil-looking.

But I'm not afraid of them.

And I'm certainly not afraid of being alone in the house. And even though it's starting to thunder, I'm perfectly safe, as long as I don't talk on the telephone, stick my toe in a light socket, or stand under a tree.

So there's nothing to be afraid of. Even if it is getting so dark that the light over the kitchen table is barely making a dent in the gloom.

So don't stay in the kitchen, dummy, I told myself. There's a whole, brightly lit house to wander around in. I'll just go check the stupid snake, I thought, then settle down in front of the TV. There's nothing like a Popeye festival to calm your nerves.

I turned on the light in the hallway and headed toward Pete's room.

One quick look into the glass tank and I could say that I'd kept my promise. Coily will be curled up on his rock, and I'll go curl up with Popeye and Olive. The rumbles of thunder that had seemed so far away a moment ago were louder now. The storm was coming closer.

That's OK, I told myself. The closest thing to a tree in this house was Coily's branch, and I would hardly climb into the tank and wedge myself under it, so there was nothing to worry about.

The door to Pete's room was wide open. This was a major violation of rules. Ever since she'd gotten the boa, Pete had strict orders to keep her door closed. That way, in case Coily ever managed to escape from his tank, he'd be confined to Petra's room and be reasonably easy to recapture.

Not that any of us, except Pete, would ever try to recapture him. My father said, "If that thing gets loose, I'm moving to a motel and putting the house up for sale."

So far the only time the snake had been out of Pete's room was when she would occasionally drape Coily around her shoulders and parade around the house so we could admire his exotic markings and alleged tameness.

When Pete "walked" her scaly pet, the rest of us found urgent business to attend to in rooms with doors that locked.

Anyway, it disturbed me that Pete's door was wide open, but I figured that in her hurry to get to the yard and climb a tree so she could fall out of it, she'd forgotten the rule.

I reached inside the room and flicked the light on. From the entrance I peered at the snake tank. It was a large, glass rectangle with gravel on the bottom and plastic mesh screening over the top. Pete had taped a little sign on the side that said COILY'S CORNER.

I couldn't see the beast at first, but that didn't throw me. As Pete had said, snakes like to hide, so I figured Coily was scrunched inside his copper pipe.

I moved into the room. A clap of thunder made me jump, but it wasn't too bad, and I hadn't seen any lightning flash.

"Kilometres away," I reassured myself. "Just get the stupid snake check over with and go watch something dumb on the tube."

OK. I cleared my throat so Coily would know I was coming and not feel he had to rear up and do anything dramatic to protect his territory. I know snakes can't hear. But why take chances?

I edged closer to the tank. I could see it all, the whole thing. But I couldn't see Coily. Inside the pipe, I reminded myself. Just squat down, look inside the pipe, barf, run out of the room, and shut the door.

The lights flickered with another burst of thunder. Lights flicker in a storm, I reminded myself. No need to panic. I squatted down and looked into the copper pipe.

I could see clear through it to the other side. There was nothing inside it but air.

"Yikes!" I straightened up, and as I did, I noticed that the plastic mesh screening on top of the tank had a jagged rip in one corner.

As if something—something with fangs—had gnawed right through it.

"Yikes!" I was repeating myself, but this was no time to worry about being clever. I raced out of Pete's room and slammed the door. I leaned against the wall, panting, even though I'd only sprinted three metres.

What a narrow escape. I could have been standing—or squatting—right there in front of the tank, with a boa lurking under a chair just waiting to slink up and constrict me.

And then it hit me.

Pete's door had been open when I went into her room. It had been open for almost an hour. The snake might not be in there at all. In fact it could be anywhere in the house by this time.

I hugged the wall, wanting to climb up it. If I could hang from the light fixture on the ceiling, chances were the creature couldn't reach me.

Don't lose it, Will, I told myself. This is stupid. I could see all the way up and down the hall, and the boa was nowhere in sight.

There are seven rooms in this house, I reminded myself. Plus the hall. The odds are eight to one that I won't be in the same place as the snake. As long as I keep my eyes open—

Two deafening bursts of thunder, one right on top of the other. Instinctively I shut my eyes and clapped my hands over my ears. Then I thought of the four-metre-long snake slithering along the hall toward me. I snapped my eyes open and did a 360 to make sure I was still alone.

Another clap of thunder. The lights went out.

"No!" I yelled. "*No! Don't let the electricity go off!*"

The lights came back on.

"Thank you."

A drenching rain began to pound the house. It sounded as if I were standing in the middle of Niagara Falls.

Flashlight! I thought. Candles. Quick, while I could still find them.

I ran for the kitchen. I opened the utility cabinet, next to the refrigerator. Something smacked against the window. It was probably a branch of the mimosa tree, driven by a sudden, howling wind that had seemed to come from nowhere.

"Just the tree," I told myself. "It happens all the time when it's windy."

As I turned around to make sure it was nothing more sinister than the tree branch, the room went black.

Another flicker. I tried to keep calm. The electricity would come back on in a moment.

But it didn't.

"Aw, no!" I begged. "Not the lights. A boa constrictor and a thunderstorm aren't enough for one night?"

As if in ironic answer, a flash of lightning—very close, *extremely close*—illuminated the room with a harsh, chalky light. For three seconds I could see as clearly as if it were daytime. The mimosa tree, the sink, the white curtains at the window...

And the giant brown reptile twined around the curtain rod flicking his forked tongue at me.

I screamed and jumped backward, crashing against the open door of the utility cabinet. Shrieking, I stumbled out of the kitchen,

flailing my arms in front of me to keep from banging into anything else.

Which didn't work. I tripped over the stepladder, bounced off a wall, and staggered into the dining room, where I met the china cabinet head-on. Every dish on the shelves clattered as I careened into it and landed on the floor. I moaned, and wondered which part of my body hurt the most.

I sat huddled there for a moment, dazed and whimpering. Now, accompanying the torrential rain, there was a loud, rattling sound, as if someone were hurling handfuls of gravel against the windows. Hail, I thought. You sometimes get hail with severe thunderstorms. And tornadoes.

Great. A tornado. Just what I need. Thunder and lightning and hail and total darkness and a wandering boa constrictor and a tornado.

Mommy!

The hail and rain were making so much noise that I could hardly hear myself think. If you could call what I was doing thinking. If I can't hear myself think, I realized, I can't hear the brown monstrosity unwind himself from the curtain rod.

I can't hear him slip down off the sink, and across the floor, and out of the kitchen, and into the dining room, where I'm curled up here on the floor like a sitting—

"Ayiee!"

I leaped to my feet—or at least I crawled to my knees and stood up as quickly as I could with an entirely black-and-blue body. *Think, Will*, I ordered myself. *Just shut the kitchen door, and—*

Good idea. Except we don't have a kitchen door, only an archway that separates the kitchen from the dining room. At this very moment Coily could be slithering past the refrigerator, heading for the dining room.

I'll go to my room. I'll go to my room and shut the door. No problem. Just grope around the table, through the living room, down the hall, and into my room. I can certainly move faster than a snake can slither—at least I can when the lights are on.

Of course there is another archway that leads from the kitchen and into the hall. The snake could be creeping out that way and into the hall just as I—

Don't even think about it.

Move.

I moved. As fast as I could, in the dark, with only an occasional flash of lightning to help me around the maze of furniture that clutters the living room.

"Why is this room so crammed?" I wondered, as I banged my shin against a footstool. "Does anyone really need this much furniture?"

I flung my arm against a plant stand. A flowerpot crashed to my feet.

"Please don't let it be my mother's African violet that didn't bloom for three years up until last week," I prayed.

I made it to my room without further damage to myself or to our overfurnished house. I slammed the door behind me. I was sure the snake couldn't have gotten to my room before I did.

Well, I was pretty sure.

Call Josh, I thought. *Maybe his parents are home by now. Maybe he can come over with a flashlight, find the boa, and put him back in his tank.*

The phone next to my bed has a lighted keypad, which is convenient if you have to call the police in the middle of the night, or if a boa constrictor gets loose in the dark.

When Josh picked up his phone, I didn't even say hello. I just shrieked.

"You have to come over and help me! I don't know where Coily is!"

"Did you check with Larry and Moe?" he asked.

"What?"

"A Three Stooges joke," he explained. "You know, Larry, Moe, and—"

"This is no time for jokes!" I yelled. "I'm alone in the house with a rampaging boa constrictor, and the lights are off, and—"

"I can't take my sister out in this storm," he cut in.

"When will your parents be home?" I asked desperately.

"Monday," he answered.

"ARRGGHH!" I slammed down the phone.

There was only one thing to do. Only one intelligent, mature way of coping with the situation.

I dived into bed and pulled the covers over my head.

The snake couldn't be in my room. He just couldn't be. I'd be perfectly safe here under the covers. If I didn't pass out from the heat or smother myself.

I cowered there, sweating and shaking, waiting for my parents to come home. Once in a while I'd think I'd heard a car door slam. Then I'd poke my head out and listen. And gasp for air. But the only sounds were the rain—softer now—and distant rumbles of thunder.

I don't know how long I stayed there, trying to breathe, feeling my clothes getting wetter and wetter with sweat, telling myself that there was no snake in my room and that even if there was, he preferred curtain rods to beds.

And then I felt something soft graze my leg.

For a moment I froze. I couldn't breathe, couldn't even scream, which is what I really wanted to do.

It can't be a four-metre boa constrictor, I told myself. It's just a beetle or a mosquito or something. But it didn't feel like a beetle or a mosquito.

It felt like a wet strand of spaghetti crawling up my leg.

I threw the covers off, howling. Just as I did, the electricity came back on. My room blazed with light. I blinked, and like a kid waking up from a nightmare, clutched my pillow to my chest. I forced myself to look down, down toward the end of the bed, where I had flung off the covers.

And saw a procession of brown, thirty-centimetre-long snakes writhing up my sheet, heads darting, tongues flicking, coming straight at me.

Screaming uncontrollably, I threw myself out of bed. I could still feel something on my leg. When I looked down, I saw that one of the creatures was hanging from my ankle like a loose boot strap.

"NO! *NO!*" I shook my leg violently, and the snake fell to the floor. I felt as if there were snakes crawling all over my body. I twisted around frantically, smacking my pillow against my legs, my arms, my chest.

What if they're in my shorts?

I screamed even louder, dropped my pillow, and scrambled out of my cutoffs. Through my screaming I heard feet pounding down the hall.

"Will! *Will!*" My father threw my door open and grabbed me by the shoulders.

"Snakes! Snakes!" I screamed. "In my pants! In my bed!"

My mother was right behind him. Dimly, through a haze of terror, I saw Pete peer into my room. She had a splint on one arm and a boa constrictor wrapped around the other.

"How come you're running around in your under—" She looked over at my bed.

"Coily!" she cried delightedly. "You're a girl!"

◆ ◆ ◆

Maybe the biggest surprise was that my hair did *not* turn completely white. Although I was afraid to look in a mirror for two days.

Coily has been adopted by one of my sister's weird friends. My mother put her foot down. She told Pete, "Look, your brother cannot live in the same house with that snake."

"So let him move," Pete said.

They think they found all the babies. But since no one knows how many snakes Coily actually gave birth to, no one is positive they're really all gone. Pete says if there are any left, they ought to come out pretty soon, because they'll be hungry. In the meantime they could be anywhere. In the pipes under the toilet, in the back of a closet, behind the refrigerator.

So I did move. I'm staying at Josh's house for a while. My parents have been very understanding about my traumatic experience. Especially my father.

He's checked into a motel for two weeks.

----

1. RESPONDING TO THE STORY

a. List three things that Will claims he's not afraid of. Do you believe him? Why?

b. Explain how the story turns out to be even worse than Will's worst fears.

c. Although the story is suspenseful, it is also meant to be funny. Find at least five humorous lines in the story. Did you think the humour was effective? Why or why not?

d. Would Will's situation be a nightmare for you, too? With a partner, think of other nightmarish situations.

2. STORY CRAFT ANALYSE SUSPENSE

"For Pete's Snake" could be classified as a **suspense** story. Locate at least three spots in the story where you think the author was trying to make the reader feel suspense. Do you think the author's efforts were successful? Explain your answer.

> **Suspense** is a feeling of excitement and uncertainty about what will happen next.

In small groups, describe some of the most suspenseful moments in TV shows and movies you have seen. What techniques were used to create the suspense? Why do you think that people enjoy feeling suspense? As a group, create a list of at least five ideas that a writer of stories or scripts could use to put an audience on the edge of its seat!

3. WRITING DEVELOP AN OUTLINE

As a class, brainstorm suspenseful situations such as exploring a cave, landing on an unexplored planet, or investigating a crime. Choose one situation the whole group would like to develop. Together, create a story outline. Focus on how your story will create suspense. Your outline should include

- an *introduction* that gives the setting, describes important characters, and relates an exciting or mysterious event to get the story going quickly
- *rising action*—a series of events that builds suspense
- a *climax,* when the suspense "explodes" in a final adventure or confrontation
- a *resolution* that explains any unanswered questions and ties up loose ends

You might work individually or in groups to draft a story based on your outline.

4. LANGUAGE CONVENTIONS DASHES

You may have noticed that Ellen Conford uses dashes (—) in a special way throughout the story. Reread the story and identify all the places where the author places a dash at the end of a sentence or line of dialogue. What meaning is communicated through these dashes? Why is this use of punctuation especially appropriate in a suspense story?

SELF-ASSESSMENT: Review a piece of your own writing. Are there places where you could use dashes to increase the effectiveness of your writing?

HOW TO WRITE A
SHORT STORY

Goals at a Glance
● Develop a story idea. ● Revise a story draft.

Choose an Idea

For many people, this is the hardest part of writing a story. Here are some ways to find an idea that's original and exciting.

- **Brainstorm.** Write as many story ideas as you can think of in a short time. Draw on places and people you know, experiences you've had, and other stories you've read.
- **Check Your Writing Folder**. Look through everything you've written this year. Can you find a character you'd like to develop? A funny incident? A favourite memory? An image of a place you love? Any one of these could turn into a short story.
- **Use Your Imagination**. Where would you like to visit? Imagine yourself there. What adventures would you like to experience? Imagine what would happen if you could really have one of those adventures!
- **Check Out the Anthology**: Quickly review the short stories in this anthology. It's always a good idea to try writing the kind of story that

you like to read. Do you enjoy funny stories? mysteries? fantasy? realism?

Develop Your Story Idea

Now that you have a story idea, what are you going to do with it? While you don't have to plan out every detail of your story in advance, there are some key parts you should try to get straight before you write.

- **Create an Interesting Setting**. Make the setting vivid for your readers by including lots of sensory details (sights, sounds, smells, and so on). Before you write, jot down some words and phrases that will help you create a sense of place.
- **Set the Plot in Motion**. Stories have to go somewhere, and they have to carry their readers along with them. Here is a list of story starters.
  - the main character has a problem to overcome or a goal to reach
  - conflict is set up between the main character and someone or something else

CHARACTER CHART:	Taslim				
Age	Appearance	Interests	Personality	Good Points	Bad Points
14	tall, dark hair and eyes	sports, music	confident, outgoing	never gives up, loyal	doesn't want advice or help

Instead, tell the most important things and let the reader fill in the gaps.

— an unexpected person or event creates difficulties for the main character

— the main character is propelled into the past, the future, or a new and dangerous place

- **Create Believable Characters**. Readers will believe in your characters if they're like real people. Try making a chart for your main characters, listing his or her qualities. You'll find an example above.

Draft Your Story

You've now done some thinking about character, setting, and plot. What comes next? Stop planning and start writing—it's as simple as that! Don't worry about grammar, spelling, or punctuation. You can fix those things later. However, there is one decision you'll have to make: How will you narrate your story? Will you use a first-person narrator ("I leaped aboard the rescue helicopter...") or a third-person narrator ("Harif leaped aboard the rescue helicopter...")?

Here are three things to keep in mind as you write your draft:

- **Focus on What's Important.** If you try to give a second-by-second account of all the action, you'll soon run out of energy and words.

Save some energy so you can make the end of your story exciting and memorable.

- **Use Dialogue**. Your characters should talk to one another just as real people do—asking and answering questions, agreeing and disagreeing, and telling important information.

- **Provide Detail**. Include enough detail so a reader can imagine what is happening, who is involved, and where the action is taking place. If the setting changes, describe the new place so the reader can picture it.

Revise Your Story

Congratulations! Now you have a story to polish. At this point, it's a good idea to read your story aloud to yourself. Use the checklist below to help you decide what parts of your story to revise.

❏ Is the opening sentence catchy?

❏ Do my characters come alive?

❏ Is there a detailed description of the setting?

❏ Does my story have tension (conflict, suspense, mystery, or problems to resolve)?

❏ Is the dialogue convincing?

❏ Does my ending bring the story to a satisfying (for example, dramatic, humorous) conclusion?

PROCESS

All is Calm

SHORT STORY BY ANN WALSH

I don't know how it happened, but I was the only one who could do it, and it was turning out to be worse than I thought it would be. I mean, I love my grandma; everyone loves their grandmother, right? But Gran had become, well, strange isn't quite the word. Mom said it was Alzheimer's, and she cried when she told me. It didn't mean much to me at the time, but believe me, as the year went by I learned more than I ever wanted to know about that disease.

It makes people forget. Not just ordinary forgetting—the square roots of numbers or your last boyfriend's phone number—but serious blanking out, like the names of your children, where you live, what you do in a bathroom, and whether your bra goes on before or after you put on your blouse. Gran didn't do those things yet, but chances were she *would* as the disease took her farther and farther away from the person she once had been. She still had good days, times when she seemed so normal, so like her old self that it made it worse when she went off into whatever strange place the Alzheimer's was taking her mind. She had always been a bit "odd"—actually "ditzy" was the word my father used—but she had been kind and funny and caring and clean. Now—well, sometimes she was really different, weird even, and I was on a bus with her at four o'clock on a Wednesday afternoon hoping that today would be one of her good days.

GOALS AT A GLANCE

- Understand some purposes of fiction.
- Analyse dialogue.

I was the only one who could do it, take Gran to the doctor's appointment. Mom was away at a conference, my brother had to get his braces adjusted, and Dad couldn't get off work in time. "Katie," Mom said before she left, "Katie, she has to go. It took us months to get this appointment, and this specialist is the one who can help us get Gran into a home—he has to classify her condition as serious so that we can get her into a place where she'll be looked after properly. I can't do it any more; I just can't. She's only lived with us a year, but I can't handle her any more."

I thought Mom was going to cry again when she said that. She'd been doing a lot of crying lately, so I put my arm around her and hugged her and said all the right things about how I didn't mind at all, and sure, it was just a short bus trip, and no, Gran wouldn't embarrass me and we'd manage just fine.

Sure. We were managing. Barely.

It started when I got home from school. Mom had left a note, reminding Gran of the appointment, and Dad had phoned her at noon reminding her again—but she hadn't picked up the phone, and I heard his anxious voice when I checked the answering machine. At 3:30, an hour before we had to be at the doctor's, Gran was sitting at the kitchen table in her nightgown writing Christmas cards. At least she thought she was writing them. She'd taken the box of cards out of the drawer where Mom had stored them until next November, and she'd written her own address on every envelope—no name, just the address. She was singing to herself when I got home, singing Christmas carols and stuffing blank cards into envelopes —in March!

It took a while, but I got her dressed and we got out of the house and down to the bus stop in record time. The bus came along right away, and everything was going to be OK, and I was sort of proud of myself—and then she started singing again. "Silent night, Holy night, All is calm..." Gran has a loud voice, loud and friendly and the kind of voice you wanted to hear singing happy birthday to you when you were nine, but on a crowded bus it didn't sound friendly but just plain strange.

People turned around to stare at us, and I said "Gran, it's not Christmas. Don't sing those songs now."

She looked at me, and the singing stopped. Her mouth stayed open for a while, sort of caught in the phrase "mother and child," and then her face crumpled and she began to cry.

Out loud. Cry as if I had kicked her, or told her her puppy had been run over. "Don't cry, Gran," I said quickly. "Listen, you can sing all you want to once we get home—really."

She clutched at my hand, and suddenly the tears were gone. "We'll go carol singing," she said. "All of us. I'll make hot chocolate and we'll all go out in the snow and sing."

"Sure, Gran," I said, trying to untangle my hands from her. "Sure, when Christmas comes we'll all go carol singing."

She smiled at me, and I gave up trying to get my hand away from hers, and just held it and squeezed it. Gran always had a nice smile. She looked at you when she smiled too, right in the eyes, and you always knew that smile was for you and not for anyone else.

"Where are we going?" she asked loudly. "Why are we going this way? We'll get lost."

"It's the way to the doctor's office, Gran." I spoke really softly, hoping she'd get the idea and lower her voice, too. Again heads were turning, as people craned their necks for a look at my...for a look at the crazy woman who used to be my grandma. I tried not to meet anyone's eyes. "Shhh, Gran. We won't get lost," I reassured her.

It didn't make any difference. "Stop the bus, stop it, right now! We're lost!" she yelled. She tried to stand up, but the bus lurched away from a stop and she sort of fell backward into her seat.

"Sit down...everything's going to be all right," I said. And then, just like the sun coming out, she smiled at me and, as if everything was normal and fine, she said, "Isn't it a lovely day, Katherine? It's so nice to spend some time with you, dear. Shall we go and have tea cakes after our appointment? You always liked those sticky buns they make at the Tea Shoppe."

She had come back again. Just like that. One moment there was this crazy woman sitting beside me, and the next moment my grandmother was back. I don't know why, but suddenly I wanted to cry too.

"Sure," I said. "We'll go for tea and goodies." We sat there, silently, for the rest of the trip.

Then it was our stop and we had to get off. "Come on, Gran," I told her. "We're here."

She turned to me, and her face changed again, and she grabbed onto the seat in front of her and said, "I'm not moving. You're just trying to trick me."

"Gran," I urged, hoping that she hadn't gone too far away into the craziness of the disease again, "Gran, come on. The bus is stopping." I took her arm and tried to gently pull her to her feet, but she just clutched the handrail tighter.

"Leave me alone," she said, her voice now louder than it had been when she was singing carols. "I don't know who you are. I don't go places with strangers."

"Come on, Gran. It's me, Katie...Katherine. We're going to see the doctor. This is where his office is. Come on, Gran." The bus had stopped now, and the other people who were getting off had already left. I stood up and tried to pull her to her feet.

"Leave me alone. Don't touch me. Help, help me someone!" I couldn't believe it. She was calling for help as if I were trying to kidnap her—me, her own granddaughter!

"Gran," I said. "Please come with me. You know who I am...you've just forgotten for a moment. Please, get off the bus."

"Everything all right back there?" called the driver, and I could see him turning around and halfway rising from his seat. "I've got a schedule to keep, miss. You'll have to get her off right now because I can't wait any longer."

"I'm never going anywhere with you," Gran said to me. "I hate you. You're a nasty little girl, and I don't know why you want me to go with you." The doors of the bus closed, and the driver pulled slowly ahead and I stood there in the aisle and wondered what on earth I could do. One thing I knew I mustn't do, though, was get angry. It wasn't my grandmother talking. It was the disease, the Alzheimer's. I must remember that; Mom had told us over and over that Gran didn't mean to be cruel or to say horrible things to us, but the disease took over her voice as it took over her mind, and she couldn't always control the words that she said.

It's the disease speaking, I told myself, only the disease, not Gran. Fine. But the stupid disease wasn't going to let her get off the bus, and what could I do about it? I put my arm around her shoulder. "Gran, Gran...please, try to remember. It's me, Katie."

The bus began to slow again, approaching the next stop. I didn't hear him come up behind me, but suddenly he was there. "Hi," he said, and then stood beside me, smiling down at my grandmother. "I have to get off at this stop," he told her. "Can I help you? Would you like to come with me?"

Gran was silent for a moment, and I was, too. I knew this guy, Kevin; he was in several of my classes this semester. He was tall, blond, and into sports, not a type I hang around with. He always seemed to be clowning around with a group of kids, and I had figured he wasn't worth the effort of getting to know—just a jock who hung around with airheads. "It's OK," I said stiffly. "We'll manage."

But Gran was smiling up at him and taking the arm he offered. "What a nice young man," she said. "Yes, please, do help me. I think I'm on the wrong bus."

Kevin helped her out of her seat, then down the stairwell, and out the doors of the bus. He held out his hand as she stepped down to the curb, and she took it and smiled at him, as gracious as the Queen Mother. "I think your doctor's office is one block back," he said. "Would you like me to walk with you and Katie?"

"Katie?" said Gran, and for a minute I thought she'd forgotten me again, but then she noticed me and the glazed look went from her eyes and she, my grandmother, not the crazy woman, was back again. "Why, Katie, come on. We don't want to be late for the doctor, and then we're going for tea. Perhaps your young man would like to join us?" She slung her handbag over her shoulder and straightened the scarf around the neck of her coat and strode off down the sidewalk, heading in the right direction, walking tall and proud and normally.

"Thanks, Kevin," I said. "I'm sorry..." And then the tears that I'd been fighting with for almost the whole bus trip won the fight and I began to bawl.

"I know," he said. "It's really hard. Go ahead and cry. I'll keep an eye on her." He gestured to my grandmother, who had stopped in front of a grocery store and was staring at a crate of oranges as if she had never seen that fruit before. Well, in the world she lived in these days, perhaps there weren't any oranges. Or any apples or bananas or granddaughters.

"I'm OK," I said, and blew my nose. "Thanks again for your help. You were really great with her. I don't know what I would have done if you hadn't helped get her off the bus." Then it struck me. Here was this guy I barely knew, big-shot jock and classroom clown—what was he doing helping out with my grandmother?

It's almost as if Kevin read my thoughts. He grinned at me. "Yeah," he said. "Didn't you know that your grandma is my type?"

I grinned back. "No. But then, I guess I don't know you well enough to know what your type is, do I?"

"We'll work on that," he said. "I think we've a lot in common, more than you realize."

"A lot in common...?" I began, then I saw him looking down the street at Gran and I remembered how patient and good he'd been with her, how he'd gotten her off the bus when I couldn't, and suddenly I understood.

"Your grandmother, too?" I asked. "Your grandmother has Alzheimer's?"

"My father," he said, and he began walking toward Gran. "The doctors say it's 'early onset,' which means it starts when someone's younger. He just turned forty-six."

"Oh," I said. "I'm sorry." And I was. Sorry for Kevin and what he had to go through as his father went away to that special hell where people with Alzheimer's live; sorry for my family and me for what we had to go through with Gran; sorry for the embarrassment and pain and ugliness that was ahead and couldn't be avoided.

I was sorry for us all, but I knew we'd get through it, we'd survive. But Gran and Kevin's father, they wouldn't get through it. They wouldn't survive except as lonely shadows of themselves in a world where nothing made sense and no one was familiar.

I went up to Gran, who was still staring at the oranges, and right there, in the middle of the sidewalk with people all around us and Kevin staring at me, I gave her a hug. "I love you, Gran," I said. "I'll always love you."

She looked me right in the eyes, and smiled. Then, from somewhere far, far away she said, "I love you too, Mary." ◆

1. RESPONDING TO THE STORY

a. What did you learn from the story about how Alzheimer's disease affects people? Summarize what you knew about the disease before you read the story.

b. Why is Katie surprised that Kevin is able to help her and understand Gran? How do her feelings about Kevin change by the end of the story?

c. Why do you think Ann Walsh used the title "All Is Calm" for this story? How is it appropriate or inappropriate?

2. READING EXPLORE PURPOSE

"All Is Calm" introduces us to characters who are trying to cope with Alzheimer's disease. In a small group, explore some reasons why an author might write a story that deals with a problem such as Alzheimer's. What influence could such stories have on readers?

In your group, think of stories, songs, movies, and TV shows that, like "All Is Calm," try to present a specific problem or issue in a realistic way. Which examples are your favourites? As a group, identify some problems or issues that you think should be dealt with through a work of fiction. Have one member of your group present your ideas to the class.

3. STORY CRAFT DIALOGUE

Dialogue is very important in story writing. One of its most important functions is to reveal character. Look closely at the excerpt below.

> "Where are we going?" she asked loudly. "Why are we going this way? We'll get lost."
> "It's the way to the doctor's office, Gran." I spoke really softly, hoping she'd get the idea and lower her voice, too.

What does this dialogue reveal about Gran? How do you think Katie feels when Gran talks this way? How does she hope to change Gran's behaviour?

With a partner, discuss some of the other functions dialogue serves in stories. Look in the story for examples of dialogue that fulfil some of these functions.

4. LANGUAGE CONVENTIONS SENTENCE TYPES

There are four basic types of sentences.

- A *statement* makes an assertion and ends with a period:

  The garbage is piling up.

- A *question* asks for information and ends with a question mark:

  Will you take out the garbage?

- A *command* gives an order or makes a request and ends with a period:

  Please take out the garbage.

- An *exclamation* expresses surprise or a strong feeling and ends with an exclamation mark to show emphasis:

  This garbage stinks!

Find one example of each sentence type in "All Is Calm," and write it in your notebook with the correct label. Create a brief dialogue in which you include each different sentence type at least once. With a partner, exchange dialogues and identify each sentence type in one another's work.

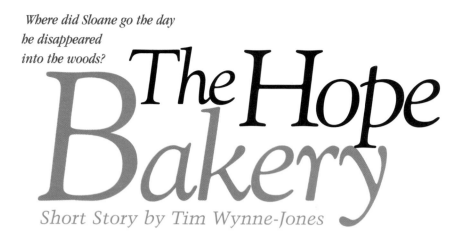

Where did Sloane go the day he disappeared into the woods?

The Hope Bakery

Short Story by Tim Wynne-Jones

When he was only five, Sloane wandered out of the back garden into the woods behind his house. He was gone for some time and everyone got horribly worried, but he arrived home before dark. He didn't understand the greeting he got when he came back out of the woods. Everyone hugged him and kissed him and lectured him between hugs and kisses about not going off like that.

Sloane asked if he was late for supper. He thought that was what all the fuss was about. Of course, nobody had bothered making supper because they were all out looking for him, and so they could only laugh between their tears and say, "No, you're not late for supper." They asked him, "What special thing would you like, sweetheart? Noodles, maybe? Hot dogs?" Sloane wanted mashed potatoes, and everyone agreed that would be very comforting.

But then came the strange part. At dinner he produced a piece of paper from his pocket with the word HOPE on it. The paper was brown; the word was written in pencil.

"Hope?" said his mother.

"It's where I was," he answered.

162

- Analyse plot.
- Identify subordinate clauses.

Mother and
Father and
Sloane's older
sister and brother
all looked question-
ingly at one another and
then at Sloane, who was too
busy with his mashed potatoes to
notice. The thing is, Sloane was only five,
and although he knew his letters pretty well, he
didn't know too many words. But the writing was
unmistakably his. He always put four crossbars on his E's.

"You were at Hope?" his father asked, looking at the wobbly
word on the very ragged piece of paper.

"I thought you'd want to know where I was." Sloane stopped
eating long enough to extract a stubby pencil from his pocket. "Good
I remembered this," he said. "There was paper there, lots of it." He
looked around at everyone staring at him. "Don't you know where it
is?" he asked. Nobody did.

Sloane said he would take them there. He tried once or twice,
but he couldn't find the right path.

So nobody ever learned where Sloane had disappeared to on
that scary afternoon when he was only five. The ragged little bit of
paper with HOPE written on it stayed on the refrigerator door for a
long time beside the shopping lists, the swimming schedules, the *Hi
& Lois* cartoon, the crayon drawings of monsters.

And then on Mother's Day, as a kind of joke, Father had that
piece of brown paper framed in a beautiful wood frame with glass
and everything. It was hung on the wall above Mother's desk where
the pictures of the kids were. And Sloane, if he ever thought about
the adventure, never mentioned it again.

◆ ◆ ◆

Sloane grew up. When he was eight, another brother came into his life, Todd. So by the time Sloane was thirteen, Todd was five.

Sloane found being thirteen difficult. Especially school. He was lost at school. He liked lunch and music and geography. He liked maps, liked filling in the sea around the continents with a blue pencil crayon. He spent a lot of time at it.

He was upset easily. One morning, waiting for the school bus, Sloane found a dead chipmunk on the front drive and got so broke up about it that he stayed home from school. His older brother, Lawren, teased him about it.

Then one morning, when he was watching TV, Sloane saw a lion killing a litter of lion cubs. He wanted to turn off the TV, but he wanted to watch it, too. The lion had already driven off the father of the cubs and was taking over the pride, which is what they call a lion family. This new lion didn't want any of the other lion's cubs around. The program didn't actually show the new lion killing anything, but there was a picture of two of the cubs crouching together looking very scared. It was worse than a horror movie. Sloane hated it. And he hated himself for having wanted to watch it.

After that he didn't watch TV for a week. He wrote a letter to the TV station about the show. He wrote about it in his journal; he talked about it with his parents and with his friend Trevor. He even brought it up in class. Everyone agreed it was pretty terrible, but no one seemed to understand just how deeply Sloane felt about it. He couldn't shake it off. It made him ache in a place inside him he hadn't known was there. He wished he had never found that place.

◆ ◆ ◆

Sometimes when things go bad, they get deeply rotten before they get better. That's what happened to Sloane. The new place inside him that ached so much for dead chipmunks and lion cubs got a real workout.

In his class, there was this girl Cynthia, who had something wrong with her. Everyone liked her well enough, but nobody really got to know her. She couldn't keep up with the class, but the teacher didn't seem to worry too much about it. Cynthia was going to be having some operation; that was all any of the kids knew.

One Thursday Sloane's mother was going to be in town on an errand and so Sloane didn't take the school bus home that afternoon. He hung out at the park instead. He met a guy on the basketball court and they got talking and playing some one-on-one. The guy's name was Billy. It turned out that Billy was Cynthia's brother. When Sloane found out, he stopped right in the middle of dribbling toward the net. It was like the lion on TV all over again. He didn't want to ask, but he couldn't stop himself.

"What's wrong with her?" he said. Billy told him. The operation was on her brain. It was pretty major. So Cynthia's family was trying to keep everything as ordinary as possible. That's why Cynthia was staying with her own age of kids in school even though she couldn't really keep up.

Billy bounced the ball a few times, watching the way the ball and its shadow met each time the ball hit the ground.

"Like last night," he said, "Mom made spaghetti and meatballs and when she gave Cyn her plate, Cyn said, 'Umm, this looks delicious. What is it?'"

Sloane wasn't sure he had heard right, wasn't sure he understood. "She never saw spaghetti and meatballs before?"

"Sure," said Billy. He bounced the ball a few times, never looking up. "We have it all the time."

Going home that night, Todd was whining a lot and Sloane was supposed to keep him entertained. Mother had a headache. Todd got more and more crotchety, and Sloane grew angrier and angrier. He was thinking about Cynthia. How could such a thing happen? He kept thinking.

At home he got into a big argument with Lawren over whose turn it was to clean their room.

Rachel, his older sister, was making dinner that night. She made pumpkin lasagna. Everybody found other things to talk about. And then, suddenly, Sloane said, "It just isn't fair!"

Lawren thought he was talking about their room. Rachel thought he was talking about her pumpkin lasagna.

"Just 'cause the edges are a bit burnt," she said, and stamped out of the dining room.

Little Todd laughed. He liked burnt edges.

Father excused himself and went to talk to Rachel.

"I meant something that happened in town," said Sloane.

"What?" said Lawren. "Did you see some more dead stuff?"

"Yeah, your brain," said Sloane.

"Boys!" said Mother.

But it was too late. Sloane couldn't hold back. He didn't want to talk about what Billy had told him. What good would talking do? He wished he had never heard of Cynthia. He wanted it all to go away.

He was sent to his room. Lawren slept somewhere else that night.

◆ ◆ ◆

The next morning, when Sloane came down for breakfast, the family was excited. Father had seen an elk at the bottom of the garden while everyone was still asleep.

Although they lived in the country, on the edge of a forest, they had never heard of an elk being seen in the area. Sloane joined his brothers and sisters looking out the window. But the elk was long gone.

"I was letting the cat in and the elk spooked when he heard the door open, took off into the brush," Father said. The family kidded him about it over breakfast, but they all knew he didn't make up stories.

"It was huge," he said. "Ten points on its rack."

"What?" Todd asked. Sloane explained to him that the elk had ten points on its antlers. It must have been a big one.

Little Todd wanted to see the elk. He asked Sloane to walk down to the bottom of the garden with him to look for it. Sloane was still depressed about Cynthia and the fight with Lawren. He hadn't slept well and he was grouchy, but he went anyway.

They went down and Sloane looked out at the forest, but he saw nothing more lively than the wind turning the leaves bellyside-up, and a few noisy bluejays playing tag.

"I found his house!" Todd cried.

Sloane went to look. Todd was crouching beside a groundhog hole in the dirt bank where the lawn slipped off into bramble and prickly ash woodland.

"Whose house?" Sloane asked.

"The elk's," said Todd.

Sloane laughed. "An elk's huge," he said.

Todd poked at the hole with a stick. "Well, some of the dirt fell in so he doesn't look so big any more."

Sloane laughed again. "No, I mean *huge* like a horse." He could see Todd staring at the hole and wondering how something as big as a horse could get into a hole so small.

"Come on," said Sloane, and he led his little brother back to the house. In an encyclopedia, he showed him a picture of the elk.

Todd beamed and grabbed the book from his brother's hands. He tore out of the house and down to the groundhog hole. When Sloane arrived, Todd was comparing the size of the picture to the hole. He looked up triumphantly.

"See! It would so fit!"

Sloane shook his head. "You goof." He grabbed the encyclopedia. "Don't be so stupid!" he said, more angrily than he meant to. Then he headed back to the house to get his stuff for school.

He spent the day being sore and trying not to look at Cynthia or think about spaghetti. He got in trouble twice for not paying attention, once more for not having done his homework. He got a detention and had to take the late bus home from school.

As the bus neared his house, Sloane saw some of his neighbours walking along the sideroad. They had megaphones. There was another one in his driveway.

He rushed up to the house. That's when he found that Todd was missing.

"He was talking all morning about finding the elk's house," said Mother. Sloane went cold all over. There were search parties everywhere. Sloane could hear them down the old logging path, in the woods. "He's never wandered away before," said Mother. "He knows better than that!"

Sloane joined the search. The coldness that gripped him was like a black belt around his chest. As he tramped through the woods behind the house, moving deeper into the forest, the strap seemed to get tighter and tighter.

He didn't usually spend much time in the woods; he hardly ever had. City cousins who visited seemed to think he was lucky to live on the edge of a forest. They always wanted to play out there, to explore. They wanted to look for arrowheads and build forts. That was about the only time Sloane went into the woods any more. He cursed it now for its rotten wildness, its thousand sharp edges, the pointlessness of it all.

And then suddenly he came to a place in the woods that he seemed to know. Maybe it was on one of those visits from city cousins that he had explored this particular part. He couldn't recall the time. Maybe, he thought later, he had known he was heading this way from the moment he left the house. The cries of the other searchers had fallen far behind, barely distinguishable now from the twittering and screeching of the birds.

An opening. There were several paths leading to it or from it depending on how you looked at things; where you had come from or where you were going. Sloane stopped. It was as if he was in a dream. He felt he knew which path to take. He didn't know why, but the certainty of his decision seemed to loosen the belt around his chest a notch or two.

The path he chose led him through the dappled late afternoon into the shadow-making sunshine at the edge of a small meadow. Memory worked in him now. *He had been here!* When or how, he couldn't recall. The familiarity of the meadow was not a knowing thing so much as a feeling thing. As he walked, however, he was quite sure that he had been here alone.

Memory, loosed in him like this, seemed to unbuckle the fear and pain a few more notches. He stopped, looked around.

"This way," he told himself. "There will be an old fence. An abandoned road. A swamp. A junkyard."

He almost forgot Todd. It was as if he wasn't looking for him any more. Almost.

Finally, Sloane saw what he had been looking for, though he could never have given it a name. In the junkyard, resting on no wheels, rusted and overgrown with thistles and harsh grasses, stood an old blue-grey panel truck. On the side of it in faded letters were the words: "The HOPE Bakery."

The words "The" and "Bakery" were in a swirly kind of script, but the word "HOPE" was printed in tall letters. There had once been a little hand painted picture under this sign: some buns and loaves and a pie, maybe. It was hard to tell now. The paint was all peeled and crumbly.

Sloane looked at the panel truck, letting the shape of it drift into a waiting puzzle hole in his memory. And as he looked, the back door of the truck opened with a loud squeaking and out stepped Todd. Todd seemed almost to have been expecting him.

"You should see this, Sloaney," he called out, waving his hand. "I think this is where that elk lives."

Sloane made himself walk very slowly to his brother, as if to run might shatter the terrifying beauty of the moment. When he got there, he resisted hugging Todd, who was too busy anyway picking up rusted bits of engine parts, a stained hat, scraps of paper. If he hugged him, he was afraid he would burst into tears himself.

"There's plenty of room here," said the five-year-old. Sloane looked around, nodded.

Yes, he thought. Plenty of room.

1. RESPONDING TO THE STORY

a. Why do you think Sloane's father puts the word *Hope* in a special frame? If you were going to frame one word, what would it be?

b. Sloane hates the TV show about the lions, but can't stop watching it. Have you ever had that experience? Why do you think a person would keep watching something that was disturbing?

c. "Sometimes when things go bad, they get deeply rotten before they get better." How would you express what is going wrong for Sloane?

d. When Sloane joined in the search, did you expect him to find his brother? What information in the story shaped your expectations?

e. With a partner, discuss the ending of the story. What do you think Sloane means when he agrees that there is "plenty of room"? Is this a good way to end the story? Why or why not?

STRATEGIES

2. STORY CRAFT ANALYSE PLOT

Plot (the pattern of events in a narrative) is an important part of a short story. The main parts of a short story plot are (a) the introduction (b) the rising action (c) the climax and (d) the resolution. To remind yourself what these terms mean, see "Develop an Outline," page 149.

Copy the chart into your notebook. Then fill in the chart to create an outline of the plot of "Hope Bakery," listing the main events from the story.

	PLOT OUTLINE
Introduction	
Rising Action	
Climax	
Resolution	

Compare your chart with a classmate's. Discuss the following questions: What is the mystery we learn about in the introduction? How is this mystery solved in the climax and resolution? What does this story say about hope?

3. READING CHARACTER DEVELOPMENT

"The Hope Bakery" is a *coming-of-age story*. In a coming-of-age story, the main character is on the brink of becoming an adult. The story follows the character's struggle with a new idea or experience. When the struggle is over, the character sees the world through different, more adult, eyes.

In a group, discuss what Sloane is struggling with in "The Hope Bakery." From Todd's perspective, what is the world like? What is the world like from Sloane's point of view? How does Sloane's viewpoint change after he finds Todd? What do you think the author is saying about the process of becoming an adult? Answer the questions as a group, finding details in the story to support your ideas, and then present your conclusions to the class.

4. LANGUAGE CONVENTIONS SUBORDINATE CLAUSES

Many sentences are made of two or more *clauses*. The opening sentence of "The Hope Bakery" is a good example:

subordinate clause		main clause

When he was only five, Sloane wandered out of the back garden into the woods behind his house.

A *main clause* is a group of words that has a subject and a verb, and can stand on its own as a sentence. A *subordinate clause* is a group of words that has a subject and a verb, but is an incomplete sentence without another clause.

Look through the story and find two other examples of sentences that have a main clause and a subordinate clause. These tips might help:

- Look for sentences that contain commas, since clauses often are separated by commas.
- Look for the words *although, because, since, when, that,* or *who,* either at the beginning of the sentence, or immediately after a comma.

In each example you find, try to identify the main and subordinate clause, and the subject and verb in each clause.

SELF-ASSESSMENT: STORY CRAFT

As you worked on this unit, what did you learn about
- story beginnings and endings?
- details that show rather than tell?
- suspense?
- dialogue?
- sentence variety?
- point of view?
- plot development?
- character development?

How has learning about these aspects of writing helped you to understand or appreciate the stories? How have they helped you in your own writing?

ORAL COMMUNICATION TALK SHOW INTERVIEW

With a partner, choose a character from one of the stories in the unit. Imagine you are doing a talk show interview. One of you is the host and the other is the character. What is interesting about this character and what should the audience learn about the character's experiences? Prepare the host's questions. When planning the answers, stay true to the way the character is presented in the story. Present your talk show.

WRITING CREATE A SHORT STORY

Choose one of your favourite genres from this unit—science fiction, humour, and so on—and write your own two-page story. Review the work you did for this unit—there may be a story idea to complete, a character you can develop, or writing techniques you want to use. See "How to Write a Short Story," page 150.

"Fall seven times
Stand up eight."
Japanese Proverb

MEDIA MIX

DISASTERS!

UNIT AT A GLANCE

It's a beautiful day in the mountains, but beware—
snow can turn deadly in the blink of an eye.

AVALANCHE!

MAGAZINE ARTICLE BY BILL CORBETT

Entombed beneath half a metre of snow, Josh McCullough figured this would be a lousy way to die. Gasping for air, an incredible weight on his chest, all he could do was wiggle his fingers to enlarge his tiny breathing hole. And think. After a few seconds of sheer panic, it seemed the 21-year-old Calgary snowboarder had a long time to think.

"I said goodbye to everyone I knew," Josh recalls. "I had really strong images of how people would react when they found out I was dead." Then everything went black.

In fact, Josh was well prepared for his expedition into mountain back country. He had taken avalanche courses. He was wearing a transceiver and carrying a shovel. When the avalanche hit, he wasn't even snowboarding. But he made two critical mistakes that day in December near Rogers Pass in the interior of British Columbia.

First, he didn't know that recent snow had made conditions much worse than the avalanche hazard signs had indicated. Second, he was alone while his friend had gone by snowmobile to pick up another friend.

Josh was snowshoeing just above the packed track on a small, 35° slope—and that's likely how he triggered his own burial. He heard a loud "whoomph" and immediately knew he was in trouble. The avalanche hit in waves—the first pinning his feet, the second buckling his knees, and the third

---

GOALS AT A GLANCE

■ Identify and sort proper nouns.
■ Draft a first-hand account.

slamming the back of his head. He was completely covered with snow.

Josh awoke to hear digging. His friend had come back 10 minutes later, seen the slide, and—luckily—turned his transceiver to "receive." Picking up a strong signal, he started digging frantically. He quickly unearthed Josh. Blue in the face, very cold and badly shaken, Josh was otherwise all right despite being buried 15 minutes.

He was lucky. Many Canadian skiers, snowboarders, and snow-mobilers do not survive avalanches. The number could be reduced, however, with more training and common sense.

Mountain lovers get caught in avalanches for two main reasons—enthusiasm and ignorance.

Some people get too enthusiastic when they reach fresh powder snow, and look for thrills on dangerous slopes. Others take shortcuts instead of following safe routes up and down the mountains.

Ignorance claims more lives, often for easily avoidable reasons. Too many people forget to check the daily avalanche forecasts, don't carry safety equipment, or don't know how to use it properly.

"One of the biggest mistakes people make is simply not realizing they are at risk, that an avalanche could happen here," says Banff avalanche consultant Clair Israelson. "Often, they don't recognize that it doesn't have to be super steep to slide, or else they wrongly think they're far enough from steep slopes to be safe."

When signs say the avalanche hazard is Extreme, people tend to be more careful. Most accidents happen when the hazard is Moderate or Considerable, because people take more chances.

So how should you minimize the risk of getting caught in an avalanche?

1. Take avalanche courses from certified instructors. You will learn how to use shovels to test the snow conditions, and how to use transceivers to locate companions, if they are buried. You will also discover how to choose safe routes for ascending and descending slopes.

2. Join an outdoor club that stresses safety first. Never go into the mountains by yourself.

3. Refer to the twice-weekly reports by the Canadian Avalanche Association for

ROUTE SELECTION IN AVALANCHE TERRAIN
GOOD ASCENT ROUTE: Through trees to ridge. Follow ridge to summit.
POOR ASCENT ROUTE: Switch backing up slide path.
CAUTIOUS ASCENT ROUTE: Avoid slide paths. Stay in open trees.

conditions in Canada's western mountains. (Currently there is no formal system of avalanche forecasts in central and eastern Canada.)

4. When the avalanche hazard is Considerable to Extreme, stay home or stick to groomed trails or ski area boundaries.

Paul Norrie is a professional ski guide based in Banff. He recommends, "Always be thinking and looking around. Always treat the mountains as if you're going to be surprised."

What if you're hit by an avalanche, despite all precautions? If there is no escape, use swimming strokes to stay as high as possible in the stream of snow. As the avalanche slows, try to fling one hand to the surface and use the other to clear an air space in front of your mouth. If you are buried, you now have to relax to preserve oxygen.

If you're unburied, you'll have to rescue the victims. Using a transceiver, an experienced

CANADIAN AVALANCHE ACCIDENT STATISTICS

- **90% of fatalities are males, typically in their twenties.**
- **43% of those killed are back country skiers.**
- **Perhaps 80% of avalanche fatalities are triggered by the people caught in them.**
- **About 25% of avalanche fatalities are caused, not by suffocation or hypothermia,* but by physical injuries.**
- **41% of recreational avalanche accidents occur in the Rocky Mountains of Alberta and British Columbia, 39% in the Interior Ranges of British Columbia, and 16% in British Columbia's Coast Mountains.**

*hypothermia: abnormally cold body temperature caused by exposure to cold air or water.

person should be able to find a victim in 2 minutes. Try to dig the person out in less than 5. With a 5-minute recovery, there's a 90% chance he or she will be alive. After 5 minutes, brain damage can start. Beyond 15 minutes, the survival rate falls below 50%.

Master these rescue skills, and one day someone like Josh McCullough could be eternally grateful.

Oh So Silent

FIRST-HAND ACCOUNT OF AN AVALANCHE INCIDENT

by Wayne Grams and Sandy Wishart

On the Haig Glacier at an elevation of 2740 m we waited, hoping for a break in the swirling clouds. My wife, Sandy, and I had spent the day, Easter Sunday, ski touring up the French Glacier to reach the plateau of the Haig. Our goal was a long, deep powder ski down the Robertson Glacier. All that kept us from that dream run now was a 150-m climb up a steep slope to the Robertson Col.

I had been this way several times before, but never had I seen the slope entirely snow-covered. Winds usually kept most of it a bare scree* slope even in winter. When visibility improved slightly, I left Sandy in a safe position on the glacier and started kicking steps directly up the slope with my skis strapped to my pack. I was struggling in the new snow about a quarter of the way up the slope when I saw a crack suddenly tear across the snow high above me. As if in slow motion, snow slabs started to slide toward me. I had no time to register anything but astonishment at this unfolding scene. Then I felt myself tumbling down in a white whirl of snow. At first I was rolling on the surface of the avalanche, but in moments it had swallowed me whole.

When it stopped there was dead silence. I felt unhurt and, thinking my left leg might be higher than the rest of my body, I tried to kick it up, perhaps to the surface. It wouldn't budge. In fact, I couldn't move at all. The snow held me in its firm grip. I was breathing fast from struggling on the slope and from sheer panic. Keep calm, slow down your breathing, I reminded myself. Easier thought than done in this situation.

Sandy, I knew, was safe and now everything depended on her finding me. Did I have enough air until then?—Unaware, I slipped into unconsciousness.

* **scree:** loose, fragmented rock lying below a cliff or bluff.

I watched in disbelief as the avalanche carried Wayne down the slope and out of sight. I waited for the avalanche to stop, then I quickly skied up and over a roll fully expecting to see him, but all I saw was snow, and it was oh so quiet.

Frantically I pulled out the earphone to my avalanche beacon and was able to clearly hear the steady signal from Wayne's beacon. He had to be near! I skied out onto the avalanche debris, pulled off my pack, took off my skis, and got out my shovel. Without

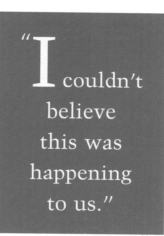

"I couldn't believe this was happening to us."

letting go of the earphone, I ran over to dig in a hollow spot that looked like a place where Wayne would be buried. After randomly shovelling for a while, I realized I wouldn't be able to find him this way. I started back toward my pack, but fell into several waist-high hollows and struggled to crawl out. I felt so helpless and cried out in desperation. I couldn't believe this was happening to us. I thought about how just last night Wayne and I

were both enjoying a visit with my family and looking forward to this trip. I briefly wondered how I would cope without Wayne in my life, and how I would be able to tell anyone that I couldn't find him.

Finally, I got focussed and realized that I had to use the avalanche beacon properly. I could hear the steady signal of Wayne's transceiver. By continually turning down the volume, I zeroed in on his location. Using a ski pole to mark the spot, I started digging.

A metre down I hit his ski tip. I had forgotten he had strapped his skis to his pack so I imagined his body to be upside down or twisted. I kept digging, then realized that I could hear Wayne's laboured breathing. I cried out, "Hang on, Wayne, I'm coming." A metre and a half down, I exposed the top of Wayne's toque. I dropped the shovel and used my hands to uncover his face. He was still breathing! I touched his cheek and felt that it was still warm and saw that his colour was good. I told him he was going to be OK. He didn't respond. I moved the snow off his chest to help him breathe easier, then kept on digging.

Finally, Wayne "woke up" and reached out his hand to mine, held it for a moment, and said, "Thank you for finding me." His voice was strained, as if he had been shouting and had gone hoarse. Though groggy and disoriented, he said he was OK. As I tried to make the hole bigger, Wayne struggled periodically to try to move, but his right side was still pinned. He was breathing very fast, and I tried to calm him down, and encourage him to breathe deeply and slowly. Finally, his right arm and right leg were free and the snow released its cement-like grip. I helped him to stand up in the cavernous pit that was about 2 m deep and 2 m wide.

Once Wayne was standing, I looked at his watch and saw that it was 6:30 p.m.! It had been an hour and a half since the avalanche happened. He was shaking uncontrollably from cold and shock. I cut steps to get out of the pit, brought my down jacket to him, then hugged and rubbed him to warm him up. Soon he was able to crawl out of the hole and stand up.

I tried to give him some water, but he was shaking so violently he couldn't bring the bottle to his mouth. We knew it was getting late, and that we had to get moving. I helped Wayne put on his skis and pack. His poles were gone so I gave him mine.

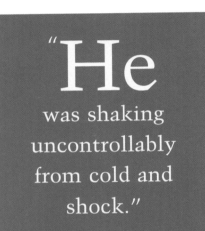

"He was shaking uncontrollably from cold and shock."

Meanwhile, the sky had cleared. The setting sun bathed a few lingering clouds in golden and purple hues. Around us the mountains stood serene and beautiful, supremely unaware of the drama that had just unfolded. To me, it felt as if someone had been watching over us, and I gave thanks. We looked for a moment at the slope that had caused us such grief, then set off for home.

Wayne Grams and Sandy Wishart both work for Kananaskis Country and live in Canmore, Alberta. They still enjoy life in the mountains.

1. RESPONDING TO THE MAGAZINE ARTICLE

a. What two mistakes did Josh McCullough make when snowshoeing? What did he do right?

b. What do you think was the main reason—enthusiasm or ignorance—that Josh was caught in an avalanche? What about Wayne Grams? Support your opinions with evidence from the article.

c. Why is "Oh So Silent" an appropriate title for Wayne and Sandy's first-hand account of an avalanche and rescue?

d. Make two lists. First, list ways to avoid being caught in an avalanche. Second, make a list of strategies to help you survive an avalanche.

2. LANGUAGE CONVENTIONS   PROPER NOUNS

List six of the **proper nouns** in this selection. Note how they've been given an initial capital letter, and how some don't have an apostrophe—like Rogers Pass—where you would expect one. Sort your list of proper nouns into the four categories in the definition: Person, Place, Organization, Period of Time. To provide an example for each category, you may have to include additional proper nouns not used in the article.

> A **proper noun** is a noun that identifies one particular person, place, organization, or period of time.

3. WRITING   A FIRST-HAND ACCOUNT

Why do you think first-hand accounts like "Oh So Silent" are commonly used in magazine articles and news stories? Create a first-hand account based on an exciting event in which you were involved. Begin your draft with a powerful opening sentence that will hook your reader. "I saw a tornado" is less interesting for your reader than a description of a swirling wind sweeping everything in its path. Describe the action you witnessed, and any emotion you experienced. Use strong verbs, specific nouns, and vivid adjectives and adverbs to make your reader believe in your story. When you are finished your draft, share your account with another classmate.

SELF-ASSESSMENT: Did your first-hand account capture the feeling of the experience? How could you make your account more exciting?

4. MEDIA   PULL QUOTES

Many magazines use a feature called a *pull quote* (see box on page 182) to catch the reader's eye and make the article seem more interesting. Reread "Avalanche!" and "Oh So Silent" and suggest two phrases or sentences that could be used as additional pull quotes. Explain to a partner why you made those particular selections.

You've seen on TV the damage an earthquake can cause.
Could the same thing happen here?

Earthquakes
Rock the World!

MAGAZINE ARTICLE FROM *YES* MAG

by Barbara Saffer

You may not be able to feel it, but the continent you live on is in constant motion.

Scientists explain continental movement by the theory of *plate tectonics*. Plates are thick slabs, like pieces of a jigsaw puzzle, which make up the crust of the Earth. These plates float—like rafts on the sea—on a layer of hot, mobile rock called the *mantle*. We don't usually notice the motion because plates move very slowly—about as fast as your fingernails grow.

Earthquake survivors in Golcuk, Turkey.

On occasion, however, we are jolted into remembering. Where one plate slides beneath another, volcanoes spit out masses of fiery lava. Where plates collide, earthquakes rock the world! As residents of Turkey well know, (see photo) an earthquake is a sudden shaking of the Earth's surface. Hundreds of thousands of earthquakes jiggle the planet every year. Most are small and do little damage. A major tremor, however, can cause enormous damage.

GOALS AT A GLANCE

■ Create a glossary of technical terms.
■ Develop a magazine article including visuals.

How Earthquakes Happen

Earthquakes occur when the thick plates of the Earth's surface crack or break suddenly or slide past one another. Most earthquakes occur near plate boundaries. This is where the slabs slide together, drift apart, or creep past each other. These motions are slow and cumbersome, and plates often get stuck as they try to scrape past each other.

If a plate is trying to move, but can't, the plate bends and builds up stress. When enough stress has built up, the plate breaks, forming a *fault*. It's like bending a pencil until it cracks. The pieces of broken plate recoil—and quickly slip up, down, or sideways along the fault. This releases the stored energy and sends shock waves in all directions.

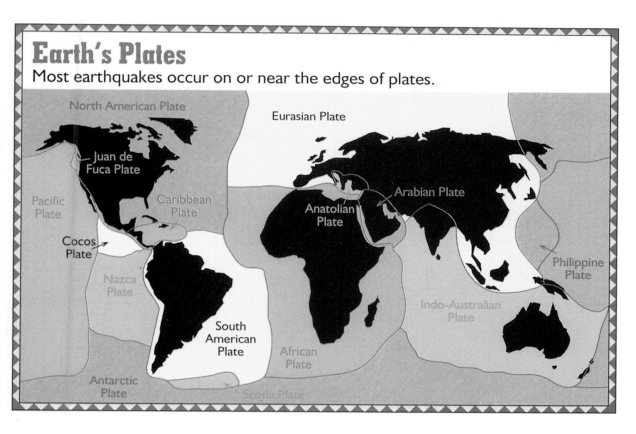

Earth's Plates
Most earthquakes occur on or near the edges of plates.

North American Plate

Eurasian Plate

Juan de Fuca Plate

Arabian Plate

Pacific Plate

Caribbean Plate

Anatolian Plate

Cocos Plate

Philippine Plate

Nazca Plate

Indo-Australian Plate

South American Plate

African Plate

Antarctic Plate

Scotia Plate

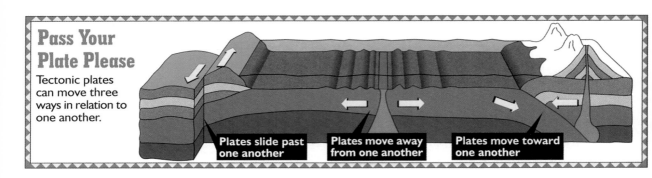

Pass Your Plate Please

Tectonic plates can move three ways in relation to one another.

Plates slide past one another

Plates move away from one another

Plates move toward one another

These *seismic* waves rattle the ground, resulting in earthquakes. Often, stress builds up along the same fault again and again, causing earthquakes to re-occur in the same area. A famous example of this is the San Andreas Fault in California.

The spot where rocks begin to move along a fault is called the focus of the earthquake. The focus may be shallow or deep, ranging from close to the Earth's surface to a depth of about 700 km. The point on the Earth's surface directly above the focus is the *epicentre*. Earthquake tremors are generally strongest near the epicentre.

After a major earthquake, the initial shock waves are often followed by a series of smaller tremors, called *aftershocks*, which can last for days or weeks. Aftershocks occur when the Earth's crust near the fault "settles" into a new position.

With all that shaking, it's no wonder earthquake tremors can be destructive. In addition to damaging buildings and other structures, earthquakes can also cause tremendous secondary damage from fires, floods, rock slides, mud slides, avalanches, and *tsunamis* (huge, destructive ocean waves).

A Quaking *Time Line*

1556 One of the most deadly earthquakes in recorded history claimed approximately 830 000 lives in China.

1700 Aboriginal accounts and geological evidence suggest that a massive earthquake of 9.0 on the Richter scale hit the Cascadia region, affecting areas from Vancouver Island to Oregon.

Measuring Earthquakes

by Kathiann M. Kowalski

While thousands of earthquakes occur every year, only a tiny percentage of them cause significant damage and injury. In fact, the vast majority can barely be felt by most people.

Scientists use two scales to measure earthquakes. The Richter scale was developed in 1935 by Charles Richter. It measures the strength (or magnitude) of an earthquake. The scale is *logarithmic*, meaning that each whole number represents a 10 times increase in strength from the previous number. For example, a 4.0 earthquake is 10 times stronger than a 3.0 earthquake, and 100 times stronger than a 2.0 earthquake.

The Modified Mercalli Intensity Scale, expressed in Roman numerals, focusses on how earthquakes are experienced by people and buildings in particular locations. At Level I, earthquakes are not even felt, while at Level XII, major damage and injuries occur.

In the year 132 Chinese geographer and astronomer Zhang Heng invented the world's first instrument to detect an earthquake and the direction from which it comes. The 2-metre-wide bronze device used a system of levers and a pendulum. When a tremor occurred, a ball was released from a sculpted dragon's jaws and dropped into the mouth of a sculpted frog below.

1856 Italian physicist Luigi Palmieri invented a sophisticated earthquake recorder that makes a permanent record, called a *seismogram*, of the earth moving.

1880 English engineer John Milne travelled to Japan where he studied earthquakes. He developed the modern *seismograph*, used to detect vibrations caused by earthquakes. In 1898, Milne's Instrument Number 10 began operating in Victoria, British Columbia, making Victoria one of the oldest seismic observatories in the world.

Where Canucks Feel Quakes

by Kathiann M. Kowalski

What time is it when everything around you starts shaking and rumbling? It's time for an earthquake. The catch to this riddle is that no one knows exactly when or where an earthquake will occur.

Scientists do know that approximately 97% of the world's earthquakes occur near plate boundaries.

Did You Know?

- The largest earthquake ever measured occurred in Chile in 1960. It hit 9.5 on the Richter scale.
- More than 1000 earthquakes are recorded every year in Canada, but we don't feel most of them.
- In 1949, the strongest earthquake in Canada so far this century rocked the area around the Queen Charlotte Islands in British Columbia. It measured 8.1 on the Richter scale.

Off Canada's west coast three plates interact with each other: the North American plate, the Pacific Plate, and the Juan de Fuca (Wan-da-Foo-ka) Plate. "About 2/3 of Canada's earthquakes are in western Canada or in the western Arctic," reports seismologist Garry Rogers of the Geological Survey of Canada in Sidney, British Columbia. "We locate and catalogue 1000 to 1200 per year in the West."

Nonetheless, notes Rogers, "Earthquakes can affect most of Canada's population." Three percent of the world's earthquakes occur within plates. Most of the earthquakes occurring away from plate boundaries occur along or near ancient fault zones, like the Ottawa valley. These represent zones of weakness where

1902 Giuseppe Mercalli, an Italian seismologist, came up with a scale to rank earthquakes based on how they affect people and structures. His scale uses Roman numerals from I—when people don't even notice the earthquake—to XII—when there is massive damage.

1935 American seismologist Charles Richter developed a scale to measure the energy released by an earthquake—its magnitude. While earthquakes measuring less than 3.0 on the Richter scale might not be felt, earthquakes measuring over 8.0 result in massive damage.

failure is most likely to occur due to *crustal stresses*. This helps explain the Ste.-Agathe-des-Monts earthquake that shook people from Ottawa to Montreal on July 30, 1998. It had a magnitude of 4.4 on the *Richter scale.*

Scientists are studying methods of predicting earthquakes, such as measuring stress along faults and observing animals, which act strangely before quakes. As of now, however, there is no reliable way to predict earthquakes.◆

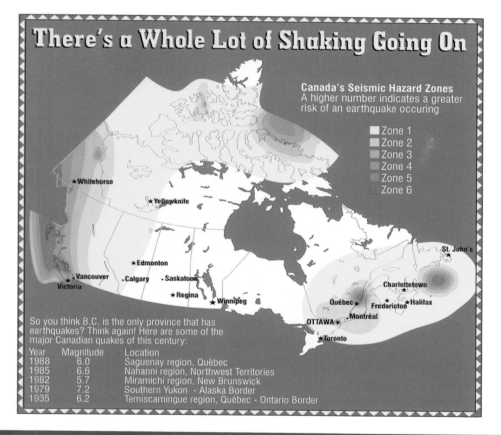

There's a Whole Lot of Shaking Going On

Canada's Seismic Hazard Zones
A higher number indicates a greater risk of an earthquake occuring

- Zone 1
- Zone 2
- Zone 3
- Zone 4
- Zone 5
- Zone 6

★ Whitehorse
★ Yellowknife
★ Edmonton
· Vancouver
Victoria
· Calgary · Saskatoon
★ Regina
★ Winnipeg
St. John's
Charlottetown
Québec ★
Fredericton ★ Halifax
★ Montréal
OTTAWA ★
★ Toronto

So you think B.C. is the only province that has earthquakes? Think again! Here are some of the major Canadian quakes of this century:

Year	Magnitude	Location
1988	6.0	Saguenay region, Québec
1985	6.6	Nahanni region, Northwest Territories
1982	5.7	Miramichi region, New Brunswick
1979	7.2	Southern Yukon - Alaska Border
1935	6.2	Temiscamingue region, Québec - Ontario Border

1960s A theory called plate tectonics was developed. This theory suggests that the Earth's crust and part of the upper mantle—called the *lithosphere*—are made up of plates that "float" on a layer of hot mobile rock.

1998 A deadly tsunami caused by an off-shore earthquake killed and injured thousands in Papua New Guinea. Tsunami hazards have prompted the United States to install sensors in the Pacific which will determine waves of tsunami height. The data will be transmitted to a satellite which will send in the information to tsunami warning centres.

1. RESPONDING TO THE MAGAZINE ARTICLE

a. List three new things you learned about earthquakes from this article. What else would you like to know?

b. The time line provides a brief history of earthquakes. Which information do you find the most interesting? Why?

c. Look at the headings and captions. Do you think the use of humour is appropriate in this context? When might it not be appropriate?

2. VISUAL COMMUNICATION EXAMINE VISUALS

Many magazine articles like "Avalanche!" on page 176 and "Earthquakes Rock the World!" include visuals such as charts, photos, diagrams, and maps. Look at the visuals included with this selection. What kind of information is presented in each one? How does each of these visuals help you understand the topic better? Next time you write a magazine article or report, include visuals to help readers understand your topic.

3. WORD CRAFT TECHNICAL TERMS

Create an illustrated Earthquake Glossary. First, find the technical terms presented in the article in italic type and write them down. Try to figure out their meaning from their context in the article. For words you are unsure of, consult an encyclopedia (book or electronic) and/or the Internet. Write your definitions so that your readers will understand the meanings easily. You may wish to illustrate your glossary.

4. MEDIA MAGAZINE ARTICLES

With a small group, discuss the two magazine articles that begin this unit. For each article, consider the purpose, intended audience, content, style, and visuals. What strengths and weaknesses do you see?

Together, choose another type of disaster, such as volcanoes, or the sinking of the *Titanic*. Develop a magazine article about the disaster. Begin by researching your subject carefully. Each group member could develop one part of the article—background information, coverage of the disaster, sidebars, visuals (illustrations, maps, charts, and so on), or the glossary. Discuss how these sections should be organized and designed for the greatest effect. Post your completed article on a Disaster bulletin board.

GROUP ASSESSMENT: Does your magazine article give enough information to answer the questions most readers would have? Is it interesting? Did you include visuals that help to tell the story? How could you improve your article?

Some of the most destructive disasters have been turned into movies for our entertainment.

CANNED CATASTROPHES

SPECIAL EFFECTS IN DISASTER MOVIES

NON-FICTION BY JAKE HAMILTON

Volcanoes. Twisters. Asteroids. Explosions... For almost as long as films have been made, audiences have flocked to see one disaster after another on the big screen.

People seem to be fascinated by images of destruction—the bigger, the noisier, and more terrifying, the better. A film director, of course, can't just wait until a real catastrophe occurs. (It's hard to predict when the next twister will whirl by!) That's why special effects are essential to every disaster movie.

Special effects (SFX) is the art of making the impossible into a fantastic reality. Since 1902, when Georges Mélies first impressed an audience with cinematic special effects, there has been a dizzying explosion of SFX breakthroughs. From camera trickery to digital technology, the history of special effects has always pushed the boundaries of human imagination, and keeps today's audiences glued to their seats in starry-eyed wonder.

GOALS AT A GLANCE

- Develop a movie proposal.
- Evaluate special effects in a movie.

NATURAL DISASTERS

A building rips apart when struck by lightning, a battered car floats down the main street in a torrential flood, tractors fall from the skies during a spectacular tornado. These are just a few of the many breathtaking set pieces conjured up by special effects experts to show the destructive power of the world's natural disasters. Miniature models, full-scale explosions, and matte paintings have all been used in films to portray the effects of violent storms, destructive earthquakes, and erupting volcanoes. For a minor effect, wind machines and rain heads are employed. For extreme effect, recent films such as *Twister* (1996) and *Dante's Peak* (1997) have used computer-generated images (CGI) to visualize the dark side of nature in all its terrifying glory.

TERRIFYING TORNADOES

Tornadoes have been made for films in various mechanical ways, including the use of fog machines. But for the film *Twister* (1996), the latest in computer-generated technology brought the power of the dark

An image from *Twister*.

side of nature to the screen. Using a combination of real weather footage shot in Tornado Alley, Texas, and some revolutionary CGI, the film captures the terror of such high winds. The digital twisters were added to real footage, filmed months in advance, of actors running for cover.

FLOODED

Filming the action scenes in huge water tanks for the disaster film *Hard Rain* (1998) was a soggy business. All the filming equipment on set, from the boom microphones to the camera cranes, had to be covered in plastic to prevent damage from the large quantities of water used. In turn, the actors were playing their roles up to their necks in water, and special safety teams were kept on standby to look after them.

Up to their necks in water on the set of *Hard Rain.*

IN THE HOT SPOT

Los Angeles, California, is one of the warmest climates in the United States, but in the film *Volcano* (1997), the temperature soars through the roof! An underground volcano engulfs the city in lava, turning it into a molten mass. Using both miniature models and full-scale buildings, the crew filmed the destruction of Los Angeles streets, later adding huge lava rivers with the aid of digital technology.

Los Angeles streets awash in lava in *Volcano.*

CREATING A STORM AT SEA

Filming disaster scenes on location is a complicated affair. For the climax to the movie *The Mosquito Coast* (1986), Harrison Ford and his screen family have to face a destructive monsoon storm as they float downriver on a makeshift raft. Even though the seas were calm, the special effects team created a

Finished scene from *The Mosquito Coast*. Harrison Ford wrestles with the raft in turbulent waters.

chaotic scene in stormy waters. They filmed with waterproofed equipment and wore waterproof or diving suits.

Huge wind machines are used.

Waterproofed cameras capture close-ups.

The sound technician has to get close to the actors.

Film crew revs boat's engine to create turbulence in the water.

FRIGHTENING LIGHTNING

Lightning is virtually impossible to capture on a film shoot. Instead, filmmakers have learned to rely on storm effects generated on the computer. Forked lightning can be created and manipulated on screen, and the accompanying thunderclaps reproduced in a sound studio. Movies such as *Ghostbusters* (1984), *Jurassic Park* (1993), and *Cape Fear* (1991) have used computer technology to good effect, producing spectacular and unforgettable storms on screen.

CGI elements let rip in *Ghostbusters*. Computerized lightning is combined with real film footage.

On the set of *The Mosquito Coast*.

NOT SO NATURAL DISASTERS

CRUISING OUT OF CONTROL

Big-budget explosions do not always have to be undertaken with huge sets, expensive cars, and detailed preparation. For the film *Speed 2: Cruise Control* (1997), a luxury boat sails head-on into a tourist resort causing widespread destruction and chaos. The filmmakers decided to use a miniature model for the climactic scene, making sure that the hotels, beach houses, and luxury boat looked completely lifelife. Tiny explosives were inserted into the models.

Attention to detail by the modelmaker makes this scene very convincing.

Stunt double leaps to safety—safely—in *Goldeneye.*

LEAP OF FAITH

The fictional hero James Bond must always be prepared to escape disaster by jumping through a window or falling off a charging tank. In *Goldeneye* (1995), Agent 007 leaps from a huge glass window to escape his killers. The stunt was performed by Pierce Brosnan's stunt double, who was outfitted in protective clothing and padding. The glass he falls through is made of sugar glass, which will not cut him. There is a soft mattress out of shot to break his fall, and the jump is timed to give the camera crew the best angles. As always with stunts, the action is meticulously planned and tested in advance.

SPECIAL EFFECTS GLOSSARY

Camera trickery: a way of creating special effects by using a variety of lenses to distort the picture.

CGI (computer-generated images): images created by a computer that take the place of real scenery or events.

Digital technology: advanced technology involving computers.

Film footage: an amount of film made for showing.

Matte paintings: background paintings used to create a setting.

Miniature models: small scenes of a movie landscape built when a film cannot take place on location.

Rain head: a device used to create rain.

Sound studio: the place where sophisticated sound effects are developed.

Stunt double: a person specially trained to perform acts that might be too difficult or dangerous for the actors.

Wind machine: a machine used within a studio to create violent weather.

----

1. RESPONDING TO THE ARTICLE

a. What are some of the special effects movie producers use to re-create disasters? What was the most surprising special effect you learned about?

b. Why are computers so important in creating convincing special effects?

c. Why do you think people are so fascinated by disasters that they spend millions of dollars making and watching movies about them?

2. LANGUAGE CONVENTIONS EXPRESSIVE ADJECTIVES

Reread the first paragraph of the "Natural Disasters" section and find five adjectives that you think are especially expressive. Why do you think Jake Hamilton uses so many adjectives in this passage, and throughout the whole piece? Is his use of adjectives appropriate and effective? Why?

Create a list of twenty expressive adjectives—ten from "Canned Catastrophes" and ten of your own. Add to your list when you encounter other strong adjectives. You can use your list to help you with your own writing.

3. MEDIA MOVIE PROPOSAL

Create a proposal for a thrilling new disaster movie. As you write, imagine that you are trying to convince a movie producer to make a film based on your idea.

Your proposal should

- describe, in an exciting way, the time and place of the disaster
- provide an exciting story line
- describe the main characters who undergo the experience (and list actors to play those parts)
- contain expressive adjectives to convey the terrifying effect of the disaster

PEER ASSESSMENT: Exchange your movie proposal with a partner. Give each other helpful feedback. Would a producer be convinced that your story line would make a good movie? Would the producer be interested in your characters? impressed by your descriptive writing? You should also explain why your film would be popular.

4. MEDIA UNDERSTAND SPECIAL EFFECTS

Watch a favourite disaster movie, or a new release you would like to see. Pay attention to the special effects. Can you figure out how they were done? You may want to focus on one or two scenes in particular. Using the information provided in "Canned Catastrophes," determine how the scenes might have been created. Were you impressed by the scenes? Why or why not? Report your findings to the class.

THE FOREST FIRE

POEM BY
CHARLES G.D. ROBERTS

The night was grim and still with dread;
    No star shone down from heaven's dome;
The ancient forest closed around
    The settler's lonely home.

There came a glare that lit the north;
    There came a wind that roused the night;
But child and father slumbered on,
    Nor felt the growing light.

There came a noise of flying feet,
    With many a strange and dreadful cry;
And sharp flames crept and leapt along
    The red verge of the sky.

There came a deep and gathering roar.
    The father raised his anxious head;
He saw the light, like a dawn of blood,
    That streamed across his bed.

GOALS AT A GLANCE

- Create a radio news report.
- Analyse ballad form.

It lit the old clock on the wall,
    It lit the room with splendour wild,
It lit the fair and tumbled hair
    Of the still sleeping child;

And zigzag fence, and rude log barn,
    And chip-strewn yard, and cabin grey,
Glowed crimson in the shuddering glare
    Of that untimely day.

The boy was hurried from his sleep;
    The horse was hurried from his stall;
Up from the pasture clearing came
    The cattle's frightened call.

The boy was snatched to the saddle-bow.
    Wildly, wildly, the father rode.
Behind him swooped the hordes of flame
    And harried their abode.

The scorching heat was at their heels;
    The huge roar hounded them in their flight;
Red smoke and many a flying brand
    Flew o'er them through the night.

And past them fled the wildwood forms—
    Far-striding moose, and leaping deer,
And bounding panther, and coursing wolf,
    Terrible-eyed with fear.

And closer drew the fiery death;
    Madly, madly, the father rode;
The horse began to heave and fail
    Beneath the double load.

The father's mouth was white and stern,
    But his eyes grew tender with long farewell.
He said: "Hold fast to your seat, Sweetheart,
    And ride Old Jerry well!

I must go back. Ride on to the river,
    Over the ford and the long marsh ride,
Straight on to the town. And I'll meet you, Sweetheart,
    Somewhere on the other side."

He slipped from the saddle. The boy rode on.
    His hand clung fast in the horse's mane;
His hair blew over the horse's neck;
    His small throat sobbed with pain.

"Father! Father!" he cried aloud.
    The howl of the fire-wind answered him
With the hiss of soaring flames, and crash
    Of shattering limb on limb.

But still the good horse galloped on,
    With sinew braced and strength renewed.
The boy came safe to the river ford,
    And out of the deadly wood.

And now with his kinsfolk, fenced from fear,
    At play in the heart of the city's hum,
He stops in his play to wonder why
    His father does not come.

1. RESPONDING TO THE POEM

a. What are some of the frightening events caused by the forest fire in the poem? Do you think the poet does a good job of describing them? Why or why not?

b. Why do you think the father sent his son on alone to escape from the forest fire? How do you feel about his decision?

2. MEDIA   RECORD A RADIO NEWS REPORT

Assume that you are preparing a radio news report about a forest fire blazing near your community. Radio news reports are much shorter than newspaper reports. The time limit is about ten seconds on air, which is about eight lines of printed script. Here are some pointers:

- Your report should cover all the five Ws: *who, what, where, when, why.*
- The first sentence should grab the listeners' interest.
- Listen to some radio news reports to get an idea of how they sound.
- Tape record your report for presentation to the class, remembering to read slowly and clearly.

SELF-ASSESSMENT: Did you include all the important details? Did your audience understand your report? Did the audience ask any questions that could have been answered in the report but were not?

3. POET'S CRAFT   BALLAD

"The Forest Fire" is a **ballad**, one of the traditional forms of poetry. Read the first two stanzas of the poem aloud to get a sense of the *rhythm*. Rhythm is the arrangement of beats in a line of poetry, created by the accented and unaccented syllables in a word. In each stanza, which lines rhyme?

> A **ballad** is a narrative poem that tells an exciting story in a series of vivid pictures. The stanzas are usually four lines each with a regular pattern of rhythm and rhyme.

With a partner, choose a sequence of four stanzas and prepare an oral reading that captures the spirit of the lines. For an extra challenge, add one extra stanza of your own. Your stanza should follow the same pattern of rhythm and rhyme, and should fit into the story at that point.

Music can't overcome a major disaster. But it can sometimes help the victims cope.

Ballad of Springhill

SONG BY EWAN MacCOLL AND PEGGY SEEGER

Ballad
of Springhill

1. In the town of Spring - hill, —
No - va Sco-tia, down in the dark of the
Cum-ber-land Mine, there's blood on the coal and the

min-ers lie in the roads that nev-er saw—
sun nor sky, — roads that nev-er saw—
sun nor sky.

2. In the town of Springhill, you don't sleep easy;
Often the earth will tremble and roll.
When the earth is restless, miners die;
Bone and blood is the price of coal,
Bone and blood is the price of coal.

GOALS AT A GLANCE

- Locate and present background information.
- Plan a music video.

3. In the town of Springhill, Nova Scotia,
    Late in the year of fifty-eight,
    Day still comes and the sun still shines
    But it's dark as the grave in the Cumberland Mine,
    Dark as the grave in the Cumberland Mine.

4. Down at the coal face, miners working,
    Rattle of the belt, and the cutter's blade.
    Rumble of rock and the walls close round;
    The living and the dead men two miles down,
    Living and the dead men two miles down.

5. Twelve men lay two miles from the pitshaft,
    Twelve men lay in the dark and sang.
    Long hot days in a miner's tomb,
    It was three feet high and a hundred long,
    Three feet high and a hundred long.

6. Three days passed and the lamps gave out,
    And Caleb Rushton, he up and said,
    "There's no more water nor light nor bread,
    So we'll live on songs and hope instead,
    We'll live on songs and hope instead."

7. Listen for the shouts of the bareface miners,
    Listen through the rubble for a rescue team—
    Six hundred feet of coal and slag,
    Hope imprisoned in a three-foot seam,
    Hope imprisoned in a three-foot seam.

8. Eight days passed and some were rescued,
    Leaving the dead to lie alone.
    Through all their lives they dug a grave,
    Two miles of earth for a marking stone,
    Two miles of earth for a marking stone.

SPRINGHILL MINER

HERITAGE MINUTE TRANSCRIPT

by Patrick Watson

Opening shot shows a stocky, generous-looking man speaking to the camera.

On-Screen Caption: Springhill, Nova Scotia

Man:
Nine of us were trapped together in the mine, after the "Bump." We lay by a pipe to breathe. My leg was broken. Percy was dying beside me. (He shakes his head as if to say it was clearly hopeless.)

But I said, "Come on boys, The Lord is watching for us." And I started singing. Then we all sang.

Eight and a half days. No food. Even drank our own—you know. And I just *happened* to shout into that pipe when the draegermen* were passing by.

Some good folks in the United States gave us survivors a free holiday in the South. Said I couldn't stay with the others cause of my colour. The boys were gonna refuse. I said, "No, we'll all have our holiday, then we'll be together again." And we were.

Seventy-four died in that bump. But that was life around the Springhill Mines. Closed now. So much death. But my! Didn't we sing those hymns. *Together.*

On-Screen Caption:
A Part of Our Heritage
Maurice Ruddick 1913-1988

---

* **draegermen:** coal miners trained in underground rescue work.

A Part of our Heritage

Springhill, Nova Scotia

Maurice Ruddick 1913–1988

THE CRB FOUNDATION
HERITAGE
PROJECT

POWER BROADCASTING

1. Responding to the Song and Script

a. Combining information from both the song and the script, explain to a partner what you think happened to the men in the Cumberland mine.

b. According to the song, who is the hero of the Springhill Disaster? According to the Heritage Minute, who is the hero? What are some possible reasons why the names are different?

c. Compare the two accounts of the Springhill Disaster, considering subject matter, purpose, and mood. In point form, note the similarities and differences.

2. Researching Locate Background Information

Working with a small group, create a list of questions you have about the Springhill Disaster—questions that aren't answered by the song or script. Together, use your research skills to find the answers to your questions. Present your findings in the form of a page of background information that would help a reader have a better appreciation of the song and script.

3. Media Plan a Music Video

What would a music video of "Ballad of Springhill" look like? In a small group, make a plan for the video. Your plan should contain a description of one or two images you would use for each stanza of the song. You might create illustrations to show what some or all of the images would look like. Join with another group and compare your plans. What are the similarities and differences between them?

Self-Assessment: After your discussion with the other group, reconsider the images you chose for your video. Would the images help the viewer understand the song? Do they reflect the meaning and the mood of the lyrics?

When disasters strike, we count on the news media to keep us informed.

TUNING *in to the* NEWS

NEWSCAST FROM CTV NEWS WITH LLOYD ROBERTSON

Opening Shot of Newscaster Sandie Rinaldo.

Sandie Rinaldo: Good evening. Many Canadians were teased with a taste of spring this weekend as the mercury rose in most parts of the country. But in Québec the sun's warm rays had a darker side. As temperatures shot up from zero to almost twenty degrees, water levels rose and rivers spilled their banks, forcing evacuations in the southern part of the province. The worst hit areas are near the Chaudière River south of Québec City, and along the Châteauguay River near Montréal. That's where CTV's Rosemary Thompson was today and she files this report.

Cut to Rosemary Thompson.

Rosemary Thompson (reporter): Flooding swept through the Châteauguay Valley leaving 500 homes under water.

Pull back camera to include unidentified man.

Unidentified Man: In some areas it looks like a big lake.

Cut to Rosemary Thompson.

Thompson: Farmers struggled to get livestock to higher ground.

Pull back camera to include Bill Bryson.

GOALS AT A GLANCE

■ Scan text to locate specific information.
■ Script and present a TV newscast.

Bill Bryson (farmer): I haven't had any sleep for twenty-four hours. One more day of this and we're going to have water in the barn, yeah. The local firefighters tell us it's rising two and a half centimetres an hour.

Close-up of Rosemary Thompson.

Thompson: Getting around isn't easy. This is the second time this season the Maloche family was forced to leave their home. In January it was the ice storm, now a surprise spring thaw. Our trees were damaged by the ice storm, he says, now this. We've had it. When the power went out in January, everyone wanted hydro crews to rescue them. Now this hydro truck needs rescuing. Helicopters are going into areas cut off by the flood water to airlift the stranded. One hundred people have left their homes. Three highways are closed. Now you've got a 4×4.

Cut to unidentified man.

Unidentified Man: Yeah. I would have continued but it's just that you can't tell where the road is or not, you know.

Close-up of Rosemary Thompson.

Thompson: This region floods every year, but never like this. In some places the river is three metres higher than usual. Last weekend there was a huge snow storm. Thirty centimetres of snow covered this field. In the space of forty-eight hours it melted. And there's rain in the forecast for Monday and Tuesday.

Cut to Jean Beaudette.

Jean Beaudette: We can't say that there won't be any problems. We cross our fingers.

Cut to Thompson.

Thompson: Hoping for a calmer passage to spring. Rosemary Thompson, CTV news, Ste.-Martine, Québec.

1. RESPONDING TO THE NEWSCAST

a. This newscast reports on a flood using the five Ws of reporting. Find answers to the following questions:

- Where did the flood take place?
- When did it happen?
- Who was affected by the flooding?
- What did people do?
- Why was the flood caused?

b. What other questions does the article answer? What other questions do you think it should have answered?

S T R A T E G I E S

2. MEDIA TV NEWSCASTS

In a small group, look at "Tuning in to the News" and list the characteristics of a typical TV newscast. How are TV newscasts different from newspaper articles or radio newscasts? How are they the same?

With your group, prepare a script for a TV newscast of a disaster. Your script should

- contain all the essential information about the disaster
- indicate who is speaking the lines
- briefly describe the camera shots

To enhance your newscast, create drawings of the physical damage caused by the disaster. Present your newscast to the class, with different group members taking the roles of the announcer, reporter, eyewitnesses, and so on. Incorporate your drawings into the newscast.

SELF-ASSESSMENT: Did your newscast answer all the questions that viewers might have? Did you help your audience understand the full impact of the disaster?

*When John Isaac travels to war zones with his camera,
he knows that danger is always part of the job.*

Photojournalist:
*In the Middle
of Disaster*

Profile by Keith Elliot Greenberg

As a photojournalist, John Isaac often finds himself in danger. In disaster zones around the world, he records the effects of war on the lives of ordinary people.

John—who lives close to UN world headquarters in New York City—didn't grow up dreaming of taking pictures of war scenes. He was raised in the city of Madras, in India, and moved to New York in 1968. After applying for a number of jobs, he became a UN messenger. Meanwhile, he spent his spare time taking pictures—a hobby he had loved since childhood.

John takes many chances as he tries to photograph the effects of war.

When the UN had a photography contest for employees, he entered a photo he had taken in India. John not only won first prize, but also a job in the UN's photography department.

GOALS AT A GLANCE

■ Evaluate photographs.
■ Create a photo report.

For several years, he worked at UN headquarters. There, he took pictures of the General Assembly—the place where United Nations representatives from around the world debate issues and vote on proposals.

In 1968, John was invited to accompany a UN mission to Lebanon in the Middle East. Israel had invaded the country and now UN forces were trying to supervise a peaceful withdrawal. Because UN soldiers were trying to calm the situation, they were known as "peacekeepers."

A man and boy support each other as they learn to walk with artificial limbs in Afghanistan.

John shown with Palestinian refugees.

John knew very little about the circumstances in Lebanon. "I didn't even realize I was going to a war," he says. "I was just happy to be flying to another country on a big assignment."

One of his first tasks was travelling with UN diplomats who were paying a visit to Yasser Arafat, head of the Palestinian Liberation Organization, or PLO. Arafat has many enemies, and he didn't want people to know the location of his hideout in Lebanon's capital of Beirut. John was blindfolded, so he wouldn't know where he was being taken. When he arrived, he immediately put his camera to his eye and started snapping.

A Nepali girl poses for the camera.

"It was my first big assignment, and I was really excited," he explains. "We were on a block of apartment buildings. There were about 150 windows on the block, and every one of them was stacked with sandbags, with machine guns pointing out. Nobody wanted me to show where Arafat was staying."

On the same trip, John had his first brush with death. As he drove down a street, a large rocket-propelled grenade shot in front of him. It blew a hole in a wall and blasted through a building.

John's camera captures the sunset on a beach in India.

"I'm not embarrassed to tell you that it was scary," John admits. "Every time something like this happens, it scares me. But I've always felt like I had a shield around me. Other war photographers have told me the same thing. It's like a guardian angel watching out for you."

❖ ❖ ❖

The next year, John found himself in Cambodia in Southeast Asia. Vietnam had invaded the country, and over forty thousand people were fleeing. John took a touching photograph of an elderly woman who'd left everything behind as she escaped to Thailand. The UN released the picture and several major magazines printed it.

One day, John received a telephone call from a woman in California. She'd seen the photo of the old lady, and recognized her. It was her grandmother, but they'd lost touch five years before. With John's help, the family was united again.

"That was one of my happiest moments," he says. "I felt that by being there and taking that picture, I helped an entire family." ◆

John's moving portrait of an elderly Cambodian refugee and child.

1. RESPONDING TO THE PROFILE

a. Why do you think John Isaac likes and continues to do such a dangerous job?

b. Discuss why a war zone can be considered a disaster area. Refer to the text and John's photos. What effects does war have on the lives of ordinary people?

c. If you were a photojournalist and you could go anywhere in the world to do a story, where would you go? Explain your choice to a partner.

2. MEDIA EVALUATE PHOTOGRAPHS

With a few of your classmates, decide which of John Isaac's photos is the best in each of these categories:

- most dramatic
- most informative
- most moving (emotional)

For each choice, write a brief description of why the photo is effective. Do you think it's true that people remember certain photos longer than they remember words they've read? Why do you think this might be so? How do photos influence our view of people and places in the news? Discuss the questions as a group, and then summarize your ideas for the class.

3. MEDIA CREATE A PHOTO REPORT

Working independently or with a partner, choose an event to cover as a photojournalist. You could bring a camera to a school field day, a holiday parade, or another local event. Take pictures from several viewpoints: wide angle shots to get the whole scene, shots from high and low angles, and close-ups to capture interesting details. Make sure to show people's faces reacting to the event. Select a variety of your best photos and arrange them in logical order to create your photo report. Add captions that will help viewers understand the five Ws: *who, what, where, when* and *why.*

SELF-ASSESSMENT: Do your photos show what you hoped they would? Is your photo report interesting and complete? Do the captions help the photos tell their story?

4. RESEARCHING CAREERS IN JOURNALISM

From reading about John Isaac, you have learned that photojournalism is a rewarding, but sometimes dangerous career. Some other careers in journalism include news reader, sports reporter, crime reporter, news reporter, and travel writer. What other journalistic careers are there? Remember that journalists work in newspapers, magazines, radio, and TV. Which job would you prefer? Explain why.

Choose one of the careers to research. Investigate what skills, education, and experience you would need. Determine the salary earned, the working hours, travel requirements, and anything else you would like to know. Write up your findings on a large card, and pin it to a class Job Board.

Linden MacIntyre, broadcast journalist on the CBC's popular program *the fifth estate.*

Olivia Ward is a journalist with the *Toronto Star.*

Kevin Newman is a popular TV journalist.

HOW TO WRITE A
NEWSPAPER ARTICLE

Goals at a Glance
- Create a newspaper article.
- Use the inverted pyramid structure.

Newspaper articles have to provide accurate information, and they also have to be interesting to read. Following a few suggestions can help give professional flair to the newspaper article you write.

Find and Learn the Story

To write a good newspaper article, the first thing you need is an interesting story. Consider telling about a current event in your school, city, or province. Once you have decided on the topic, the next thing to do is to find good sources of information about it. If your story covers a local event, try to interview those who are involved. Take notes as you collect the information.

Analyse the Information

Now that you have the information, sort through it to find the answers to the five Ws— *who, what, where, when,* and *why.*

Newspaper articles should be *objective*, which means they should give facts, not opinions. Remember, it's your job as a journalist to find answers for the questions your readers will have.

Write the Article

Your news article should begin with a *lead*— an introductory paragraph that tells the most important details about the news story. It answers the five Ws. Next comes the *body* of the article. This part is where you develop or explain the main facts given in the lead. The details in a newspaper article are given in what is called the *inverted pyramid* (right) structure. The most important and interesting information comes first in the article since most people read only the first parts of it. Less important details come at the end. Read the following newspaper article to help you understand the inverted pyramid structure.

PROCESS

Nine Killed in New Year Tragedy

BY NUNAVIK.NET
KANGIKSUALUJJUAQ, QUÉBEC/JAN.2/99

A deadly avalanche swept through the northern Québec village of Kangiksualujjuaq in the early morning hours of New Year's Day. It has left at least nine people dead.

About 500 hundred people were in the town's gymnasium, celebrating New Year's Eve, when the avalanche hit. The avalanche smashed down one of the walls, leaving one to three metres of snow in the gymnasium.

Most people were able to get out by themselves. But the avalanche killed nine and injured about twenty-five people. Some of the injured are reported to be in serious condition. Fifteen of them will be transported to hospitals in Montréal and Québec City for treatment.

The village has two nurses and one doctor. Some of the residents have medical training, but more qualified personnel are needed. A small plane

Deadly avalanche sweeps through Quebec village

with supplies and medical personnel landed the day of the tragedy, and two other aircraft carrying rescuers and search dogs are on their way. A blizzard has made getting other aid into the community difficult.

Kangiksualujjuaq is an Inuit village of about 700 inhabitants, roughly 1500 km north of Montréal.

Include a Byline and Placeline

The byline tells who wrote the article, and the placeline tells where the story takes place. These are written underneath the headline in a smaller font.

Photographs and Captions

If possible, include a photo, or perhaps a drawing, to attract attention, and to help tell your story at a glance. The *caption*, usually a short sentence, explains the photograph.

Self-Assessment

Review your article, using the checklist below:

❏ Is my headline eye-catching?
❏ Does my lead include the answers to the five Ws?
❏ Does the body of my article adequately develop the details of the story?
❏ Is the information arranged in the inverted pyramid structure?
❏ Are any important facts or details missing?
❏ Is my article objective? Does it report the events fairly without stressing one opinion?

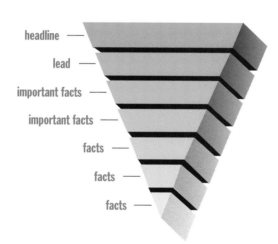

headline
lead
important facts
important facts
facts
facts
facts

Write a Headline

The headline is what will attract the reader's attention, so it needs to be written as a large, bold-print title. A clever headline will draw more readers to your article.

PROCESS

Gwaii Haanas*

Poem by Jenny Nelson
Painting by Emily Carr

When I grow up, my father says,
the Big Trees will be gone.

I want to see the trees
my father's seen.

I want to travel on the water
Watch the otter
slide into the sea.
I want to see how small I am
beside old Chini Cedar Tree.
I want to see the things
Grandfather's seen.

I want to know the forest
through my toes, as my foot goes,
on moss, on beach, on rock,
on rotting wood.
I want to feel the forest
with my eyes and hands and nose,
wet clothes.

Sounds of tree-bird,
sounds of silence,
smell of mushroom, smell of
cedar,
following the creeks that run
red and quiet.
Water falls.
The forest calls.

I have a need
to see the Trees.
My father's seen.
Leave some for me.

GOALS AT A GLANCE

■ Compare ideas suggested by a poem and a painting.
■ Make connection between literature and
  personal experience.

Plumed Firs

RESPONDING TO THE POEM AND PAINTING

a. What is the speaker in this poem pleading for? What do you think has motivated this plea?

b. In what ways are the poem and painting well suited to one another? Are there aspects of the poem that are not represented in the painting? If so, what are they?

c. Are there natural environments in your local community or elsewhere in the world that you think may be gone when you grow up? Discuss how you feel about this.

---

*Gwaii Haanas: the name for the South Moresby area in the Queen Charlotte Islands of British Columbia.

How much does it matter if the banana slug
from Borneo is an endangered species? Not
at all, if you ask Francine Scrounge.

Every Day Is Earth Day

**Play by
Steven Pricone**

CHARACTERS

Francine Scrounge
Her Employees
> **Michael**
> **Lynette**

Students
> **Michelle**
> **Candice**
> **Melissa**

Dodo Bird
Martha, *passenger pigeon*
Banana Slug
Box Turtle
Old Francine
Four Cockroaches
Off-Stage Voice

SETTING: *Francine Scrounge's office, with large desk and chair centre.
On it are vase with artificial flowers, stacks of paper, and intercom.
Huge window behind desk on rear wall shows city skyline.*

AT RISE: *Standing with her back to audience, Francine
Scrounge looks out through window. She turns and faces audience,
leaning on desk, arms wide apart.*

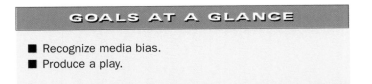

GOALS AT A GLANCE

222

■ Recognize media bias.
■ Produce a play.

Francine *(Proudly)*: It's like a dream—*my* office, *my* building, *my* company. When I think how I started out, making Air Jaguar sneakers out of endangered jungle cat hides—and now this! I'm powerful! *(Michael enters.)*

Michael *(Sheepishly)*: Ms. Scrounge, tomorrow is Earth Day, and well...I promised my little boy Anthony that I'd take him on a hike in the woods and show him a day of appreciation for nature. May I...

Francine *(Interrupting; sharply)*: Earth Day? Little boy? *(Angrily)* You listen to me, you little loser. You get paid a good salary to work here, don't you?

Michael *(Meekly)*: Yes, ma'am.

Francine: Our business is to make this world a better place!

Michael: *(Ironically)*: By manufacturing endangered sneakers, ivory toothpicks, and plastic containers for insecticides?

Francine *(Fiercely)*: Be proud of it! *(Excitedly)* Michael, I'm working now on a deal with an auto maker to bring back leaded gasoline engines. Think of it—we'll make millions!

Michael: But we can't go back to leaded gas—it pollutes the air!

Francine *(Sarcastically)*: Perhaps you didn't hear me, Michael. Millions! "Money Day" is what you should be celebrating! Every day is Money Day around here.

Michael: But...

Francine *(Intensely)*: Don't forget, Michael. Play your cards right, and you and your little boy will never have to worry about money. *(Michael nods sadly and exits in defeat.)*

Lynette *(Entering)*: Ms. Scrounge, your ten o'clock appointment is here. It's those school kids.

Francine *(Annoyed)*: Oh. Well, send the little brats in. *(Lynette exits. Francine shakes head.)* Public relations. I hate it. *(Michele, Candice, and Melissa enter.)*

Candice: Thank you for letting us see you today, Ms. Scrounge. We know you're busy.

Francine *(Annoyed)*: Well, of course I'm busy. What is it— some dumb school newspaper interview? Autographs? The secret of my success?

Michele: Actually, we understand you bought four hundred hectares in the rain forest, and your company is chopping it down to build a plantation. *(Pulls out long sheet of paper)* We have this petition.

Francine *(Ignoring Michele)*: Oh! It's a beautiful sight! All those trees lying on their sides, clear, vacant land as far as the eye can see. It's part of my newest marketing brainstorm— cigarettes for dogs. It'll make millions!

Melissa: Ms. Scrounge, do you know how important those trees are to the Earth? To us?

Candice *(Pleading)*: You can't destroy the rain forest!

Melissa: It's the home of endangered species, like the jaguar and the howler monkey.

Francine *(Who has been listening without interest)*: Oh! That reminds me...*(Into intercom)* Lynette, make a note that I need a stuffed howler monkey to put next to my mounted condor. *(Girls look at each other in disbelief.)*

Michele *(Upset)*: Ms. Scrounge, I'm appalled. As human beings we have a responsibility to all life forms on Earth. Especially endangered life forms.

Francine: No, you're wrong. We have a responsibility to ourselves. Whoever has the most toys wins. *(Sarcastically)* Well, this has been a rare pleasure. I'm sure your science teacher is very proud of you. Now, if you'll excuse me I have to return to the "real" world. The world where humans win.

Candice *(Passionately)*: Humans don't have to win. We all can win!

Francine: What are you, a bumper sticker? Get out! All of you! I've lost my patience with you.

Candice: I'll leave this petition with your secretary.

Francine: You do that. *(As girls exit, Francine speaks into intercom.)* Lynette, these little do-gooders will be giving you a petition. Shred it! *(Girls look at each other in amazement, glare at Francine.)* Then call Brazil and buy four hundred hectares and have them put up a factory to manufacture spotted owl repellent. *(Disgusted, girls exit. Francine falls into chair, spins around gleefully.)*: Power! I love it! *(Yawns)* It takes a lot out of a woman to run the planet with such gusto. I'm exhausted. *(Leans back in chair, putting her hands behind her head. Musing)*: I wonder how panda fur oven mitts would sell...*(Closes eyes, goes to sleep)*

Off-Stage Voice: And with that, Francine Scrounge fell into a deep sleep. She didn't usually nap during business hours, but this was a special day...a special nap...with a special dream. *(After a few moments, Dodo Bird enters.)*

Francine: What? Who? *(Stares at Dodo)* Who the dickens are you?

Dodo: I am the ghost of endangered animals past.

Francine *(Amazed)*: Why, you're a dodo bird! You're extinct!

Dodo *(Insulted)*: I beg your pardon! I do not stink.

Francine: No, no! *Extinct!* *(Peering more closely at Dodo)* What are you doing here?

Dodo: I am an apparition. This day you shall be visited by three apparitions who will show you the error of your ways. You have done wrong, Francine Scrounge.

Francine: Error of my ways? Done wrong? I think not, bird.

Dodo: You don't see that all life resonates as one. There is a web of life that links us all, a spirit...

Francine *(Breezily)*: Listen, dodo, as I always say—and you may

quote me in the spirit world—adapt or become extinct.

Dodo: As a human, the most highly evolved creature, you have a responsibility to the planet...a responsibility to use not only your considerable intelligence, but your common sense and compassion.

Francine: Hey, don't blame *me* for extinction. Extinction is the way of nature. Animals disappeared long before we humans appeared. It clears out the losers for us winners!

Dodo: But in this century even the "winners" are dying out. Extinction is at an all-time high.

Francine: So is the stock market!

Dodo *(In sombre tone)*: Humans are messing things up. *(Points across stage)* Francine Scrounge, look at the past. *(Martha enters.)* This is Martha, the passenger pigeon.

Martha *(Opening wings wide)*: I was once the most abundant bird in North America. We numbered in the billions.

Our nesting colonies measured thirty-three kilometres across. John Audubon reported once that we made the sky "black with birds" for three days straight. *(Drops wings)* Then in the mid-1800s, the humans chopped down our nesting sites and we were hunted, *slaughtered* by the millions for food...I was the very last bird of my kind. I was kept in the Cincinnati Zoo until I died in 1914—*(Ominously)* the last of my species, never to be seen again.

Francine *(Callously)*: How much did they get for a barrel of birds back then?

Dodo *(Disgusted)*: Is your heart a change purse?

Francine: Look, Martha bird, your story is really sad—especially the part about having to live in Cincinnati—but in case you haven't noticed, my life has not been affected one bit by your extinction. I can still sit by the pool on hot days and sip cool drinks.

Martha: In the last two hundred years, hundreds of species have

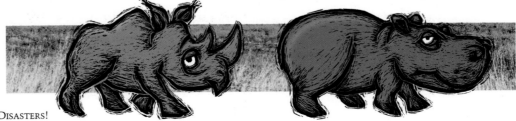

been erased from history just in North America alone—the Eastern elk, the Wisconsin cougar, the...

Francine *(Dismissively)*: Yeah, yeah. I'm telling you guys, adapt or become extinct.

Dodo: The world is slowly being affected by the loss of plant and animal species, at a rate of hundreds per year. You just don't see it...yet! *(Dodo and Martha exit.)*

Francine *(As they exit)*: Go! Good riddance! Who needs your guilt? I have a world to control. *(To herself)* Wow! This is some dream. I wonder if I could do a hostile takeover in my dreams? *(Goes to desk and presses intercom)* Lynette, get in touch with those two big companies and ah...the entire country of Italy. Tell them I'm offering sixteen dollars and seven lire as a takeover bid for a whole bunch of them.

Banana Slug *(Off-stage)*: Francine Scrounge...this is the ghost of endangered animals present. You are greedy, selfish, and you cheat at games.

Francine *(Looking about; confused)*: Who said that? *(Banana Slug enters.)*

Slug: I am the ghost of endangered animals present.

Francine: *What* on earth are you?

Slug: I'm a banana slug! Haven't you ever seen a banana slug?

Francine: Can't say that I have. You look like a skinny pickle.

Slug: You are the one in a pickle, Francine Scrounge. Over one hundred organisms are becoming extinct each year. And you care not.

Francine: Why should I?

Slug *(Philosophically)*: Each life form is a note in the symphony of life. As each note disappears, the music is less beautiful. With each falling note it's more empty...until...silence.

Francine *(With an attitude)*: So tell me, what's endangered? Is it the redheaded slithy tove from the jungles of Borneo? That's real significant.

Slug: Try the tiger!

Francine *(Genuinely surprised)*: The tiger? Tony the Tiger? Tigger?

Slug *(Nodding)*: Only six thousand left. Poachers kill them and they're losing their habitats.

Francine: But there have always been tigers.

Slug: There were always passenger pigeons.

Francine: Who else is endangered?

Slug: The black rhino and giant panda number less than two thousand apiece. Unless drastic conservation measures are taken, they both can be gone in just five years.

Francine *(Wistfully)*: You're making me remember all those animals I loved so as a little girl.

Slug: Like box turtles?

Francine *(Excited)*: I had a box turtle! I named her Leona. I fed her worms and blackberries.

Slug: They're endangered, too.

Francine *(Shocked)*: No! *(Box Turtle enters.)*

Francine: Leona?

Turtle: No, sorry. My name is Ferdinand. My kind used to be so common. Now our habitats are shrinking and we're sold off into the slavery of being pets. We're all going, right before your eyes, Francine. Will you do nothing?

Francine *(Flatly)*: I merge, I invest, I manufacture. I don't have time to think about...are you sure *tigers* are endangered?

Slug *(Nodding)*: Along with the African grey parrot and the hippopotamus.

Francine *(Surprised)*: The hippo!

Slug: Its teeth are being used as a substitute for elephant ivory.

Francine: Gosh, I have a bicycle made of ivory. It's giving me a little tinge of guilt, to see these animals, hear their stories. When I was a little girl I had a stuffed hippo. I slept with it, and...*(Snaps out of it)* Hey, wait a minute, slug. You know all about my childhood. You're telling me all this to make me feel guilty! How dare you invade my memories!

Slug (*Shrugging*): Be that as it may, they are still endangered—each one. More notes going...going...(*Slug and Turtle exit.*) going, until all you can do is whistle alone. (*Exits*)

Francine: What a downer! Dumb slug, ruining all my fun. How can I enjoy all my power, when... (*Crunching sound is heard*) Who's there? (*More crunching*) Who is that? (*1st Cockroach enters, crunching on celery stalk and reading from paper. Cockroaches are constantly crunching on something as they speak their lines throughout the rest of the play.*)

1st Cockroach: Is this the Scrounge Building, 17 Centre Street? I'm looking for a Francine Scrounge. (*Looks up*) Is that you?

Francine (*Haughtily*): Don't tell me. You're the ghost of endangered animals future. Well, I'm ready for you. That banana slug made me a little sentimental by tapping into my memories, but I'm ready for you, bug! You're not going to intimidate me! I'm *Homo sapiens*, and I run things around here!

1st Cockroach (*Impatiently*): Sure, sure, whatever you say. (*Looks at watch*) Look, let's get on with this.

Francine (*On intercom*): Lynette, bring me a can of industrial-strength bug spray...Lynette? Lynette?

1st Cockroach: Save your voice. This is the future, remember? There've been some changes. (*He walks to window, beckons Francine.*) Come here. (*She goes to window.*) Remember that symphony the banana slug referred to? Well, look what you guys have done to it. (*Points out window*)

Francine (*Looking out*): It's a mess! Where are all the people?

1st Cockroach: You mean the *Homo sapiens*? Sorry, you've all been driven underground. You can't handle the air any more. The ozone layer is gone...lead is at a level of two percent.

(2nd, 3rd, and 4th Cockroaches enter during 1st Cockroach's speech. Francine turns toward them, with a start.) Yes, we have *you* to thank for that. (Cockroaches applaud, then look out window.)

2nd Cockroach (Enchanted): Isn't it beautiful?

3rd Cockroach: I love the air.

1st Cockroach (To FRANCINE): You guys are manufacturing your own air and water. Most species are gone. Plants are rare now, so you must also manufacture your food.

Francine (With disdain): And you cockroaches have taken over, I suppose?

1st Cockroach: You say that as if it were a bad thing.

2nd Cockroach: Listen, we *always* ran things.

3rd Cockroach: We were here before the dinosaurs.

4th Cockroach: Nice sort of creatures. Clean. Dominating without being boorish.

(Shakes head) A shame about that asteroid.

3rd Cockroach: And we'll be here long after the likes of you is gone.

2nd Cockroach (Looking at his watch): Which could be any time now.

Francine: And just *how* is it that you have survived?

3rd Cockroach: Oh, we don't ask for much. A little garbage here, a little decaying matter there. We've even adapted to eating plastic. (Rubs stomach) Yum! What I wouldn't give for an empty pop bottle right about now.

Francine: Plastic?

1st Cockroach: Sure. As we always say, "Adapt or become an appetizer." (2nd Cockroach exits.)

Francine (Fearfully): But what about me? What has become of me?

1st Cockroach: You? (Checks paper) Oh, you're still around.

Francine *(Relieved)*: Thank goodness.

3rd Cockroach *(Pointing)*: See? *(2nd Cockroach pushes in wheelchair in which Old Francine sits.)*

Francine *(Horrified)*: Oh, no! That can't be me!

1st Cockroach *(Nodding)*: But it is. Seems your illness was traced to environmental contamination, something to do with the lead content in the air.

3rd Cockroach: It's serious, but curable.

Francine *(Desperately)*: Then cure me! Cure me!

Old Francine *(Hoarsely)*: They can't. The cure would have come from a tropical plant that was never discovered.

Francine: Why not?

Old Francine: It grew in the tropical rain forests of the Amazon. One construction site destroyed the very last ones. It's gone now *(Sighs)* like so much else.

2nd Cockroach: Ironic, isn't it?

Francine *(Shaken)*: But we humans are so smart, so powerful.

1st Cockroach: Oh, "power" doesn't last long, Francine.

Francine *(Moving away from window, meekly)*: Does this have to be? Must this be our future?

1st Cockroach: The future is what you make it, sister. It's changing all the time. Everything you do *now* shapes it.

3rd Cockroach: So, do your thing. We don't care. We're not going anywhere. We're adapting masters.

1st Cockroach *(Checking watch)*: Well, we're done here. I hope we brought a little ray of sunshine into your day. *(Cockroaches exit, pushing Old Francine off. Francine watches for a moment, then shakes head mournfully. She takes another disbelieving look out window,*

then sits down at desk. She stares out into audience and puts her head down on her hands and goes back to sleep. After a moment, Michael enters.)

Michael: Ms. Scrounge...(*Notices her asleep*) Oh! (*Francine awakens with a start.*)

Francine: Michael! Are you a ghost? I mean...

Michael: I'm sorry, I didn't know you were asleep.

Francine (*Flustered*): I wasn't. I was just resting my eyes. (*Rubs eyes wearily*) What is it, Michael?

Michael (*Boldly*): Well, this Earth Day deal with my little boy, it really means a lot to me—and to him. I know your feelings on it, but I'd like you to consider changing your mind. (*Eagerly*) I'll make it up to you. I'll work a holiday, a double shift, if you'd prefer—

Francine (*Rushing to window and looking out; to herself*): It's all still here. (*Sighs in relief*)

Michael (*Quizzically*): Ms. Scrounge? Is something wrong?

Francine: No, nothing, Michael. It's just—ah—the weather seems brighter than they forecasted today.

Michael: Um...so what about Earth Day, Ms. Scrounge?

Francine (*Hesitating*): I need to think about it, Michael. I'll get back to you if I...change my mind.

Michael: I'll be waiting, Ms. Scrounge. (*Checking watch*) But it is getting late.

Francine (*Thoughtfully*): Yes, I realize time may be running out. (*Michael looks at her, confused, then exits. Francine remains with back to audience as curtain slowly closes.*)

1. RESPONDING TO THE PLAY

a. This play is a **parody** of the famous Charles Dickens story *A Christmas Carol*. Discuss with your class how understanding that story helps to explain Francine Scrounge's name, the appearance of endangered animals past, present, and future, and the role of Michael and his little boy, Anthony.

> A **parody** is a humorous imitation of serious writing.

b. Why does Francine Scrounge prefer to forget about Earth Day? What finally makes her more aware of the seriousness of environmental problems?

c. What parts of this script did you find amusing? Do you think humour helps Steven Pricone get his message across to audiences? Were you convinced by his message? Explain.

d. Do you think Francine's attitude toward the environment has changed by the end of the play? With a partner, discuss some positive things Francine could do if her attitude has changed and she wants to take responsibility for the environment.

2. MEDIA BIAS IN THE NEWS

In groups of three or four, check your local and national newspapers, listen to the radio news, and watch the news on TV for about a week. How many news items concern environmental issues? After each group presents its findings on this question, hold a class discussion. For items you read, heard, or saw, which side did the media take on the issue? Did you recognize any **bias** on the part of the media? Draw a conclusion from your findings.

> **Bias** is an opinion that may interfere with a fair judgment on an event or situation.

3. LANGUAGE CONVENTIONS PARENTHESES

Steven Pricone uses parentheses ( ) to provide directions to the actors and set designer in "Every Day Is Earth Day." Writers use parentheses for other purposes as well. Look through the selections in this book, and in other pieces of published writing, to discover some other examples of how parentheses are used. Create some sentences of your own that show the functions parentheses can perform. Make sure your sentences are punctuated properly.

4. ORAL COMMUNICATION PRODUCE A PLAY

With your classmates, prepare a dramatization of the play "Every Day Is Earth Day" using the following suggestions:

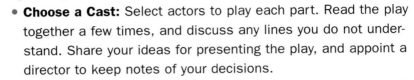

- **Choose a Cast:** Select actors to play each part. Read the play together a few times, and discuss any lines you do not understand. Share your ideas for presenting the play, and appoint a director to keep notes of your decisions.

- **Rehearse Your Parts:** Learn your lines well by reading them aloud over and over. (This will take extra work if you decide to memorize them completely.) Pay careful attention to the stage directions (notes in italics and parentheses). They will help you interpret your character properly. Practise your lines often with other actors so that you learn which words come immediately before each of your lines—these are your cues.

- **Make Costumes and Find Props:** At least two people should be in charge of making costumes and finding props—furniture, books, telephones, and so on. The actors should begin practising with costumes and props as soon as possible.

- **Rehearse the Play:** With your director, decide where each actor should enter, stand, move, and exit. Your actions should be consistent from practice to practice, and your voices should be loud enough to be heard by the whole audience. Be careful to deliver your lines at the right time so that everyone stays on track.

- **Dress Rehearsal and Performance:** Have your classmates watch your final, fully costumed rehearsal to give you feedback about how you're doing. Then polish your play and present it to your audience with confidence!

PEER ASSESSMENT: Ask for feedback from your audience. Could all the actors be heard? Were their facial expressions and gestures in character? Were the costumes and set funny? Did the production run smoothly? What could have been improved?

SELF-ASSESSMENT: MEDIA

As you worked on the unit, what did you learn about
- analysing visual information?
- writing a newspaper article?
- special effects in movies?
- writing and presenting a TV news script?
- using technical terms?
- evaluating media bias?
- creating slogans?
- using the five Ws of journalism?
- preparing and conducting an interview?
- producing a play?

MEDIA ANALYSE MEDIA COVERAGE

Disasters get a lot of attention. Do you think this is a good or a bad thing? With a partner, make a list of the positive and negative aspects of the way disasters are covered in the media. Together, create a short opinion piece that summarizes your point of view about media coverage of disasters. Read your opinion piece aloud as part of a Speaker's Corner on this topic.

WORD CRAFT TECHNICAL TERMS

Review your illustrated glossary of technical terms. Research other technical terms that are related to the subjects of the unit, and add those terms and definitions to your glossary. Compare your glossary with one prepared by a classmate. Did you select the same terms? Are your definitions logical and easy to understand?

ORAL COMMUNICATION DEVELOP STRATEGIES

As a class, discuss the different types of disasters you learned about in this unit—natural events and those caused by humans. What causes these disasters? What can be done to prevent them? Create a list of five strategies for preventing and/or dealing with one particular kind of disaster.

HUMOUR

Ha

Ha

Ha

Ha

Comics

free!

Why did chicken th'

"Laughter is the shortest distance between two people."

Victor Borge

ON THE FUNNY SIDE

Satire

Some comedians use events and people in their own lives to create their stand-up comedy. Others take on new roles, inventing funnier versions of themselves.

Just for a Laugh

TWO STAND-UP COMEDIANS SPEAK UP

They Just Don't Get It—
COMEDY SKETCH BY JANE WAGNER

I wish I had a quarter for every time my parents said, "Edith, you are being childish." Excuse me, but shouldn't a kid my age have the right to be childish? It's one of the few perks we have left. Not that I blame them for wanting us kids to act more like grown-ups. I wish my parents would act more like grown-ups, too. But it just does not seem to work. Acting childish seems to come naturally, but acting like an adult, no matter how old we are, just doesn't come easy to us.

Fire and Bad Clothes
COMEDY SKETCH BY DENNY DILLON

One of my most vivid memories is that when I was a kid our house burned down. "Oh my, you poor thing!" It always gets quite a reaction. Especially if you say "burned down." It's so dramatic. People even try to trip you up... *"To the ground...?"*

> **GOALS AT A GLANCE**
> ■ Analyse the use of informal language.
> ■ Follow instructions to perform a comedy sketch.

Let me tell you about my house on fire. I was doing my homework and I saw smoke coming out of the closet…I should have done like the movies and yelled "FIRE!!!" Instead I was a *very cool, laidback preteen.* "Oh Mom, there's smoke coming out of the closet." With that signature preteen disgust…"Just thought you might like to know." My mother raced downstairs. "Oh my God!!! KIDS! Grab your coats and get your hat…there's a fire in the basement"…Sounded like a song cue. My mother always loved musicals.

Now this next moment crystallizes my childhood. We all ran to the closet to get our coats. But being good kids, we all chose our bad coats. Is this a Midwest thing or what? I was always taught, you come home from school and you take off your good clothes and put on your bad clothes. I never understood this philosophy. But I got so used to wearing my bad clothes that my entire childhood was spent in hand-me-downs, and anything nice was reserved for an audience. In fact, that's why I became a performer. So I could wear my good clothes.

So that night, February 1, 1963 (I have a great memory), *we ran out of our burning house into a one hundred centimetre snowdrift* with our one possession: our bad coats. My brother even picked a bad hat. We didn't think to wear gloves or scarves. It was our first fire. You make mistakes.

I knocked on Helen Fortney's door: "Hi, Mrs. Fortney. Can we come in your house because our house is on fire." Once again, my attitude was a very cool preteen kind of "Sorry for the cheap drama, Helen, but we're in a bind." "Holy Toledo, Earl, did ya hear, did ya hear, did ya hear. The Dillon kids say their house is on fire." Earl Fortney said: "Did you call the fire department?" Duh. Thanks a lot Earl.

Then the fire trucks came roaring down my boring dead-end street. I sat in Earl's recliner chair where the footrest shoots out and stared out the huge living-room window. It was very exciting. The perfect seat to watch my house burn. It was like watching a Fellini movie. The fire trucks, the flashing lights, my hysterical optimist mother screaming: "This means we'll get all new furniture." Positive Thinking or Denial Queen…You decide…

The next day I went to school and told my teacher Sister Boniface: "Hi, Sister. I'm sorry I'm wearing my bad clothes, but last night my house burned down." She stared at me in pity: "To the ground?!"

Then my classmate, Beanie Gallagher, showed me a newspaper. My house was on the front page! "House on fire…Survivors are Mr. & Mrs. Dillon…and their children Kathe, Laurie, Sean, & Denny Dillon…"

I lit up!!! *My name was in the paper!!* I know it was just a survival mention, but…*my name was in the paper.* It looked great. I imagined the letters popping off the page and onto a marquee:

Broadway Tonight: DENNY DILLON—SURVIVOR!!!

----

1. RESPONDING TO THE COMEDY SKETCHES

a. Do you think these comedians capture what it's like to be a kid? Why or why not?

b. Reread the teaser, and discuss with a partner which of these comedians has invented her identity. What makes you think so?

c. With a small group, compare the two sketches. What words would you use to describe either style of humour? Which sketch is the funnier? Why?

d. What other styles of humour have you encountered?

e. Who is your favourite comedian or comic actor? What do you like most about his or her style of humour?

2. LANGUAGE CONVENTIONS INFORMAL LANGUAGE

Denny Dillon and Jane Wagner have written their comedy sketches using *informal language,* the kind of language most people use in a casual conversation with a friend. Informal language uses slang expressions, sentence fragments, and exclamations.

With a partner, find five specific examples of informal language in this selection. Why do you think the comedians have chosen to use informal language rather than a more formal form of expression? Share your ideas with the class.

3. ORAL COMMUNICATION PERFORM A SKETCH

Choose one of the sketches from "Just for a Laugh" and perform it as a stand-up sketch. (For "Fire and Bad Clothes" you could work with a group, with each group member performing a paragraph, or you could perform just a few paragraphs of it independently.) Try to analyse why the sketch is funny, then practise delivering it with a humorous tone of voice and gestures. Comedians generate humour by

- varying their pacing (the speed at which they speak)
- pausing before and/or after an interesting word or phrase
- emphasizing key words
- exaggerating facial expressions and body language

Most stand-up comics work only with a microphone, but you may want to use other props, such as a "bad" coat or hat, or a newspaper. Perform your sketch for your classmates when you're ready.

SELF-ASSESSMENT: What was the hardest part of performing the sketch? What special performance techniques did you use to be funny?

4. WRITING HUMOROUS SKETCH

Let these stand-up comics inspire you as you write your own humorous sketch, based on incidents or feelings from your own life. Keep the sketch short and use informal language. Some possible topics include

- a funny incident during your last vacation
- something that happened during your last ball game
- crazy things your siblings do
- a conversation with a parent or other relative

For extra amusement, you and a classmate can read one another's sketches. Perform your sketch for the class, using the tips in Activity 3.

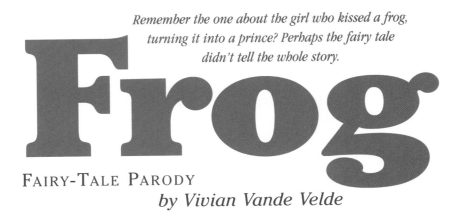

Remember the one about the girl who kissed a frog,
turning it into a prince? Perhaps the fairy tale
didn't tell the whole story.

Frog

FAIRY-TALE PARODY
by Vivian Vande Velde

Once upon a time, when princes still set out to seek their fortunes, a prince named Sidney came to a well where an old woman asked him for help in getting water.

Now the old woman didn't have a bucket and Sidney didn't have a bucket. But he'd heard enough fairy tales about three sons setting off down the road and meeting a strange old woman, and the first two sons were always rude and got into trouble, and the youngest son was always polite and then the old woman would give him whatever it was that he needed to fulfil his quest. So—being a middle son—Sidney always did his best to be polite to everybody, even when he wasn't on a quest.

But his best wasn't enough for this old woman, and the next thing he knew he was a bulgy-eyed green frog, which just goes to show that sometimes having a bucket is more important than being polite.

"There, you loathsome thing," the old woman said, which was hardly fair since she was the one who had made him into what he was, "stay a frog until a beautiful princess feeds you from her plate and lets you sleep on her pillow."

Travel goes a lot faster when you're riding a horse than when you're hopping, especially if your feet are less than thirty centimetres long. It took several days for Sidney to find the nearest castle, and when he got there, he didn't even know whose castle it was.

GOALS AT A GLANCE

- Suggest alternative verbs for *said*.
- Write a parody of a fairy tale.

Everything looked different from grass level, but he was still pretty sure he didn't know the people who lived here. He hoped there was a princess.

Sidney hopped across the drawbridge and into the dusty courtyard. There were horses and dogs and chickens. People, too, way, way high up. And lots and lots of legs. Many of them were walking so fast that he knew he was in danger of getting stepped on. He saw a well in the courtyard, but Sidney had had quite enough of wells for the time being. Hurriedly, he hopped off to the side, where there was a quiet and well-tended garden.

In the garden was a lively, cool-looking reflecting pool, with fresh, clear water and lily pads. Sidney jumped in and it felt like heaven.

Until something bonked him on the head and dunked him.

Sidney came up sputtering, just as a beautiful girl of about his own age came running up to the pool.

"Oh, no!" the girl cried. "My golden ball."

"Excuse me," Sidney said, "are you a princess?"

The girl didn't answer. She just flung herself onto the bench by the pool's edge and began to weep.

Sidney, in the middle of the pool, looked down and could see the ball just settling into the soft mud below him. He paddled closer to the girl. "Excuse me," he said again, "are you a princess?"

"What a twit," the girl snapped, never even looking up. "Of course I am. Don't I look like one?"

"Yes, you do," Sidney admitted apologetically. "And a very lovely one at that. I think the two of us can help each other out."

"I don't want to help you out," the princess said. "I want to have my ball back."

"That's what I mean," Sidney said.

The princess finally looked at him. "You can get my ball?" she asked. Sidney nodded.

"Well, then, do it."

"Yes," Sidney said, "but then, afterward, will you let me eat from your plate and sleep on your pillow? I'm a prince, you see, and I have a magic spell on me, and that's the only way to break it."

The princess's lip curled in disgust. "I need that ball. It's my father's paperweight and I wasn't supposed to be playing with it."

"I don't have to eat a *lot* from your plate," Sidney told her, "and I can sleep *way over* on the side of the pillow and not take up much room at all."

"Oh, all right," the princess said.

Sidney dove into the water. The ball was heavy, but with a great deal of struggling he finally managed to get it up close enough that the princess could reach over and grasp it. As she turned the ball over in her hands to make sure it wasn't damaged, Sidney jumped up onto the bench next to her.

"Now," he said just as she shook the water off the ball, drenching him all over again. He coughed a little bit, and when he looked up again, she was gone.

"Wait," he called, catching sight of her leaving the garden. But she didn't. By the time he made it out of the garden, across the courtyard, and into the castle, the princess was sitting down to dinner with her family.

Sidney kicked on the dining room door. "Hey," he yelled. "Hey, princess!"

He heard the king ask, "What's that noise?"

"Nothing," the princess answered.

"Princess!" Sidney yelled. "It's me, the frog prince. You accidentally left me behind."

The king's voice said, "He says he's

a frog prince. What does he mean, you left him behind?"

"I don't know," the princess said.

"You promised you'd help me." Sidney wasn't used to yelling, and his throat was getting sore.

"You promised you'd help him?" the king asked.

"No," the princess said.

There was no other way. Sidney called out, "In return for getting back your father's golden ball paperweight that you were playing with and dropped into the pool in the garden."

"The golden paperweight that left a wet spot on my papers this afternoon?" the king asked.

"I don't know anything about it," the princess said.

The king must have brought his fist down on the table. Sidney could hear the dishes rattle. "A promise," the king said, "is a promise. Let the frog in."

Servants came and opened the big golden doors.

Sidney hopped into the dining room, which was decorated with mirrors and crystal chandeliers and hundreds of flickering candles. He hopped until he came to the princess's chair.

"What, exactly," the king asked his daughter, "did you promise him?"

"I can't remember," the princess said.

"That I could eat from your plate," Sidney reminded her. "That I could sleep on your pillow. I promised not to eat too much and to use only the corner of the pillow."

"A promise is a promise," the king repeated.

The princess lifted Sidney, not very gently, and plunked him down on the white linen tablecloth beside her china dish.

Sidney nibbled on a piece of lettuce that was hanging off the edge of the dish.

The princess put her napkin up to her mouth and made gagging sounds. "I'm all finished," she announced, shoving the plate away.

"Then you may leave the table," the king said. "Don't forget your little friend."

The princess scooped up Sidney and brought him up the stairs to her bedroom, stamping her feet all the way.

"Thank you," Sidney yelled back down the stairs to the king.

"You horrid beast," the princess growled at Sidney. "You told him about the paperweight. Now I'm going to be in trouble."

"It was your own fault for walking away so fast that I couldn't keep up," Sidney said. "Are you going to put me on your pillow now?"

"I'll put you on my pillow!" the princess shouted. "But I'll put you on my wall first."

She flung Sidney with all her might against the wall.

"Ow!" Sidney cried, landing in a heap on the floor.

"Now here's the pillow," the princess said, throwing that on top of him.

But as soon as the pillow touched Sidney's head, he instantly regained his normal shape.

"Oh my!" the princess gasped. She was going to be in serious trouble with her father now, she thought. Here she had a man in her room, and her father was never going to believe that this was the same person who had come into her room as a frog. Even now she could hear her father coming up the stairs, demanding, "What's all the commotion?"

But the prince—he was obviously a prince—who stood before her was incredibly handsome, and she was falling in love already, which surely would balance out the trouble she'd be in with her father.

"Oh," she said, clapping her hands together. "I'm so sorry. But my father will make it worth your while. We can get married, and he'll give you half the kingdom and—"

"Are you out of your mind?" Sidney said. "First you break your promise to me, then you lie about it until your father forces you to keep it, then you try to kill me. No, thank you, princess." He strode out of the door, out of the castle, out of the kingdom, returning home, where he eventually married the goose girl.

And the princess was right: her father didn't believe her story.

1. RESPONDING TO THE PARODY

a. "Frog" is a *parody* (a humorous imitation) of a fairy tale called *The Frog Prince*. Working in a small group, make a list of the ways in which "Frog" makes fun of the characters and plot of a typical fairy tale.

b. Do you think this parody version of the fairy tale has a more up-to-date message than the original? Explain.

2. LANGUAGE CONVENTIONS VERBS TO REPLACE *SAID*

When she writes dialogue, Vivian Vande Velde uses many different verbs to replace the verb *said*, for example, "'Oh my!' the princess *gasped*." (page 246). Make a list of the other verbs Vivian uses in place of *said*. What does she achieve by using these different verbs?

Rewrite the following dialogue in your notebook, using vivid verbs to replace *said*. In each case, try to choose a verb that expresses the speaker's emotion.

Excuses, Excuses

"I was only coming to borrow the lawnmower," said Mr. Wolf.

"Yeah, sure! That's why you blew down my straw house!" said the First Little Pig.

"I have bad allergies. I just couldn't stop sneezing," said the Wolf.

The Second Little Pig said, "Oh, right! Then explain how you blew down my house of twigs."

Mr. Wolf said, "Well, a bee flew up my nose and I was simply trying to snort it out. Besides, I still needed to borrow a lawnmower."

"Then how do you explain the fact," said the Third Little Pig, "that you tried to blow down my brick house?"

"Oh, that's easy," said the Wolf. "A huge, ugly, hairy spider was crawling on your front door. I raised my paw to knock, saw it, and instantly began hyperventilating— I mean, huffing and puffing!"

---

3. WRITING PARODY

Write your own parody of a well-known fairy tale to give it a fresh perspective. In your parody you might use some or all of the following techniques:

- Change the point of view to that of another character.
- Give the characters contemporary attitudes and behaviours.
- Use a modern setting.
- Give the story a new message and a different ending.

When you have written your parody, share it with the class.

*When it comes to jokes, nothing beats one-liners—
unless it's a rhyme by Ogden Nash or that no-name comedian,
Anonymous.*

Quips & Quotes

VERSES AND JOKES
BY OGDEN NASH AND OTHERS

*Light Verse
by Ogden Nash*

The Fly
God in His wisdom made the fly
And then forgot to tell us why.

The Baby
A bit of talcum
Is always walcum.

The Jellyfish
Who wants my jellyfish?
I'm not sellyfish!

GOALS AT A GLANCE

■ Experiment with rhyme in light verse.
■ Revise statements to eliminate ambiguity.

Unsigned Advice

On Tomato Ketchup
**If you do not shake the bottle,
None'll come, and then a lot'll.**
Anonymous

Be Careful
I'm careful of the words I say,
To keep them soft and sweet,
I never know from day to day
Which ones I'll have to eat.

Anonymous

Sound Advice
When in danger or in doubt,
Run in circles, scream and shout.
Anonymous

And By That You Mean...?

For those who like this sort of thing, this is the sort of thing they like.
Abraham Lincoln

I wouldn't be paranoid
if everyone didn't pick on me.
Anonymous

People have one thing
in common: they
are all different.
Anonymous

He lived his life
to the end.
Anonymous

I must follow the people.
Am I not their leader?
*Benjamin Disraeli,
British Prime Minister*

Nobody goes
to that restaurant
any more—
it's too crowded.
Anonymous

That shoe fits him like a glove.
Anonymous

CLASSIFIED GOOFS

Taken from the classified sections of newspapers from across the country:

Now is your chance to have your ears pierced and get an extra pair to take home, too.

VACATION SPECIAL: Have your home exterminated.

DOG FOR SALE: Eats anything and is fond of children.

USED CARS: Why go elsewhere to be cheated? Come here first!

---

1. RESPONDING TO THE VERSES AND JOKES

a. What is your favourite joke or verse in the selection? Why?

b. Which jokes can you imagine using in a speech to amuse an audience?

2. READING CATEGORIZE BLOOPERS

The quotations in "And by That You Mean?" were not meant to be jokes; they are actually funny mistakes called bloopers. They fall into two main categories:

- **stating the obvious** (for example, "He lived his life to the end.")
- **logical impossibilities** (for example, "That shoe fits him like a glove.")

For each of the other bloopers, decide which type of mistake it is. When you read the newspaper or listen to politicians, watch out for similar bloopers.

3. WORD CRAFT RHYME

Ogden Nash and the anonymous poets who wrote "Unsigned Advice" use rhyme to create humour. Read the verses aloud to hear the rhymes better. Which are the funniest, in your opinion?

Try making up your own funny rhymes. If you like, coin new words the way Ogden Nash did with "sellyfish" and "walcum." Make a class display board of your humorous rhymes.

Post your funniest rhymes on the school's Web site, asking visitors to add their own.

4. LANGUAGE CONVENTIONS AMBIGUITY

The bloopers in "Classified Goofs" can be described as ambiguous because they appear to mean something other than what the writers intended. Working with a partner, decide

- what each statement actually means as written
- what the writer wanted it to mean
- how you could rewrite it so that it actually says what the writer intended

Now, rewrite each statement and share your results with your classmates.

SELF-ASSESSMENT: Check your rewritten version of each statement. Are you sure you have eliminated all ambiguity?

GOALS AT A GLANCE

■ Analyse visual humour in comic strips.
■ Research biographical information.

1. RESPONDING TO THE COMIC STRIPS

a. Have you ever had a serious disagreement with a best friend? Do you think Lynn Johnston has captured the teens' feelings well?

b. Lynn Johnston's daily comic strips each have four panels. In each strip, which of the four panels contains the punch line? Which punch line is funniest, in your opinion?

c. How would you describe the relationship between Elizabeth and her teacher? Do you think it's realistic? Why or why not?

d. Do you have a favourite newspaper comic strip? Tell why you enjoy it. Which characters do you like the best?

2. VISUAL COMMUNICATION ANALYSE COMIC STRIPS

In comic strips, the humour and interest come as much from the drawings as from the words—even the way individual words are drawn can be important. Choose one of Lynn Johnston's comic strips. For each panel, make notes about how she creates humour and interest visually. Consider such things as

- drawing style (simple or complex)
- point of view (close-ups, medium shots, long shots)
- facial expressions
- body language
- size and position of words and speech balloons

Compare your ideas with those of a partner.

3. RESEARCHING BIOGRAPHICAL INFORMATION

Lynn Johnston is a popular Canadian cartoonist. Find out what you can about her work, her interests, and her family by exploring the library and the Internet. (As an alternative, you might conduct the same kind of research about a favourite cartoonist of your choice.) Present your findings in the form of a brief written report. Be sure to include examples of the cartoonist's work.

So you've always wanted to create your own comic strip? This article could be just the help you've been waiting for.

WRITING on THE FUNNY SIDE of THE BRAIN

How-to Article
by Christopher Hart

I'm not going to dissect humour here. Anyone who asks the question, "What is humour?" isn't funny. Trust me on this. I had a professor in college who taught a course in film comedy. In my opinion, he was the dullest man in the history of the world. Thought I was going to die midway through each lecture. This guy spent all of his pitiful waking hours trying to explain humour. Can't be done. Want to know why? OK, here's my treatise on what humour is: If something's funny. That's it. That's the complete answer. We're done.

So, I'm not going to talk about humour, but I am going to talk about jokes—about how to craft them and how to make them pay off—because unlike humour, joke structure is a skill that can be taught.

GOALS AT A GLANCE

■ Summarize an article.
■ Create a comic strip.

What Should I Write About?

Generally, it's easier to write about people your own age and younger, because you've been there. This doesn't mean that if you're a teenager, you must only write about teenage things. However, you'd have an advantage if you approached your subject from an angle that's familiar to you. You could write a comic strip about parents raising kids, but you'd have a better slant if you wrote from the kid's point of view, rather than that of the parents.

You can also write about anything with which you're obsessed. If you've never known a lawyer in your life, you could still write about lawyers if you've watched just about every courtroom drama on television.

Which Comes First—The Drawing or the Joke?

The Joke. You thought it would be more complicated than that? Sorry. It's the joke. You were hoping, maybe, that it was the drawing? Nope. The joke always comes first. It's just not possible to craft a funny joke based on a few randomly drawn panels. The artist won't have a single visual idea until the writer comes up with the premise for the joke.

The All-Important "Hook"

Any good comic strip needs a hook— a humorous premise that draws readers in. You can create all the funny characters you want, but without a hook, your strip will never sustain itself. The hook should be a one-or two-sentence description of the premise. The best place to find good examples of hooks is in any TV guide. Read the descriptions of the sitcoms. Notice how brief they are, yet everything you need to know is there.

Here's an example of a hook that could launch a comic strip: A teenage girl is always falling in love with guys her parents can't stand. If it takes longer than that to explain it, you don't have the hook yet.

Conflict in Humour

Humour is based on conflict. Whenever possible, make the conflict visual. There's a saying in comedy screenwriting that works equally well for illustrated jokes and gags: Squeeze your characters. Stir things up; raise the stakes.

So, if you have a character who's off to work, make her late. If you've got a character who's going on a date, have him go to the wrong address to meet her. If you've got a character who's going to ask the boss for a raise, have her do it on the day her boss got yelled at by his wife.

Assembling a Cast

All right. You've got your idea for a comic strip. What do you do next? Start assembling a cast. You've probably thought about the main characters, and maybe one or two supporting characters. However, in order to create a world into which your readers can dive, you're going to have to weave together a few more players.

SISTER—SUPPORTING

DY/OWNER—LEAD

BOY's MOTHER—
SUPPORTING

DOG—LEAD

There are three types of characters: lead, supporting, and ancillary. Leads appear in almost every comic strip. Supporting characters appear less often, but regularly. Ancillary characters may not appear for weeks at a time, but must re-occur with enough frequency so that they won't be forgotten. Pages 257 and 258 show some typical cast members for an animal comic strip. There should be many more supporting and ancillary characters than there are leads. If you have too many lead characters, your strip will lose its focus. You must determine who the strip is about.

NEIGHBOURHOOD CAT—
ANCILLARY

NEIGHBOUR —
ANCILLARY

The Set-up Line: The Key to Writing Jokes

Everyone "knows" that a good punch line is the key to a funny joke, and everyone is wrong. The punch line is the easy part. It's the set-up that's really the key. Given the right set-up, anyone can think up a punch line.

Hard Punch Lines vs. Soft Punch Lines

There are two basic types of punch lines: hard and soft. The *hard punch line* has a sharp edge. It's the "You mean blah, blah?"/ "No, I mean, blah, blah," type of joke. The hard punch line panel is preceded by the all-important *set-up line* in the panel before.

The second type of joke makes use of the *soft punch line*. The soft punch line typically derives its humour more from character and quirkiness than from situations. It has a softer edge to it and usually presents itself in the form of a comment, rather than a strong retort. The soft punch line is set up by a preceding weak punch line, which is mildly funny or ironic, but not funny enough to carry the joke. It needs a "topper." So the soft punch line in the last panel tops it.

THE HARD PUNCH LINE

Here's an example of the hard punch line in use. Notice that the first panel establishes the premise: kid wants to borrow money from Dad. The next panels develop the joke. The second-last panel delivers the set-up, which begs for the punch line. And, the last panel contains the hard punch line. (Note that jokes are basically composed of two different things happening simultaneously on different levels. Here, the kid's dialogue progresses in one direction, while the father's goes in another.)

THE SOFT PUNCH LINE

On the next page is an example of the soft punch line. Again, the first panel establishes the premise. You see that the scene is in the living room of a couple who are couch potatoes. The second panel is the weak punch line. It's funny but not funny enough to sustain the whole joke. It needs a topper, the soft punch line, which occurs in the last panel.

THE SILENT PUNCH LINE
Sometimes a silent punch line is the funniest. If you can say it with pictures, don't say it again by adding redundant dialogue. Note the economy of words in this example. In addition, note that the strip ends exactly where it began, with the parents reading the book on the couch.

Last Laugh: Funny Words

Some words are funnier than others. Always search for the funnier word to express what you want your characters to say. Listen to stand-up comedians; they're masters at selecting funny-sounding words with which to pepper their routines. The difference between regular and funny words is that funny words are more specific, funny or zippy sounding, and/or slightly gross.

Ordinary	Funnier
full	bloated (slightly gross)
four	five (odd numbers are always funnier)
food	snack (zippy sounding)
house	condo (more specific)
child	kid (zippier sounding)
foot	toes (slightly gross)
smart	genius (more specific)
sandwich	pizza (more specific)
money	credit cards (more specific)
spot	smudge (funny sounding)
person	guy (funny sounding)

----

1. RESPONDING TO THE ARTICLE

a. Do you agree with the author that humour can't be explained? Why, or why not?

b. What was the most interesting thing about how to write comic strips you learned from this article?

c. You could think of a comic strip as a very short story. What are some of the elements that comic strips and stories have in common?

d. Summarize the information in the article, jotting down the main points in your notebook. Use your notes to create a short, step-by-step outline that someone else could easily follow.

e. Christopher Hart says that "joke structure is a skill that can be taught." Do you think his article successfully teaches people how jokes work? Explain.

2. READING COLLECT COMIC STRIPS

Clip examples of comic strips you enjoy from the newspapers. Make a class display with the headings "Hard Punch Line," "Soft Punch Line," and "Silent Punch Line." Pin each comic strip you clipped under the appropriate heading. If you're unsure of which category a strip belongs to, discuss the punch line with a classmate. Add other headings to your display if necessary. How would you categorize Lynn Johnston's comic strips in the previous selection?

3. VISUAL COMMUNICATION CREATE A COMIC STRIP

Work with a partner for this activity; one of you is the writer, and the other is the artist. Follow the advice in the article and in your own summary to create a four-panel comic strip. When you dream up a cast of characters and a story line, remember to stick to things you know well. Once you have your story line, turn it into a joke with a punch line. Plan your four panels. To complete the strip, the artist draws the characters (in black and white or colour), and the writer fills in the speech balloons. Exchange your finished comic strip with one created by another pair of students.

PEER ASSESSMENT: Does the comic strip have a hook? conflict? a good set-up line? A funny punch line? Is it clear who the main and supporting characters are? Are the pictures and words easy to see and understand? What suggestions would you make for improvements?

4. WORD CRAFT HUMOROUS WORDS

Discuss the list of funny words on page 261. According to Christopher Hart, what makes some words funnier than others? Do you disagree with any of his specific choices? Add your own examples of funny and not-so-funny words to the list.

The Friends of Kwan Ming

FOLK TALE BY PAUL YEE

When his father died, the peasant Kwan Ming was forced to sell his
little plot of paddy and the old family house to pay for the burial.
After the funeral, Kwan Ming looked around at the banana trees
surrounding his village, and saw that he had nothing left to his
name—not even one chipped roof tile. He had just enough money
to buy a steamship ticket to the New World, where he had heard jobs
were plentiful.

"I can start a new life there," he told his mother. "I will send
money home."

The voyage lasted six weeks, over rocky waves and through
screaming storms. Kwan Ming huddled together with hundreds of
other Chinese deep in the ship's hold. There he became fast friends
with Chew Lap, Tam Yim, and Wong Foon—men from neighbouring
villages. If one friend took sick, the others fetched him food and
water. If one friend had bad luck gambling, the others lent him
money to recover his losses. Together the four men ate, told jokes,
and shared their dreams for the future.

GOALS AT A GLANCE

■ Identify the elements of a folk tale.
■ Design a movie poster.

When they arrived in the New World, everyone scattered throughout the port city to search for work. Kwan Ming hurried to the warehouse district, to the train station, and to the waterfront, but doors slammed in his face because he was Chinese. So he went to every store and laundry in Chinatown, and to every farm outside town. But there was not a job to be found anywhere, for there were too many men looking for work in a country that was still too young.

Every night Kwan Ming trudged back to the inn where he was staying with his three friends. Like him, they, too, had been searching for work but had found nothing. Every night, as they ate their meagre meal of rice dotted with soya sauce, the friends shared information about the places they had visited and the people they had met. And every night Kwan Ming worried more and more about his mother, and how she was faring.

"If I don't find work soon, I'm going back to China," Chew Lap declared one evening.

"What for, fool?" asked Tam Yim. "Things are worse there!"

"But at least I will be with my family!" retorted Chew Lap.

"Your family needs money for food more than they need your company," Wong Foon commented, "Don't forget that."

Then a knock was heard at the door, and the innkeeper pushed his way into the tiny attic room.

"Good news!" he cried out. "I have found a job for each of you!"

The men leaped eagerly to their feet.

"Three of the jobs are well-paying and decent," announced the innkeeper. "But the fourth job is, well..." He coughed sadly.

For the first time since they had met, the four men eyed one another warily, like four hungry cats about to pounce on a bird.

"The biggest bakery in Chinatown needs a worker," said the innkeeper. "You'll always be warm next to the oven. Who will go?"

"You go, Chew Lap," Kwan Ming said firmly. "Your parents are ill and need money for medicine."

"The finest tailor in Chinatown wants an apprentice," continued the innkeeper. "The man who takes this job will be able to throw away those thin rags you wear."

"That's for you, Tam Yim," declared Kwan Ming. "You have four little ones waiting for food in China."

"The best shoemaker in Chinatown needs an assistant," said the innkeeper. "He pays good wages. Who wants to cut leather and stitch boots?"

"You go, Wong Foon," Kwan Ming stated. "You said the roof of your house in China needs repair. Better get new tiles before the rainy season starts."

"The last job is for a houseboy." The innkeeper shook his head. "The pay is low. The boss owns the biggest mansion in town, but he is also the stingiest man around!"

Kwan Ming had no choice but to take this job, for he knew his mother would be desperate for money. So off he went.

The boss was larger than a cast-iron stove and as cruel as a blizzard at midnight. Kwan Ming's room was next to the furnace, so black soot and coal dust covered his pillow and blankets. It was difficult to save money, and the servants had to fight over the leftovers for their meals.

Every day Kwan Ming swept and washed every floor in the mansion. He moved the heavy oak tables and rolled up the carpets. The house was so big, that when Kwan Ming finally finished cleaning the last room, the first one was dirty all over again.

One afternoon Kwan Ming was mopping the front porch when his boss came running out. In his hurry, he slipped and crashed down the stairs. Kwan Ming ran over to help, but the huge man turned on him.

"You turtle!" he screamed, as his neck purpled and swelled. "You lazy oaf! You doorknob! You rock-brain! You're fired!"

Kwan Ming stood silently for a long moment. Then he spoke. "Please, sir, give me another chance. I will work even harder if you let me stay."

The boss listened and his eyes narrowed. Then he coughed loudly. "Very well, Kwan Ming, I won't fire you," he said. "But I will have to punish you, for you have ruined this suit, and scuffed my boots, and made me miss my dinner."

Kwan Ming nodded miserably.

"Then find me the following things in three days' time!" the boss ordered. "Bring me a fine woollen suit that will never tear. Bring me a pair of leather boots that will never wear out. And bring me forty loaves of bread that will never go stale. Otherwise you are finished here, and I will see that you never find another job!"

Kwan Ming shuddered as he ran off. The old man's demands sounded impossible. Where would he find such items?

In despair, Kwan Ming wandered through the crowded streets of Chinatown. He sat on the raised wooden sidewalk because he had nowhere else to go.

Suddenly, familiar voices surrounded him.

"Kwan Ming, where have you been?"

"Kwan Ming, how is your job?"

"Kwan Ming, why do you never visit us?"

Kwan Ming looked up and saw his three friends smiling down at him. They pulled him up and pulled him off to the teahouse, where they ate and drank. When Kwan Ming told his friends about his predicament, the men clapped him on the shoulder.

"Don't worry!" exclaimed Tam Yim. "I'll make the woollen suit you need."

"I'll make the boots," added Wong Foon.

"And I'll make the bread," exclaimed Chew Lap.

Three days later, Kwan Ming's friends delivered the goods they had promised. An elegant suit of wool hung over a gleaming pair of leather boots, and forty loaves of fresh-baked bread were lined up in neat rows on the dining-room table.

Kwan Ming's boss waddled into the room and his eyes lit up. He put on the suit, and his eyebrows arched in surprise at how well it fit. Then he sat down and tried on the boots, which slid onto his feet as if they had been buttered.

Then the boss sliced into the bread and started eating. The bread was so soft, so sweet, and so moist that he couldn't stop. Faster and faster he chewed. He ate twelve loaves, then thirteen, then twenty.

The boss's stomach swelled like a circus tent, and his feet bloated out like balloons. But the well-sewn suit and sturdy boots held him tight like a gigantic sausage. The man shouted for help. He tried to stand up, but he couldn't even get out of his chair. He kicked his feet about like a baby throwing a tantrum.

But before anyone could do a thing, there was a shattering *Bang!*

Kwan Ming stared at the chair and blinked his eyes in astonishment. For there was nothing left of his boss.

He had exploded into a million little pieces.

1. RESPONDING TO THE FOLK TALE

a. Why do you think the four men became such good friends during the voyage to the New World?

b. What do you think of Kwan Ming's selflessness towards his friends? Would you have been so generous in the same situation? Explain your reasons.

c. As a class, make a list of the elements of a typical folk tale, for example, one-dimensional characters that are all good or all bad. Reread "The Friends of Kwan Ming" looking for examples of the elements you listed.

d. What are the humorous moments in this folk tale? What words would you use to describe the humour?

2. ORAL COMMUNICATION PERFORM A SCENE

Working in groups of five, develop a scene that takes place after Kwan Ming's boss explodes. In this scene, the four friends explain to a police officer what happened to the boss. Write out the dialogue in script form. Assign a part to each member of the group, memorize your lines, and perform your scene for the class. You might use a video recorder to tape your performance.

3. MEDIA DESIGN A POSTER

Imagine that you are helping to promote a movie version of "The Friends of Kwan Ming." Your job is to create a poster for the movie that will intrigue people, but not give away the explosive ending. Successful posters have one powerful image, bold colours, and a few well-chosen words that can be easily read from a distance. Enter your poster in a class poster contest!

SELF-ASSESSMENT: After you have finished a rough sketch of your poster, take a step back to have a critical look at it. Is the title prominent and easy to read? Have you chosen an eye-catching image that tells something about the movie? Will your poster make a strong impression?

On The Red Green Show, *Red runs Possum Lodge, and Harold is his goofy sidekick.*

Red's Mail Call

TV Comedy Sketch from *The Red Green Show*

Harold is sitting in the den in his chair with a mailsack beside him and a couple of opened letters in his hand. He starts to talk when he sees Red coming in.

Harold: We have a really interesting letter today, Uncle Red. Came from the Yukon. I put the stamp in my time capsule.

Red: The Yukon—the land of the Midnight Sun. Dog sleds. Six months of daylight. Gold Rush. Polar bears and penguins. Quite a place.

Harold: Yeah, oh yeah. "Dear Red, Living up here in the Yukon is real great. The only problem is the people from the South who stereotype us Northerners. They think of the Yukon as the Land of the Midnight Sun, with everyone on dog sleds, and hunting seals for six months of daylight. Tourists ask us where the Gold Rush is or where they can find the polar bears and penguins. What kind of idiot doesn't know that penguins are only at the South Pole? How can we break away from these stupid stereotypes?"

GOALS AT A GLANCE

■ Recognize stereotypes and explore their effects.
■ Analyse TV comedy shows.

Red: I think the main problem is the foreigners. They come here expecting to see nothing but snowmobiles and Mounties. When was the last time you saw a Mountie? I mean, I wonder if there even is such a thing as a Mountie. Have you ever seen one? Mr....did he sign his name?

Harold: Yeah, oh yeah. Corporal H. Benson of the Royal Canadian Mounted Police, Whitehorse Detachment.

Red: Oh. Sorry, Corporal Benson, nothing against the Mounties, you're a great bunch of guys. You men carry on a great Canadian tradition, and Corporal H. Benson, if we do have one stereotype, let it be the Canadian Mountie in his bright red uniform. I salute you, sir.

Harold: The *H* stands for Helen.

----

1. RESPONDING TO THE COMEDY SKETCH

a. The humour in this skit could be called "putting your foot in your mouth." What are the places in the skit where Red says something foolish?

b. Do people from other countries or other regions of Canada have stereotyped ideas about the place where you live? What are the stereotypes, and how do you know they exist?

c. What are some possible negative results of misconceptions Canadians might hold about other countries?

2. MEDIA ANALYSE TV SHOWS

Make a list of comedy shows that are currently running on TV. Sort the shows into categories, such as sketch comedy (*The Red Green Show*), situation comedy (*Third Rock from the Sun*), and animation (*The Simpsons*). Add other categories if necessary, and write an explanation of how each category is different from the others. Which category seems to be most popular? How would you account for this? Finally, choose your favourite comedy and tell why you enjoy it.

Goals at a Glance
● Analyse character throughly. ● Prepare to perform in role.

What's the difference between acting a part in a play, and role-playing or improvising a character? When you act a part, you have a script that tells you exactly what to say. Many scripts contain stage directions that suggest what tone of voice and gestures you should use, and even how you should use facial expressions. When you role-play or improvise, you don't have a script to help! You have to rely on your imagination to create your character. Even so, there are some practical strategies you can use to make improvising easier.

Get to Know Your Character

In most cases, you'll have time to prepare before you improvise. Use some of that time to think about the character you will be playing. Your goal is to become that character so that your audience will believe you are that person and not yourself. Answering the following questions will help you to get to know your character:

- What adjectives would you use to describe your character's personality? Try to find words that truly capture what your character is like, such as confident, generous, angry.
- What is your character's background? Where does she live? How old is she? What are her family and friends like? How does this background affect her feelings and attitudes?
- What skills, education, and interests does your character have? What is his position in society?
- What motivates your character? Does she have specific goals?
- Is your character a likable person? Why or why not?
- Does your character have specific mannerisms? What do they reveal about him?
- What kinds of relationships does your character have with the others in the scene?

Set the Scene

When you have a good idea of your character, start to think about the scene you are going to improvise. Usually you'll be working with one

PROCESS

or more of your classmates. Although you won't be writing a script, it's a good idea to plan the scene with your partners.

- Identify the central idea or message of your scene. How can you best communicate your message to the audience?
- Determine what mood you want to create, for example, comic, serious, or mysterious. This will help you decide how to deliver your lines.
- Make a general plan about what your char-acters are going to say to each other at different moments of the scene. Decide on the actions the characters will perform, and what gestures and facial expressions they might use.

Practise Improvising

Practice will boost your confidence. When you practise improvising, your goal isn't to memorize a series of lines. Instead, focus on becoming comfortable in the role. With your partners, improvise a variety of situations in which your characters interact. This will give you a chance to experiment with different lines and actions.

If you have lots of time for practice, you might try the following suggestions:

- Practise on your own. Throughout the day, slip into role to help you imagine how your character would behave in different situations.
- Get your friends and family involved! Tell them about your character, then interact with them in your role.

Focus Your Performance

When you improvise, try to keep your performance focussed. Here are some tips that can help:

- Professional actors say makeup and costume help them get into role. Find at least one item of costume that your character would wear — for example, a pair of shoes, a hat, or a piece of jewellery. Choose an item that gives a strong impression of who your char-acter is.
- A single prop, such as an umbrella or a tool kit, can reveal your character and help you stay in role.
- Most people have expressions and gestures that they often use. Choose one or two behaviours that will characterize the person you are playing—for example, your character might have an obnoxious laugh or a funny way of blinking.

Self-Assessment

Use the following checklist to determine whether you are well prepared for your improvisation:

- ❏ I got to know my character by imagining his or her appearance, background, relation-ships, and goals.
- ❏ With my partners, I planned the scene to be improvised.
- ❏ I strengthened my improvising skills by practising with my partners and on my own.
- ❏ I identified costume items, props, and behaviours that will help me bring my character to life.

PROCESS

Have you ever met the
penetrating gaze
of a cow's big brown eyes?
What was it
trying to tell you?

Great Cows of History

ART CONCEPT BY MARC GALLANT

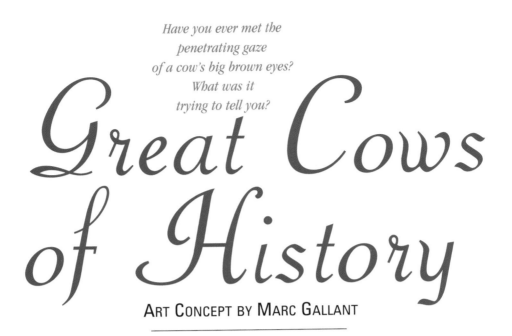

Cows Visiting the British Museum
Wayne Anderson, Great Britain

In *The Cow Book*, Marc Gallant of Prince Edward Island has created a tongue-in-cheek portrayal of important cows throughout history. His book is illustrated with paintings created by artists from around the world. No longer just a silent witness to events, the cow takes a bow at the centre of the canvas of history.

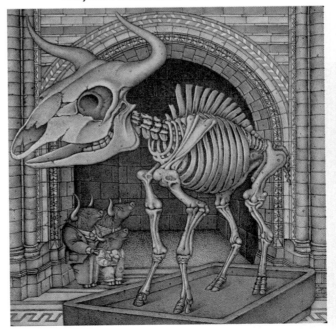

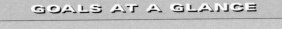

GOALS AT A GLANCE

- Recognize humour in a painting.
- Analyse a painting in terms of basic visual elements.

272

Viking Cows on Their Way to the New World
Jean-Christian Knaff, Canada

American Cowboy on Texas Longhorn
Boris Vallejo, United States

Tanzanian Cow in Moonlight
Bushiri, Tanzania

Elsie Borden in a 1950s Kitchen
Mark Hess, United States

1. Responding to the Art

a. Which painting do you find to be the most humorous? Why?

b. Suggest a subject for an additional humorous cow painting. What style of art would you recommend for your painting?

STRATEGIES

2. Visual Communication   Analyse a Painting

When you look at a painting, you might feel at a loss for the right words to describe why you like it. There are a number of elements an artist plays with when creating a painting. Knowing what these elements are can help you to understand and describe your response.

- Artists use lines to create edges, borders, outlines, and shapes. Lines can be thick or narrow, sharp or fuzzy, straight or curving.
- Artists choose their colours carefully to help them communicate emotion. Soft pastel colours, for example, have a different effect from rich, deep colours.
- Through perspective, artists create the illusion of three dimensions on the two-dimensional surface of a canvas.
- Composition refers to the arrangement of the different parts of a painting. For example, through the arrangement of shapes and colours, artists can create a sense of balance or imbalance in a painting.

Choose one of the cow paintings and explain why you like or dislike it. Your explanation should include some of the terms defined above, or other technical terms about painting with which you are familiar.

SELF-ASSESSMENT: Did you consider the different elements of the painting when you were thinking about your response to it? Were you able to mention these elements in your explanation? What was the hardest thing about writing the explanation?

It's a thankless task, writing a thank-you note
for a gift you wish you'd never received.

Thank You, Uncle Ben

SHORT STORY BY MAGGIE GRANT

I usually manage to finish writing my Christmas thank-you
notes by January 31 at worst, but this year I've bogged down
on Uncle Ben. That's my rich uncle, the one who's going to
leave me a nice legacy if I survive him. Which seems doubtful at
the moment.

There is also this about Uncle Ben: he's the type who would
cut a person out of his will if that person failed to thank him for
a Christmas present, or even failed to be adequately enthusiastic
about it. My problem this year is that—well, just glance at these
unfinished notes and perhaps you'll understand.

GOALS AT A GLANCE

■ Write a letter in role.
■ Create an illustrated how-to manual.

December 28
Dear Uncle Ben:
We had a lovely Christmas with all sorts of exciting presents, particularly yours. At first we were puzzled about its use, since no instruction sheet was enclosed, but suddenly light dawned—an electric bean pot, what a marvellous idea! To be able to plug in and bake old-fashioned beans right at the table is such an innovation we've invited a few friends in to participate in your gift's debut. At this very moment the feast is hissing away in the dining room and...

January 3
Dear Uncle Ben:
I know you'll be amused to learn that when we opened your lovely present we jumped to the conclusion it was a bean pot. We realized the error of our ways when some beans we were cooking exploded all over the dining room. The pattern they made on the ceiling looked exactly like Santa Claus and his eight tiny reindeer! Fortunately our insurance covers the cost of repainting the room and repairing the chandelier.
    Now our neighbour has told us your present is actually a bed-warmer and we're pleased as punch because both John and I suffer from cold feet these winter nights, and as a matter of fact he is now snoring peacefully in bed with the warmer toasting his...

January 5
Dear Uncle Ben:
Excuse the scribble, but I'm writing this in my lap so I can stay close to John's bed in case he needs anything. He's under sedation after burning both his feet (I won't bother you with the details of how it happened), but will soon be able to get about on crutches. Luckily a personal injury clause in our insurance policy will pay his salary while he's off work.
    I must delay no longer in thanking you for the lovely humidifier; it was so generous of you. About an hour ago I set it going in the living room and already...

January 20

Dear Uncle Ben:

At last a peaceful moment to write you! We've been higgledy-piggledy lately due to the living room broadloom having to be torn up and taken away to be dyed. It got badly stained in a foolish little mishap we had with steam and boiling water, and my Sheraton table had to be refinished. But it's an ill wind, etc., because I love the rug's new colour and insurance paid for everything.

Now to business! We are simply delighted with your Christmas present though I'm going to confess that at first we were unsure about its function. Then John's office manager dropped in and told us it's an outdoor barbecue. How silly of us not to realize it at once! To celebrate the new look in the living room we're going to prepare dinner there tonight, with John acting as chef. As I write he is fussing around with steaks and things...

January 31

Dear Uncle Ben:

As you can see by this letterhead, we are staying at a hotel. We had a fire at the house, but don't be alarmed, it wasn't too bad, mostly smoke damage. A marvellous cleaning crew is at work busily washing walls, shampooing furniture, and so forth. I understand this is a frightfully costly operation so thank goodness we were covered by insurance. In connection with this, I am expecting the company's adjuster to call at any moment, but meanwhile am dashing this off to thank you for...

February 1

Dear Uncle Ben:

If a Mr. Smither, an insurance adjuster, should try to get in touch with you in any way, I do beg you to disregard him. He called in to see me about some claims we've had recently, and suddenly started screaming and shouting dreadful things about the lovely Christmas present you sent us. Well, really! No man in his right mind would act that way about an inanimate object! The only thing to do is ignore him. And now, my darling uncle, I hope you are going to forgive the long delay in writing to thank you for the...for the... ◆

1. RESPONDING TO THE STORY

a. Were you able to figure out what Uncle Ben's gift might have been? Do you think the author did have a specific gift in mind? What are your reasons?

b. Why do you think Maggie Grant chose to write her story using a one-sided series of letters? In your opinion, was her approach funny? Explain.

c. Have you ever received a gift that you didn't really want? How did you handle this awkward situation? Would you do the same thing again?

2. WRITING HUMOROUS LETTERS

Write the letter Uncle Ben might have sent in reply to one of the thank-you letters from his niece, if she had actually mailed it. Before you begin, reread the first paragraph of the story to get an idea of Uncle Ben's circumstances and character. Share your letter with a partner. After one of you reads the narrator's letter aloud, the other could read Uncle Ben's reply.

3. VISUAL COMMUNICATION EXCUSES MANUAL

Create a humorous, illustrated Excuses Manual that offers great excuses and/or polite tricks to help people handle three difficult social situations, such as

- being invited somewhere you don't want to go
- coming home later than you said you would
- explaining why your homework is not finished

When your Manual is complete (no excuses!), share it with your class and your friends.

SELF-ASSESSMENT: Does your Excuses Manual offer advice that is funny but polite? Did you include humorous illustrations? Will you be able to use some of your own advice in real life?

Introducing Norbert

Short Story by Richard Scrimger

It sounds like an easy topic for a science report. The Moons of Jupiter. Lots of books on Jupiter in the library, lots of stuff on CD-ROM. Pictures, articles. Might even be interesting. But I'm having just a heck of a time writing it, because Norbert is very sensitive on the topic.

—*I am not sensitive*, says Norbert.

"Yes you are," I tell him. "You're very sensitive. All I have to do is mention the word Jupiter and you start to twitch."

—*That's because I know so much about it. After all, it's where I come from*, he says.

◆ ◆ ◆

I'd better introduce myself. I'm Alan. I live in a small town in Ontario. Actually my notebook reads Cobourg Ontario Canada North America The World. I'm thirteen years old and in Grade Seven. I have brown hair, and brown eyes, and a big mouth, at least that's what my friend Victor tells me. And just above my mouth, in the regular place, I have a nose. Not a regular sort of nose though. Oh, it looks normal enough—couple of freckles, occasional smudge of dirt.

GOALS AT A GLANCE

- Perform dialogue in role.
- Prepare a TV series proposal.

It drips when I have a cold, and wrinkles up when I'm thinking hard, or when there's cabbage for dinner, but...well...I don't know how to put it, except to say I'm trying to do some research for this science project only my nose won't let me. His name is Norbert.

—*Do I say hello now?*

"If you like," I say.

—*Hello. My name is Norbert Nose. I'm from the biggest planet. And the nicest.*

Norbert is talking about Jupiter. He usually ends up talking about Jupiter. And he says the craziest things.

—*Craziest?*

"Oops. Sorry, Norbert," I say. I forgot he was reading this.

—*What kind of crazy things?*

"Well, you said that Jupiter is full of noses."

—*It is.*

"The noses have little feet apparently, and no arms. And they hop everywhere. They have telephones, and spaceships, and all sorts of technology, but all they want to do is hop. And when they get tired of hopping, they put up their feet and take a nap. I'm sorry, Norbert, but it really does sound crazy to me."

Norbert gives a little satirical laugh: it sounds like this—*heu heu. You should know about crazy*, he says, *you're the one talking to his own nose!*

He may have a point there.

◆ ◆ ◆

I found out about my nose about a year ago, when he sneezed (that's what I think now; at the time I thought I was the one sneezing) and then said—*Bless me.* In a little tiny voice. Norbert isn't very old, three or four years, but as he's constantly reminding me, a year on Jupiter is really four or five of ours, so Norbert is really almost twenty years old. Quite old, to be drinking cocoa and taking afternoon naps.

—*I like cocoa. On Jupiter everyone drinks cocoa. It's our national drink.*

Can you guess what I asked him first? No, nothing about colds, or sunburns, or what it feels like to have a fingernail poking in your living room. I asked him what had happened to my own nose. I mean my real nose, the one I had until he came along.

—*Your nose is still there. That's why you look the same as before. And I'm here too. It's a big place, your nose. There's a back room, and a kitchen and bathroom, and a garage.*

I still have trouble understanding this. But my nose wrinkles up the way it used to, and feels itchy in the summer. It's still my nose— but it's Norbert too. I don't know how to explain it, and neither does Norbert.

"What's in the garage?" I had to ask.

—*A spaceship, you fish!* Norbert can be quite arrogant. He thinks a fish is the ultimate insult—maybe because fish don't have noses. I must remember to show him a picture of a swordfish one of these days. *How else do you think I got here from Jupiter?*

I asked him about other people. Do their noses come from Jupiter too? He snorted, unless it was a sigh.

—*No no, I'm kind of a gypsy. Most noses are happy on Jupiter, but ever since I lost Nerissa I've wanted to travel.*

"Oh," I said, kind of serious, because he seemed so sad. He sniffed a bit—usually he hates sniffing. I wondered about his story. An unhappy love affair, it sounded like. Forget Nerissa, I wanted to tell him. No nose is worth it. What is she?—a rag and a cartilage and a hank of hair. But I never did tell him.

◆ ◆ ◆

Let's get back to the project. I'm in the library now, staring at the cover of a book about Jupiter. I've been staring at it for a while.

—*A beautiful picture,* Norbert comments. *I think I can see the street where I used to live.*

"Come on, Norbert. The project is due tomorrow." I open the book to the chapter on Jupiter's moons and start reading. Pretty soon Norbert is twitching and making funny noises. "What is it?" I whisper.

—*Wrong,* he says. *All wrong. Wrong wrong wrong.*

I ask what's all wrong.

—*Everything. The part you have your finger on right now.*

"Where it says there are at least thirteen moons?" I whisper. "What's wrong with that?"

—*There are only three moons.*

"Norbert," I say, "this is a picture from the *Voyager* spaceship. There are lots of moons circling Jupiter."

—*Three. I know.*

"Then what are the other moons all doing in the picture?" I ask.

—*They're there for a birthday party.*

"That's ridiculous."

—*There are pictures from your last birthday party, Alan. A dozen kids, waving at the camera and holding balloons. Are they all in your family?*

"Wait a minute. You're saying that if *Voyager* had taken the pictures later on, there'd have been only three moons?"

—*That's right. Ganymede, Hyperion, and Sid.*

"One of the moons on Jupiter is named Sid? I can't believe it."

—*That's what we call him. In Jupiter's legends Sid is known as the Bringer of Cocoa.*

"Norbert, I cannot report to my class that one of Jupiter's moons is called Sid. Remember, we have to read these projects out loud. Can you imagine what Ms. Scathely would say?"

—*What if I read that part?* he says.

"No," I say firmly. "Remember the bath."

Norbert has a charming voice (I have to be nice because he's reading this), but it's a little bit high and squeaky. I was taking a bath, and my mom came right up to the door and asked if everything was all right. "I heard two voices," she said. I don't know what she thought was going on. I told her I was fine, and then Norbert said that actually he preferred showers. *Everyone on Jupiter takes showers*, he said. There was this long silence from outside and then Mom said, "Oh." She didn't come in, but I heard her muttering to herself about puberty.

◆ ◆ ◆

"Oh, hi, Alan," I look up from my book. It's Miranda. She's in my class at school.

"Hi," I say. I must be more worried than I thought because I didn't notice her coming over to talk to me. I usually notice Miranda. She has these great big eyes and a really pretty smile. She's taller than I am, and she can run faster and jump higher and hit a baseball farther than I can. And she's smarter.

Actually, I kind of like her. But I didn't think she even knew I was around.

"Still working on your project?" she asks.

"Huh?"

"Jupiter." She points to the book in my hand.

The librarian frowns over at us. You wonder if maybe they were born with that expression on their faces. I've never seen them look any other way.

"Oh." I smile at Miranda. "Right." Silver tongue, that's me. I remind myself of those teenage guys on afternoon TV. "How about you? You're finished your project, I bet." I'm smiling so hard my face hurts.

"Yes. Last week." She turns away, touches the tip of her nose. Her eyes are closed. She looks like she's going to sneeze. "Excuse me." She sneezes.

—*Bless you*, says Norbert.

"Shut up," I tell him in a furious whisper.

"What was that, Alan?"

"Nothing." She stares at me. I can feel myself getting red.

"Young man." It's the librarian. Who else calls you "young man"? She points to her lips. "I must ask you to be quiet."

◆ ◆ ◆

I don't know how long I sit there reading the book. Not very long. I try to pay attention to what I'm reading, but Norbert won't let me. He starts fizzing and spitting and getting all worked up. The librarian tells me to be quiet again. I tell her I'm sorry, and whisper at Norbert to be quiet. People are staring at me from behind their books. I now know how a mom feels when her baby is acting up. I lose my temper and threaten Norbert with a Kleenex—but nothing works. He starts shouting.

I'm reading about the poisonous atmosphere of Jupiter and its moons, and Norbert is screaming at the top of his voice, telling me what a great atmosphere it was, that noses come from all over Jupiter to breathe in the atmosphere of the moons. That's when the librarian kicks me out. She says she's sorry, but she isn't, not really.

Miranda is waiting for me at the door. "Alan, I'd like to talk to you," she says.

Ordinarily I'd have fallen over myself at this point, but I'm really upset. Also, I'm mad at Norbert. "I'll see you at school," I say, brushing past her and jumping on my bike. Ever had an argument with your nose? Don't try it, you'll lose. I yell at Norbert, and he drips on me. I pinch him, and he sneezes, explodes all over me. Yuck. I give up. "All right, Norbert," I say, finally. "You win. Just answer me this. What am I going to do now? I have to hand in the project tomorrow. I'll have to write it all tonight. I'll have to stay up late, and I'm already tired. And I have no idea what I'm going to say. There's no data at home on Jupiter, no encyclopedias or *National Geographics*. We have an old computer—no Internet, no CD-ROM. And they won't let me back in the library. What am I going to do? You got me into this mess—now get me out of it!"

—*All right*, he says, *I will.*

◆ ◆ ◆

"Did you finish your project?" Mom asks me at dinner time. Liver and cabbage. Not my favourite, but I know Norbert likes it. Nice and smelly. I hope he's happy.

"No," I say. "I'll have to work some more on it after dinner."

I yawn. Her face softens. She knows it's due tomorrow. She knows I'm tired. "Is there anything I can do to help?" she asks.

I smile at her. She means well but she has no idea. "You could get me a cup of cocoa," I say.

"I didn't know you liked cocoa, Alan."

"Just trying to get in a Jupiter frame of mind," I tell her.

◆ ◆ ◆

Norbert is so confident. —*Don't worry*, he says. *I know more about Jupiter than any encyclopedia. Your space probe took pictures of the moons, but I was there.*

"You were?" I must be crazy, I'm believing him here.

—*Of course. Just sit back and type what I tell you.* He sounds like he really does know what he's talking about. I relax a little bit. I turn on the computer, take a sip of cocoa, and flex my typing fingers—both of them.

"Ready when you are," I say.

He clears his throat—that sounds silly, a nose clearing its throat, but that's what it sounds like—*Hmm hmm. Ganymede, the largest of Jupiter's satellites, is a forbidding place*, he says. That sounds pretty good. I start to type. He keeps talking and I keep typing. At the back of my mind I'm a little worried about what's going to happen when we get to Sid, but I'll go along for now. It doesn't sound bad. —*High basalt cliffs and barren dusty plains are sterile and lifeless...*I type away. I'm yawning like crazy, I make a couple of mistakes, blink a bit. I hear Norbert's voice as a kind of singsong. —*Lullaby, and good night.* I sit up straight. Did he say that, or did I dream it? Mom comes in to wish me good night and good luck. Back to the keyboard. I concentrate on my typing. Norbert drones on. I'm paying more attention to my two fingers than to my ears, typing without listening. I shake my head and blink. Sleepy. So sleepy...

◆ ◆ ◆

I wake up with my face on the keyboard. Two in the morning. I've been asleep. I'm tired, and I have to go to the bathroom. I look up at the screen—and I can't believe my eyes. Somehow the project is done. I've printed up ten pages and the words at the bottom of the last page are THE END. Wow. I yawn.

My nose hurts. Last time it felt like that was a couple of years ago when I walked into a glass door. Poor Norbert has been wearing himself out, working so hard. He must be sleeping now, with his feet up in the back room. I wash my face in cold water, and he wakes up briefly. "Thanks," I tell him.

—*Ouch.*

◆ ◆ ◆

If Mom hadn't knocked on my door next morning I'd probably still be sleeping. "School bus in ten minutes," she says.

I almost forget the project in my rush to get ready. Norbert reminds me. There's just time to staple the sheets together and cram them into my knapsack.

"Did you get it done, Alan?" asks Victor, as we're bouncing over the railway tracks.

"Oh sure," I say. "No problem." What a liar I am.

"I tell you, I am not looking forward to reading mine out loud," says Victor. "My project is so...*boring*. Everyone is going to fall asleep."

◆ ◆ ◆

No one falls asleep during my reading.

No one looks bored. No one coughs or fidgets. For the first minute or so, the only sound apart from my voice is a collective intake of breath.

And then the whole class starts to laugh.

Ms. Scathely leads the way with a restrained little tee-hee, hand over her face, then a couple of girls in the front row snicker to each other. When I get to the part about the beaches on Hyperion, with fountains of cocoa and bright warm sun every day except Thursday, when Ganymede gets in the way, Ms. Scathely's shoulders are shaking. She's trying to control herself but she can't, she's laughing too hard, and she slips right off her chair and falls to the floor going, "Whoop...whoop...whoop." The class erupts like a one-room volcano, shouts of laughter, pencils and notebooks flying in the air. I stop reading at about this time, because no one can hear me. I'm about done anyway. My face is red and glowing, like lava, I guess. Appropriate. I'm not embarrassed though—well, I am of course, but that's not all I am. I'm mad. Ms. Scathely is on the floor, sobbing with mirth, my friends are shouting and carrying on, and I'm wondering how I go about punching myself in the nose. Wait until I get Norbert alone: I'll blow his ears off, I'll put a clothespin on him, I'll stick an entire box of Kleenex—yes, it is pretty funny, I suppose, but I'm not in the mood.

If only I'd stayed awake. If only I'd checked the project last night, or this morning.

—What's a clothespin?

"Never mind." I keep forgetting Norbert can read.

—You aren't really angry, are you, Alan? Not now that it's all turned out so well. If it weren't for me writing your project, think what you'd have missed!

"You too," I say.

—Yes. Me too.

◆ ◆ ◆

"How did it go today?" Mom asks.

I'm not mad any more. If you want to know, I'm bursting with excitement and happiness inside, but I don't tell Mom. I'm casual. "Got an A+," I say. Like this happens all the time.

"ALAN!"

"Ms. Scathely said it was the most...original piece of work she'd ever heard." She also said it was the goofiest, but I didn't pass that on. "She wants me to send it to a magazine. Maybe it'll be published."

"Oh Alan, I'm so proud of you!"

I perch myself on the counter, push back my hair. "What's for dinner?"

"What would you like?"

"Spaghetti," I say. "And," very cool now, "I'd like to...um...invite someone over."

"Miranda?"

How do moms do that? I haven't talked about her more than a couple of times. I close my mouth, nod. "She's asking her parents. She doesn't think there'll be a problem."

◆ ◆ ◆

Miranda came up to me in the hallway after class, her eyes shining. I was still mad and embarrassed. The rest of the class was on its way to history, still laughing. The bell rang. "I knew it, Alan," she said. "I knew it yesterday in the library."

"Huh?" I may have mentioned how suave I get around Miranda. "Knew what?"

"Knew you were like me." She put her hands on my shoulders.

"That stuff about Jupiter. I know about it too. I was too scared to put it in my project, but you weren't."

"Huh?"

"Oh, Alan, I know. I know where your data base is." She arched her eyebrows and gave a squiggly smile. Modern flirting. When they're interested in your data base, you've got them.

"Oh yeah?" I say.

"Yeah." And right there in the empty hallway, though we were both going to be late for our history class, she leaned down and, well, we rubbed noses.

—*Hey!* Norbert must have been napping. I'd forgotten about him.

Miranda giggled. And this teeny weeny little voice shrieked out —*Norbert! Norbert, is it you? Oh Norbert I've missed you so.*

Another nose from Jupiter.

—*Nerissa! I've missed you too.*

We walked down the hall, the four of us, talking all the time. The late bell rang. Nerissa and Norbert exchanged telephone numbers. Miranda and I ran to class. ◆

1. RESPONDING TO THE STORY

a. How did Alan feel about having an alien living in his nose? How would you feel?

b. Were you surprised that Miranda also had an alien guest? Why or why not?

c. Who was your favourite character in the story? What did you like about him, her, or it?

d. Do you think "Introducing Norbert" could be the start of a good science fiction novel? Give reasons for your answer.

2. ORAL COMMUNICATION PERFORM DIALOGUE

In groups of four, discuss what Norbert and Nerissa might talk about after their long separation. What will Alan and Miranda say to each other and to their alien friends? Develop a humorous conversation these four characters might have. Remember that the characters have distinct personalities, which should be reflected in their words. Choose roles and practise your lines, then present your dialogue to an audience.

GROUP-ASSESSMENT: Did your dialogue capture the different personalities of the four characters? Did you practise your lines so your performance sounded like a natural conversation?

3. MEDIA TV SERIES PROPOSAL

Brainstorm some ideas about what makes a good TV series for young people. Try using a web like this for your ideas:

Your task is to convince a producer to make a TV show starring Norbert and his pals. Decide whether the show should be live or animated. Write a short memo to the producer, in which you

- summarize the plot of the *pilot* (the first show) based on "Introducing Norbert"
- give at least three good reasons why this story could be turned into a successful series
- describe each of the main characters
- suggest the names of actors who could play the various roles (or do the voices if your series is animated)

What special features could you add to your memo to make it even more persuasive?

SELF-ASSESSMENT: VISUAL COMMUNICATION

As you worked on this unit, what did you learn about
- analysing drawings?
- creating a comic strip?
- designing a poster?
- expressing your response to a painting?
- illustrating your writing?

Do you find it easier to express yourself in visuals or through words? Why?

ORAL COMMUNICATION TELL A JOKE

Step up to the microphone...it's your turn to be a comedian! Memorize a favourite joke and prepare your own unique way of telling it. You might find it helpful to write your joke down so you can make notes about emphasizing particular words, pausing in key places, and using humorous gestures. When you've perfected your performance, tell your joke to the class.

MEDIA HUMOUR IN ADVERTISING

Gather several different magazines and flip through the pages looking for humorous ads. Choose the two ads you think are funniest, and write an explanation of how the humour is created. In your explanation, comment on both the visual and text components of the ads. Why do you think advertisers use humour to sell products? Do you think humour is an effective advertising technique? Explain.

ISSUES

"How wonderful it is
that nobody need
wait a single moment
before starting to
improve the world"
Anne Frank

ISSUES

A BETTER WORLD

Plenty

Poem by **Jean Little**

I have plenty of everything
    but want.
I try to imagine hunger,
Try to imagine that I have not eaten today,
That I must stand in line for a bowl of soup.
That my cheekbones angle out of my hollowed face;
But I smell the roast in the oven.
I hear the laden refrigerator hum.

I think of people whose walls are made of wind.
I stand outside in the cold.
I tell myself I am homeless and dressed in rags;
But my shiver lacks conviction.
I stand in fleece-lined boots and winter coat.
Home is a block away.

I leave my wallet at home.
Pretending I have no money,
I walk past stores and wish.
"I have no money, no money at all, no money—"
I turn my head in shame as I pass the bank.

I pay for a parcel of food. I gather clothes.
I adopt a child under a foster parent plan.
I do what I can. I am generous. I am kind—

I still have plenty of everything
        but want.

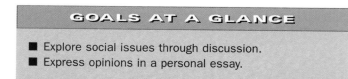

GOALS AT A GLANCE

- Explore social issues through discussion.
- Express opinions in a personal essay.

1. RESPONDING TO THE POEM

a. Explain the meaning of the word "want" in the first and last lines of the poem.

b. Why do you think the speaker in the poem is trying so hard to imagine what it's like to be poor and hungry? What obstacles does the speaker encounter?

c. Do you think it is important for people to make the effort to understand what life is like for those who are less fortunate? Why or why not?

2. ORAL COMMUNICATION EXPLORE SOCIAL ISSUES

In small groups, discuss the following questions:

- What are some of the reasons why people in Canada and in other countries live in poverty?
- In a truly just world, would there be homelessness and poverty? Why?
- Do you think something should be done to get rid of poverty in the world?
- What would you do to make changes happen?

Choose one person to take notes, and another to present your group's ideas to the class.

3. WRITING PERSONAL ESSAY

Write a short essay (3–5 paragraphs) in which you express your personal opinion about the issue of poverty. You could begin your personal essay with a sentence such as, "In a truly just world..." Support your opinions with reasons and examples. Make sure your personal essay has both an introduction and a conclusion.

SELF-ASSESSMENT: Reread your completed personal essay. Did you explain the reasons behind your opinions? What could you do to make your argument more persuasive?

It was the middle of winter, and the woman had no shoes.
Frank looked down at his sneakers and made a decision.

Reaching Out
to a Stranger

Article by Barbara Lewis

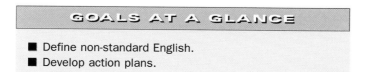

Frank Daily stared down at the
frozen ground. He kicked chunks
of snow, blackened with car
exhaust, to the side. He only
pretended to listen to the chatter of his friends, Norm
and Ed, as they all clambered aboard the Number 10 bus
after school. He spouted out automatic answers to their questions:
"Yeah, I aced the Milton test...No, I can't tonight. I've got to hit the
books."

Frank and his friends flopped down in the back of the Milwaukee
city bus, along with several other high school boys, some from other
schools. The bus belched a grey cloud out the back and headed west
on Blue Mound Road.

Frank slouched into his seat. His hands hung from his two
thumbs stuffed in the centre of his belt. It had been another cold,
grey day just a month ago in November when his world had come
crashing down around him. He knew that his basketball skills were
as good as the other boys'. His mom used to call him "the athlete of

┌─────────────────────────────────────┐
│   GOALS AT A GLANCE   │
└─────────────────────────────────────┘
■ Define non-standard English.
■ Develop action plans.

297

the season." When he was smaller, she nicknamed him "Search and Destroy." He smiled at the memory.

The bus lurched away from a curb, and Frank instinctively braced his basketball shoes against the floor. "It must have been my size," he thought. "That had to be it. One hundred and sixty centimetres. Since I'm new at Marquette High and only a freshman, the coach must have taken one look at me and decided I was too small to make the basketball team."

It wasn't easy starting a new school, especially an all-boys' Catholic school. The older boys tended to be a bit clannish. It was especially hard for Frank, because he had been a star athlete in all the sports in elementary school. Now, it seemed, he was a nothing.

Not only had he excelled in athletics before arriving at Marquette; he had also come alive to politics and history in Grades Five and Six. He recalled the advice his teacher, Don Anderson, had given him: "Look, Frank, if you'd put as much time into books as you do into basketball, you can do great in both."

"Well," Frank thought, "Anderson was right about the books, at least. My grades have been A's and B's ever since. Basketball is another story."

A loud horn and a screech of brakes somewhere behind the bus startled Frank. He looked at Norm and Ed. Norm was leaning his head against the window with half-shut eyes, his warm breath creating a circle of fog on the glass.

Frank rubbed his own eyes. He still remembered his stomach chilling into a frozen knot as he approached the locker room door, hoping, searching frantically for his name. It hadn't been there. It was missing. No name. He had felt suddenly as if he had ceased to exist. Become invisible.

The bus jerked to a stop at the County Institutions grounds. The bus driver called to some noisy boys at the back to settle down. Frank glanced up at the driver, who had been dubbed "Kojak" by some of the guys on the bus because of his bald head.

A very pregnant woman hung onto the silver handrail and slowly pulled herself onto the bus. As she fell backward into the seat behind the bus driver, her feet kicked up, and Frank saw that she was in stocking feet.

As Kojak steered the bus back into traffic, he yelled over his shoulder, "Where are your shoes? It ain't more than ten below zero out there."

"I can't afford shoes," the woman answered. She pulled her fraying coat collar around her neck. Some of the boys at the back exchanged glances and smirked.

"I got on the bus just to get my feet warm," the woman continued. "If you don't mind, I'll just ride around with you for a bit."

Kojak scratched his bald head and shouted, "Now, just tell me how come you can't afford shoes?"

"I got eight kids. They all got shoes. There's not enough left for me. But it's OK, the Lord'll take care of me."

Frank looked down at his new basketball shoes. His feet were warm and snug, always had been. And then he looked back at the woman. Her socks were ripped. Her coat, missing buttons, hung open around her

Bus driver John Williams ("Kojak") and Frank Daily stand before the Number 10 bus.

stomach, as swollen as a basketball and covered by a smudgy dress.

Frank didn't hear anything around him after that. He wasn't aware of Norm or Ed. He just felt a warm thawing in his gut. The word "invisible" popped into his mind again. "An invisible person, marginal, forgotten by society, but for a different reason," he thought.

He would probably always be able to afford shoes. She probably never would. Under his seat, he pried the toe of one shoe into the heel of the other and slipped it off. Then the other shoe. He looked around. Nobody had noticed. He would have to walk three blocks in the snow. But the cold had never bothered him much.

When the bus stopped at the end of the line, Frank waited until everyone else had emptied off. Then he reached under his seat and picked up his basketball shoes. He walked quickly up to the woman and handed them to her, looking down and saying, "Here, you need these more than I do."

And then Frank hurried to the door and stepped down. He managed to land in a puddle. It didn't matter. He wasn't at all cold. He heard the woman exclaim, "See, they fit just perfect."

Then he heard Kojak call, "Hey, come back here, kid! What's your name?"

Frank turned around to face Kojak. At the same time, Norm and Ed asked where his shoes were.

Frank's cheeks burned. He looked in confusion at Kojak, his friends, and the woman. "Frank Daily," he said quietly. "My name is Frank Daily."

"Well, Frank," Kojak said, "I've never seen anything like that in the twenty years I've been driving this bus."

The woman was crying. "Thank you, young man," she said. She turned to Kojak. "See, I told you the Lord would take care of me."

Frank mumbled, "You're welcome." He smiled at the woman. "It's no big deal. Besides, it's Christmas."

He hurried off after Norm and Ed. It seemed to him that the greyness had lifted. On the way home, he hardly felt the cold beneath his feet at all.

◆ ◆ ◆

Frank Daily was fourteen when this story took place. He never saw the woman again. Frank is modest about what he did, and he doesn't consider it anything special. In his words: "We all have the potential to be heroic in some way."

1. RESPONDING TO THE ARTICLE

a. Why did Frank feel that both he and the woman on the bus were "invisible" people?

b. What motivated Frank to give the woman his shoes? Have you, or has someone you know, ever done something like this? Explain.

c. Do you agree with Frank's statement that, "We all have the potential to be heroic in some way?" Give reasons for your opinion.

d. Compare this story with the poem "Plenty." What did Frank do that was different from what the speaker of the poem did? In the end, who felt better, Frank, or the speaker of the poem? Why?

2. LANGUAGE CONVENTIONS NON-STANDARD ENGLISH

With a partner, look at the following sentences, spoken by the shoeless woman in "Reaching Out to a Stranger." How would you change the sentences to make them grammatically correct?

"I got eight kids. They all got shoes."

The sentences above are examples of *non-standard English. Standard English* is defined as "the kind of English widely accepted as the spoken and written language used by educated speakers." What do you think the definition of non-standard English might be? With the class, discuss how people who use non-standard English might be judged by others. Are these judgments fair? Why or why not?

3. ORAL COMMUNICATION ACTION PLANS

Working with a small group, find out whether there are organizations in your community that help the poor or homeless. What are they, and what assistance do they provide? What could your group, class, and/or school do to offer more help? Come up with a list of possibilities. Choose one or two of your ideas and see if you can put them into action. Plan carefully so that your ideas will be successful.

GROUP ASSESSMENT: Did you make a list of good possibilities? Did everyone in the group contribute ideas? Were you able to carry out one or more of the ideas?

The Winner

Monologue by Peg Kehret

There was a competition at our school last year. A poetry competition. Anyone who wanted to could write a poem and enter it in the contest. The best ten were printed in a booklet and the first-prize winner received twenty-five dollars and a framed certificate.

I wanted to win that contest more than I ever wanted anything in my life. Not for the twenty-five dollars, although I could have used the money. I wanted to win because deep down inside me I wanted to be a writer and I wasn't sure if I had any talent. I thought if I won first prize in a poetry competition, it would mean I do have some ability.

GOALS AT A GLANCE

- Design a questionnaire.
- Identify adverbial phrases of time.

I'm not real good at most other things. Especially sports. Everyone else jogs and works out. They lift weights and play tennis or volleyball. I hate exercising. I'm always the last one to be chosen when we pick teams for baseball or basketball. And the only reason I passed Physical Education last year was because my gym partner lied for me and said I'd done the required three push-ups when I could barely manage one.

Maybe that's why the poetry contest was so important to me. When you're really rotten at most things, you want to be extra-good at the few things you care about.

I worked on my contest entry every day for two weeks. I wrote seven different poems and threw all of them away. I wrote about butterflies and kittens and the way I feel when I hear certain kinds of music. None of my poems was any good. I wanted them to be beautiful, and instead, they were awkward and crude.

But I didn't give up. I kept writing. I revised and changed the words around, and thought up new ideas for poems.

And then, on the last night before the contest deadline, I wrote a poem that I knew was good. It was a simple poem, but every time I read it, I got goose bumps on my arms. I knew it was the best writing I'd ever done. I called it "Unicorn Magic," and entered it in the contest the next morning.

The winner was not announced until two weeks later. During those two weeks, I floated in a special dream, imagining how it would be to sit at the awards program in the school auditorium and hear my name announced as the first-prize winner in the poetry competition.

On the day of the awards, I couldn't eat breakfast. I wore my new grey pants, the ones that make me look thinner than I am. I got up half an hour early so I'd have time to wash my hair.

Before the winner was announced, the principal read the names of the authors of the ten best poems. Mine was one of them. My heart began to pound and my mouth got all dry. Then he announced the winner: first prize to Kathy Enderson for her poem titled "Goldfish Jubilee."

When Kathy's name was called, she shrieked and jumped up and all her friends screamed and cheered. I just sat there, stunned. I couldn't believe "Unicorn Magic" had lost when it made me get goose bumps every time I read it. Maybe I wasn't going to be a writer after all. Maybe I had no talent. If Kathy Enderson, who laughs at dirty jokes and flirts with all the guys and thinks being a cheerleader is the most important thing in the world, if Kathy Enderson can write better poetry than I can, then I might as well give it up forever.

Except I couldn't. I went home that day and wrote a poem about how much it hurt to lose the competition. When I read the poem again the next morning, I got goose bumps on my arms and I knew I would keep on writing, even if I never won any awards.

I studied Kathy's poem in the booklet. I had to admit it was good.

That summer, long after the poetry competition was over and school was out, I was looking through some magazines in the public library and I came across a poem titled "Goldfish Jubilee." For one awful moment, I thought Kathy had not only won the contest, she'd actually had her poem published. Then I saw the author's name. Andrew Billings. "Goldfish Jubilee" by Andrew Billings. The poem was the same; the author was not.

I looked at the date on the magazine. It was published a month before our poetry competition.

Should I show it to the principal and demand that the poems be judged again? Should I call Kathy Enderson and tell her I knew she'd cheated? What good would it do?

That special moment in the school auditorium, when the winner's name was announced, was over. It was too late.

I hate Kathy Enderson for what she did, but I feel sorry for her too. She has a certificate that says First Prize, Poetry Competition, and she has the twenty-five dollars, but she doesn't know how it feels to read her very own poem and get goose bumps on her arms.

And she'll never know. ◆

1. RESPONDING TO THE MONOLOGUE

a. Do you think the person speaking the monologue is a boy or a girl? Why?

b. Why was the poetry contest so important to the speaker?

c. Do you think "Unicorn Magic" really was a good poem? Explain your opinion.

d. Read the monologue aloud. Do you think the author has captured the way a teenager would actually tell this story? Explain.

e. What moral dilemma does the speaker of the monologue face at the end? What decision does the speaker make? Would you have made the same decision? Why?

2. RESEARCHING DESIGN A QUESTIONNAIRE

Do you think cheating is a big problem in your school? Hold a class discussion about this topic. As a class, create a questionnaire to investigate different aspects of the topic. In a questionnaire, each question should be easy to understand and should give people a simple way to record their opinion, for example:

The statement is: "Cheating is a big problem in our school." Do you...

Strongly Disagree   Disagree   Don't Know   Agree   Strongly Agree

Ask students who are not in your class to complete the questionnaire. As a class, tabulate the results. What has your questionnaire revealed about attitudes toward cheating?

3. LANGUAGE CONVENTIONS TIME PHRASES

"The Winner" tells a story that happened in the past and covered several months. Author Peg Kehret uses many phrases that tell when or for how long something happened, for example: "last year," "for two weeks," "On the day of the awards." These adverbial phrases are known as *time phrases*.

Find three more examples of time phrases in the monologue. How do they help the reader?

SELF-ASSESSMENT: Examine a piece of your own writing. Did you include time phrases? If not, could you help readers by adding some? Revise your writing appropriately.

1. RESPONDING TO THE COMIC STRIP

a. In your opinion, what makes this comic strip funny?

b. Why do you think the cartoonist deliberately chose to discuss human nature while his characters were speeding downhill?

c. Is there a final answer to Calvin's question? What are some other examples of hard-to-answer questions? Share your ideas with the class.

2. VISUAL COMMUNICATION ANALYSE DRAWINGS

In comic strips, the words and the drawings work together. In this particular comic strip, how do the drawings help to hold the reader's interest?
Consider such things as

- layout of the panels
- point of view used in each panel
- use of line, colour, and composition

SELF-ASSESSMENT: Compare your ideas with those of a classmate. Did both of you notice the same aspects of the drawings? What have you learned that could increase your appreciation of comic strips in future?

STRATEGIES

3. ORAL COMMUNICATION DEBATE

As a class, conduct an informal debate on the following resolution: "People are basically good."
For your debate, you will need

- two debating teams, one to argue in support of the resolution, the other to argue against it
- a moderator to introduce and time the speakers and to keep order
- a panel of judges
- a plan that shows the order of speakers and the times allowed for arguments and rebuttals
- rules regarding interruptions

Each team should be given time to plan its arguments and gather supporting evidence. Conduct the debate. The audience can help the judges come to a fair conclusion about which team's arguments were most persuasive.

Some people say there's nothing one person can do to change things. Fortunately, Craig Kielburger had a different opinion.

Free the Children

Memoir by Craig Kielburger | with Kevin Major

My mind goes back to April 19, 1995. I woke to sun streaming through my window, a welcome sign that summer was on its way. It was Wednesday, another school day, one I was looking forward to, in fact. Today were the tryouts for the cross-country running team.

As I stretched my way from under the blankets, I watched my dog go through her own waking-up ritual at the foot of my bed. I hauled on a pair of jeans and a sweatshirt.

"Hey, Muffin. Let's go, girl." I gave her a playful rub about her neck and off she went, racing ahead of me and down the stairs.

My mother, up for an hour or more already, was in the kitchen making lunches. The Kielburger household would soon be heading off to school. Both my parents are teachers. There were just the three of us; my older brother, Marc, had gone away to a junior college in January.

GOALS AT A GLANCE

■ Prepare and deliver a speech.
■ Prepare a press release.

"Hi, Mom. The paper arrived yet?" I said, pouring cereal into a bowl.

"It's on the chair."

Every morning I read the comics before heading off to school. *Doonesbury. Calvin and Hobbes. Wizard of Id.* These are my favourites. If I find one particularly funny, sometimes I'll cut it out and post it on my bulletin board, or tape it to one of my school books. We all can use a good laugh every day.

I picked up the *Toronto Star* and put it on the table. But I didn't make it past the front page. Staring back at me was the headline "BATTLED CHILD LABOUR, BOY, 12, MURDERED." It was a jolt. Twelve, the same age as I was. My eyes fixed on the picture of a boy in a bright-red vest. He had a broad smile, his arm raised straight in the air, a fist clenched.

I read on. "Defied members of 'carpet mafia.'" Scenes from old movies came to my mind. But this wasn't any such mafia; the date line was Pakistan. The boy was someone named Iqbal Masih.

I read quickly through the article, hardly believing the words before me.

Battled Child Labour, Boy, 12, Murdered

ISLAMABAD, Pakistan (AP)— When Iqbal Masih was four years old, his parents sold him into slavery for less than sixteen dollars.

For the next six years, he remained shackled to a carpet-weaving loom most of the time, tying tiny knots hour after hour.

By the age of twelve, he was free and travelling the world in his crusade against the horrors of child labour.

On Sunday, Iqbal was shot dead while he and two friends were riding their bikes in their village of Muridke, thirty-five kilometres outside the eastern city of Lahore. Some believe his murder was carried out by angry members of the carpet industry who had made repeated threats to silence the young activist.

I turned to my mother. "Have you read this? What exactly is child labour? Do you think he was really killed for standing up to this 'carpet mafia,' whatever that is?"

She was as lost for answers as I was. "Try the library at school," she suggested. "Maybe you'll find some information there."

Riding the bus to school later that morning, I could think of nothing but the article I read on the front page. What kind of parents would sell their child into slavery at four years of age? And who would ever chain a child to a carpet loom?

Throughout the day I was consumed by Iqbal's story. In my grade seven class we had studied the American Civil War, and Abraham Lincoln, and how some of the slaves in the United States had escaped into Canada. But that was history from centuries ago. Surely slavery had been abolished throughout the world by now. If it wasn't, why had I never heard about it?

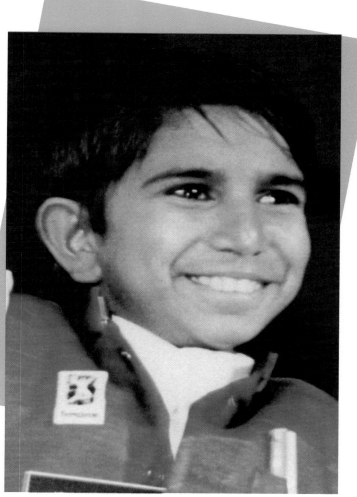

Iqbal Masih travelled to Boston to accept the Reebok Human Rights Award. He called upon everyone in the audience to celebrate his freedom by chanting with him, "We are free! We are free!"

The school library was no help. After a thorough search I still hadn't found a scrap of information. After school, I decided to make the trek to the public library.

The librarian knew me from my previous visits. Luckily, she had read the same article that morning and was just as intrigued. Together, we searched out more information on child labour. We found a few newspaper and magazine articles, and made copies.

Children working in the carpet industry often suffer many health problems, including breathing difficulties, arthritis in their fingers, and growth deformities.

By the time I returned home, images of child labour had embedded themselves in my mind: children younger than me forced to make carpets for endless hours in dimly lit rooms; others toiling in underground pits, struggling to get coal to the surface; others maimed or killed by explosions raging through fireworks factories. I was angry at the world for letting these things happen to children. Why was nothing being done to stop such cruelty?

As I walked through my middle-class neighbourhood, my thoughts were on the other side of the world. And my own world seemed a shade darker.

That evening I had great difficulty concentrating on my homework. I pulled out the articles I had brought from the library and read them over, again and again. I had often seen the faces of poverty and malnutrition on TV. At school we had discussed the famines whole nations have been forced to endure. But this was different. For some reason these descriptions of child labour had moved me like no other story of injustice.

Perhaps it was because the stories were of people my own age, and many even younger. Perhaps it was because these few words had shattered my ideas of what childhood was all about—carrying out the garbage, cleaning up the backyard—but it all seemed so trivial compared to what these children had to do.

I thought of how I would react if I found myself in their place. I felt sure I would rebel, gather everyone together, and stand up to the cruelty. But I wasn't in their place; I could only imagine what I would do.

I opened our world atlas on the kitchen table and searched the index until it led me to a map of Pakistan. I discovered it wedged between Iran, Afghanistan, and India, with the Arabian Sea along its southern edge. My eyes ran over a maze of names I had never heard before, and some I could barely pronounce. I searched for the places mentioned in the story on Iqbal. I couldn't locate Muridke; it was too small to be on the map. I did find Lahore,

Getting twenty thousand names on a petition to stop child labour was the first taste of activism for the group who founded Free the Children.

and repeated the word several times out loud. It seemed so far away, a world I didn't know at all.

I had to find out more.

"I have a friend who worked overseas, in Africa," my mother told me. "Why don't you give her a call? If she can't answer your questions, I'm sure she'll know of someone who can."

That first telephone conversation led to calls to several human-rights organizations. Little did I think, in the months to come, it would lead to hundreds of other calls and faxes around the world, all in a quest to get to the heart of the issue of child labour.

Two things struck me right away. First of all, none of the organizations I talked to seemed to know much about child labour. But equally amazing—every person who tried to answer my questions was an adult. Without a single exception. Even though the issue was all about children, there were no young people involved in these organizations. I could hardly believe it. Shouldn't other children be speaking out in defence of children?

I'm always fascinated by coincidences, how one random event can come on the heels of another and together alter the whole direction of a person's life. Early the following week, in the Life section of the *Toronto Star*, there was a full-page article in celebration of Youth Week. As part of the activities, an organization called Youth Action Network was sponsoring an event at a downtown convention centre that coming Friday. Youth organizations were invited to set up displays and distribute information.

I'm not sure why, in the end, I decided to call the number in the article. I guess it was because I was tired of being able to speak only to organizations run by adults.

By a stroke of good fortune, my call was directed to Alam Rahman. Alam, whose parents were from Bangladesh, was a recent university graduate. I had no way of knowing it at the time, but Alam would become a very central figure in my life. I spoke to him for more than an hour about Iqbal and child labour. I tested the idea of getting some friends together and starting a children's group to fight such cruelty.

Alam didn't hesitate. "It's a great idea, Craig. You should try it!"

That was all I needed. The following day I asked my grade seven teacher, Mr. Fedrigoni, if I could have a few minutes to speak to the students before class began. I'm sure he must have thought it was about some social function or a football game I was organizing during lunch break.

As usual, we stood by our desks while the morning announcements came over the public-address system, followed faithfully by the national anthem. Then we sat down and quietly listened to

Free the children

Free the Children International, 16 Thornbank Road, Thornhill, Ontario, Canada L4J 2A2
Tel: (905) 881-0863 Fax: (905) 881-1849 E-mail: freechild@clo.com
Web site: http://www.freethechildren.org
Free The Children USA, 12 East 48TH Street, New York, NY 10017

Mr. Fedrigoni say how there had been a few problems with discipline the day before, but that he hoped this would be a better day. When he had finished, he simply said, "Craig has a few comments he would like to make to you." He looked at me and nodded.

I walked to the front and turned to face the thirty students in my class. The room was silent except for a couple of boys whispering in a back row. When I began they, too, were quiet. But I was still nervous; I always found speaking in front of my peers a tough thing to do, and I still had no idea how they would react to what I would say.

"I was wondering if anyone saw this article on the front page of last Wednesday's *Toronto Star*," I began.

I had made photocopies of it, which I passed around the classroom. As I did so, I started to tell Iqbal's story. I described his struggles and his dream, and how that dream had been cut short by an assassin's bullet. I presented the alarming statistics on child labour. As I spoke, I could see that many of my classmates were just as shocked as I was by the story. Anger, sympathy, disbelief filled the room.

"So this is the issue," I said. "I don't know a lot about it, but I want to learn more. Maybe some of us could start a group to look at it together." And then came the fateful question, "Who wants to join?"

About eighteen hands shot up, and I very quickly jotted down their names. I thanked Mr. Fedrigoni and the class for the half-hour of their time I had taken.

And through that simple action, it began.

At lunchtime that day, some of us got together and talked about what we could do. I was amazed at how enthusiastic they all were. I told them about the youth fair on Friday.

"Do you think we could put together a display?" I asked. "We haven't got much time."

"Sure. Let's do it."

"We can all meet at my house," I said.

That night, twelve of us got together. It was a very tight deadline, with just two days to prepare. We found an old science-fair board, and we covered it with coloured paper, pasting on all the information I had found on child labour in the library, then drawing pictures to illustrate it.

We had determined that our first objective should be to inform people of the plight of child labourers. Armed with such knowledge, they might be willing to help. We decided to draw up a petition to present to the government, and called on the expertise of a couple of human-rights groups to refine the wording for us.

But we were still without a name for our group. For more than an hour we struggled to come up with something suitable. We flipped through the newspaper clippings for inspiration. One of them reported on a demonstration in Delhi, India, where 250 children had marched through the streets with placards, chanting, "We want an education," "We want freedom," "Free the children!"

"That's it!" someone shouted. "Free the Children!"

"Perfect," I said. "We're using their words. Children speaking for children."

"Exactly."

We had found a name. Marilyn Davis, the best artist among us, had earlier drawn a picture of children chained to a carpet loom. Before pasting the picture onto our information board, across the top she had written slogans, including "Break the Chains" and "Save the Children." Now we pasted a piece of paper over the word "SAVE" and wrote "FREE" in big letters.

Free the Children was born. We hoisted our board like a giant placard, in solidarity with the children who had marched through the streets of Delhi.

I remember lying awake that Thursday night, thinking about what we had gotten ourselves into. Here we were, just a group of friends, a ragtag lot compared to all the other organizations sure to be taking part in the youth fair. Yet we had worked hard, read all the information I had collected, and felt confident we could get our point across to anyone who was willing to listen.

As I slowly drifted off to sleep, I could only think, Ready or not, here we go. And the next morning, that's exactly what happened—off we went, the start of something that would take over my life and catch the world's attention to an extent that none of us could ever have imagined. ◆

1. RESPONDING TO THE MEMOIR

a. How did you respond to the story of Iqbal Masih? Were you surprised that some children are exploited and mistreated in this way?

b. Why do you suppose this story moved Craig Kielburger "like no other story of injustice"?

c. Craig tells us he would rebel if he were forced to be a child labourer. What might discourage children in that situation from being rebellious?

d. Do you agree with Craig that children should speak out in defence of children? Explain.

e. Would you join an organization such as Free the Children that is trying to make a better world? Why or why not? What issue is most important to you?

2. ORAL COMMUNICATION SPEECH

Craig got things started by delivering an informal speech to his classmates. Do some research about a cause or person that interests you. Your goal is to prepare a brief speech that will grab your classmates' attention. Borrow Craig's idea of telling an important or moving story. Prepare your speech and deliver it to the class. (For advice on delivering a speech, see page 320.)

SELF-ASSESSMENT: Did your speech focus on a particular cause or issue? Were you able to use a powerful story to generate interest in your issue? What aspects of your speech do you think you could improve?

3. MEDIA PREPARE A PRESS RELEASE

A *press release* gives key information about an event or story, and is sent to the media to encourage their interest. You can use a press release to get free publicity for an event such as a fund-raiser or peace rally. Here's how.

- At the top of your press release, give the name of the main contact person, a telephone number a reporter can call, and the date of the release.
- The body of the release should answer the five Ws (*who*, *what*, *when where*, and *why*). Try to come up with a "hook" that will catch a reporter's attention.
- Send the release to local newspapers and radio and TV stations.

Here is a sample:

PRESS RELEASE

For immediate release   Contact: Kirsten Novak, Teacher
                                         Lower Heights Junior High School
                                         Tel. 000-000-0000

April 8, 200_

What: Lower Heights Jr. High students will plant 50 maple trees on the
          school playground.
Who: Grade Seven students are spearheading the project.
When: April 25, 200-. The opening ceremony commences at 10:00 a.m.
          Students will explain the purpose of the tree-planting.
          Mayor Jassie Singh is planning to deliver a short speech.
          The planting will continue until 3:00 p.m.
Where: The south side of the school playground, entrance on Seventh Street.
Details: The students raised $1500 to finance the project through several car
          washes, a bake sale, a grant from the town, and the donation of 15
          trees by the Greenshade Nursery. The students have given the
          maples unique names such as Dog's Favourite and Spring Re-Leaf.

Write a press release for an event you are organizing—or would like to organize. Make it one page in length, and use a computer to produce it.

HOW TO DELIVER A SPEECH

Goals at a Glance

● Plan and deliver a speech. ● Use visuals to convey information.

People deliver speeches for different reasons. You may have heard a speech by a visiting speaker during a school assembly. Its purpose was probably to inform you about an important subject. Politicians regularly give speeches, especially during election campaigns, to convince people to vote a certain way. After-dinner speeches at weddings are designed to entertain the guests. Speeches generally have three purposes: to inform, to persuade, or to entertain.

Prepare Your Speech

Preparing a speech is a two-stage process:
● Stage 1: developing the content (what you will say)
● Stage 2: planning the delivery of the speech (how you say it)

In school, most of the speeches you'll give will be meant to inform or persuade. Developing the content is similar to other work you've done—writing a personal narrative or a report, for example. You'll have to choose a topic, gather your information, organize the informa-

tion, write a draft, and revise it. Other process pages in this book can help you with these tasks—see "How to Conduct Research" on page 86 or "How to Write a Personal Narrative" on page 54.

Connect with your Audience

When you deliver a speech, look at your audience as much as possible. If you read every word of your speech, your eyes will be looking down at the page. Two methods will help you use your eyes for communicating, not just reading.

1. Write your speech out in full, but learn it so well that you can look up frequently without losing your place.
2. Make notes instead of writing out every word. Your notes can be on cue cards that you hold in your hand.

The first method may be better if you're nervous. Experienced speakers prefer the second method because the speech sounds spontaneous and natural. Whatever method you choose, use big lettering to make reading easier.

PROCESS

Provide an Outline

Making a brief outline of your speech can be very helpful. Write it out ahead of time on the chalkboard. As you are speaking, refer to your outline. Set it up as follows:

- *Title of your speech*
- *Topic* (if the title doesn't express your topic)
- *Point-form notes giving your key facts, in order*
- *Summing-up statement*

Use Visuals

Your audience will be more attentive if they have something to look at while listening to your speech. Maps, charts, illustrations, posters, and models are typical visuals. Other visuals are more complicated, and involve the use of overhead projectors, slide projectors, audio and video equipment, or computers.

A good visual presents important information in a way that is easy to read and understand. Visuals need to be large enough to be seen from the back of the room. It's also important that your visuals are prepared in advance and well-organized, and that you know how to operate any technology you are using.

Polish Your Delivery

These hints can help you deliver your speech smoothly and with confidence:

- Practise your speech in front of a mirror to reduce anxiety. You'll see yourself as others see you, plus you'll get used to looking at your audience as well as your notes.
- If possible, practise delivering your speech in the room where you'll be speaking. Practise with your visuals so you are comfortable referring to them.
- Learn your speech very well. You'll feel and sound more confident.
- Stand straight and keep your head up as much as possible. Avoid fidgeting.
- Smile at your audience and sound enthusiastic about your topic.
- Make eye contact with specific individuals in the audience. Focus on different parts of the audience throughout your speech.
- Speak slowly, clearly, and loudly enough so that your message is heard at the back of the room.
- Speak expressively, varying your tone of voice.
- Use gestures and movements to emphasize key points.
- Display visuals so that everyone can see them.

Self-Assessment

Use this checklist to analyse how successfully you prepared and delivered your speech.

- ❏ I wrote my speech in full or as a set of notes.
- ❏ I used an outline and/or other visuals to help communicate my message.
- ❏ I practised delivering my speech.
- ❏ I spoke enthusiastically in a loud voice so that everyone could hear.
- ❏ I looked at my audience and not just at my speech.

PROCESS

*When you're a student
in a new country—and
you have to learn a new language—
it can be hard to look
on the bright side.*

Laughter and Tears: ADJUSTING TO CANADA

Reflections by Students

People come to live in Canada for many different reasons. Some families want better opportunities for their children. Others are escaping danger or injustice in their home countries. But wherever they come from and why, new students are often dismayed by the difficulties they face in Canada—especially if they speak English as a second language.

If you have recently arrived in Canada, you may recognize many of the situations these students describe. If you are not a recent immigrant but have classmates who are, the following stories will help you to understand their feelings.

PRONUNCIATION PROBLEM

Whenever I make a mistake in English, I am anxious that my English will improve quickly. A couple of months ago, maybe my second day in Canada, I went to Niagara Falls with my family.

After we had finished our sightseeing, we were waiting for my father to open the door of our car. When I stood beside the car, someone in a car approached me and asked, "Are you leaving?"

I was confused. I thought he said, "Are you living here?" So I confidently said, "No!"

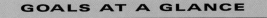

GOALS AT A GLANCE

322

■ Reflect on a personal experience.
■ Explore diversity through discussion.

But once we left there, the stranger looked at me strangely. I didn't know why he did, but my sister explained the reasons to me.

I didn't know the man wanted to park in our spot. I was very embarrassed. It was the first time that I had tried to speak English with a Canadian.

Sung Ja Hong

AFRAID OF EVERYTHING

When I registered at school, I felt like an alien. I was afraid of everything. I was afraid the principal wouldn't let me study in Grade Nine, afraid that my terrible speaking of English would make the teachers laugh, afraid of possible racial tension in the school.

Fortunately, I was put in a special class for new immigrants learning English. There I met many Chinese friends, and if I had problems in homework, I could ask them. At first I felt embarrassed to see the different colour of people around me, but later I got used to it.

Now my English is better, but sometimes I still don't understand what the teachers say. I always ask the teachers for extra help after school. I am glad that my teachers are very kind, and they don't look down on me or laugh at me. Now I like my teachers, my classmates, and my school.

Amy Tam

A Letter Home

Dear Xin:

In Canada everything seems all right, but I still miss you and my other classmates. Do you remember that night when we finished the last math test and we played cards in my home through the whole night? When we were tired playing, we even went out to play soccer in the street. What a happy night we spent! I'll never forget that.

Don't think I am enjoying a rich life. In your mind, Canada must have lots of gold in the streets. So when I reached Canada, I would not need to work and study at all. Even I indulged in that fantasy before I arrived here. I imagined that my parents would have a furnished room for me. In my own room, I used to fantasize a few times, there would be a TV and a video machine. I had seen how developed the Western countries are and how rich these foreigners are on TV in China. Since my parents wanted to stay in Canada, and even take me there, I thought life would be much better than in China.

When I got to Canada and saw my home, I was very disappointed. I could not find my own TV or video machine or record player. I did not even have my own room. I began to wonder why I had come here, why I had left my classmates, my teachers, my friends. I felt I had lost myself.

However, as soon as I knew some special Chinese friends, I changed. They are the same age as I. They have come to Canada by themselves. Some of them didn't even know where they would live when they got off the airplane with only $400 to $500 in their pockets. In Canada, they have to work long hours each day to support themselves while they are in school. They only can sleep four to five hours and cannot find a good job. They, in fact, could live well in China; however, they saved up everything in China to come here because they want experience and knowledge.

Then I look back at myself. I used to be proud of reaching Canada by myself. Since I am luckier than they, I think I must study harder. I'll never complain about what kind of living condition I am in. After all, my situation is much better than that of lots of others. In some ways in Canada there is more chance for people to have a good future. There is more freedom of choice, but for me, there is only one choice—science. In China we are forced to study science because in the eyes of our parents, only people who specialize in science or math are considered clever. Since I did not want to be thought of as stupid, and since I was good at math and science, I studied science. But my greatest interest was history. In Canada I must study science because it is impossible to learn English as well as Canadians in a short time; therefore, even here I cannot study history, the subject I love best.

When I first arrived, some Canadians said sympathetically, "Oh, you come from China. How lucky you are. There must be lots of teenagers the same age as you who are suffering."

I could not say anything. People believe that China is a hell, and I had just escaped from hell. How could I explain to them? China is a poor country, and it is not a democratic country, but they are not cruel people. Although there is great suffering in this country, the Chinese also know how to laugh and joke. The Chinese are poor. That does not mean we are homeless and always hungry. China is not democratic. That does not mean the Chinese are in prison.

At present I have no time to experience society. What I am supposed to do and must do is study, study, study in order that I can go to university. It's supposed to be the most important goal for me. What I have learned so far almost all comes from school. It is very limited. Although I know most new ideas should be absorbed from society, I don't have time to participate in society.

Sincerely,

Su Wang

SHOULD I CHANGE MY NAME?

My parents tell me that when I was born, my father looked at me for about half an hour. My mother asked my father, "What's the matter with you? Why are you looking so puzzled?"

My father did not hear what she was saying because he was thinking about what to call me. My father said, "My son. No, no, our son! He is very beautiful—like a moon! And very bright—like a sun!" So my parents decided to give me the name Matheyalagan—*Mathey* means "moon," "beauty," "sun," and "stars." Another meaning is "good," "intelligent," and "brave. *Alagan* means "beauty."

When I was old enough to learn the meaning of my name, I asked my parents, "Why did you choose this name? It embarrasses me. Could you please change it?"

My mom was angry with me. She said, "Don't ever be ashamed of your name. It will bring you good luck in your life." I remember my mother's advice now. When Canadians get impatient with my name because it is hard to say and it is too long, I remember what my name means, and I never consider changing it.

Matheyalagan Nagaranthy

VALENTINE'S DAY

There was a Canadian girl who played an important role in my life. She was the one who raised my confidence. It was a wonderful feeling to have a Canadian friend. After many months of depression I was able to think positively that life was not that bad. She was friendly, but whenever she tried to communicate with me, I would tremble with fear. Because I couldn't reply to her, I felt angry with myself. During school recesses, we would play games together and she would always make an effort to explain the rules to me carefully and slowly. I liked her, but I didn't think she liked me. Then on Valentine's Day she gave me a card which said, "I love you."

Tong Ang

DO YOU WANT TO DANCE?

After a while Joe became my best friend, and he asked me why I never went to the school dances. I told him that I didn't even know there were any. As soon as I got to the gymnasium, I recognized the same songs they had played in Hungary.

I asked Joe, "What do you say to a girl to ask her to dance?"

He replied, "Do you want to dance?"

It took me one hour to get up my courage and ask a girl to dance. Hey, it was not bad, not bad at all!

Joseph Csermak ◆

1. RESPONDING TO THE REFLECTIONS

a. Which of the students' stories made the biggest impression on you? Why?

b. Why do you think language is such an important factor for students newly arrived in Canada?

c. Would most of the students who wrote these reflections say that Canada is "a better world" than the home countries they left behind? Give reasons for your opinion.

d. What do you think is the single best thing Canadians can do to help new-comers adjust to life in Canada?

2. WRITING REFLECTION

In a piece of reflective writing, such as a journal entry or a letter to a friend, describe a time when you found yourself in an unfamiliar environment. Your reflection should describe the situation vividly to help your reader imagine it. It should also tell what you were feeling at the time, and what you feel now as you look back on the experience. What advice would have helped you deal with the situation?

3. ORAL COMMUNICATION EXPLORE DIVERSITY

How many languages do you and your classmates use or understand? In a class discussion, find out

- the first language of each student
- the second language, for those who know one (English or another language)
- other languages students can speak, read, or understand

Those who speak English as a second language might talk about which language they speak at home, whether or not their families speak English, and what language-related challenges they have faced.

As a class, create a bulletin board display that shows written examples of the different languages you mentioned in your discussion.

During World War II,
Canada was at war with Japan.
Did that justify treating
Japanese Canadians as
the enemy?

Remember, Chrysanthemum

Short Story by Kathryn Hatashita-Lee

I n the school hallways, the kids call her "Speedbump" Woodley due to a rollerblading accident that summer when she had broken her arm, but her real name is Allison Kiku Woodley, an identity that hints at her dual heritage. Her father is of English descent and reads about samurai* swords; her mother of Japanese descent and studies Victorian literature. *Kiku* is Japanese for chrysanthemum, a flower that blooms for many days and graces pottery and kimono** fabrics.

When Allison leaves her home near Vancouver's English Bay and skates across town to visit her Grandmother Tanaka, she is met by a white ceramic cat with one raised paw. The cat is a *maneki neko,* or a beckoning cat, bringing good fortune to homes and businesses.

---

* **samurai:** Japanese warrior class from eleventh to nineteenth century.
** **kimono:** a loose outer garment held by a sash.

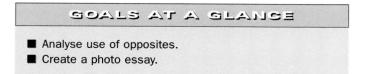

GOALS AT A GLANCE

■ Analyse use of opposites.
■ Create a photo essay.

On bookshelves, and on the television stand, are many albums of family photos. Every photo on their pages is held in place with silver corners. Allison liked leafing through their pages: her grandmother as a girl and a young woman, the giant trees of Lynn Valley, where the family often picnicked on a sushi* lunch...

◆ ◆ ◆

Allison thought she had seen every album in the collection, but one day Grandma Tanaka pulled out a black case tucked under some old hat boxes. Allison quietly opened the latches and pulled back the top. Inside were piled more black-and-white photos waiting for her fingers to sift through their filmy images.

"Take your time, Allison Kiku," said her grandmother.

Allison spread the photos on the floor and let the blue carpet disappear beneath the white borders of the prints. "Is that you and Great-Grandma and Great-Grandpa?" she asked.

"Yes. You can see my seven brothers and sisters all lined up. Your great-grandmother is holding my brother, Tosh. He was just a baby," said Allison's grandmother. "The old frame house still stands in East Vancouver."

Allison picked up a photo of a class with rows of students holding long needles from which dangled partially completed pieces of knitting. Almost all the students looked Japanese.

---

* **sushi:** Japanese dish made from cold, cooked rice, and raw fish or vegetables.

"My grade six teacher at Lord Strathcona Elementary took that photo in January 1942," Mrs. Tanaka began. "During the war, World War II I mean, our whole class knitted sweaters to clothe the British schoolchildren. The girl beside me knitted one sleeve, and I knitted the other one. My sleeve came out a few centimetres shorter. I still feel sorry for the British schoolgirl who received our lopsided gift."

"Mom says your whole family left Vancouver by train that spring," said Allison. "You lost your home and all your things and went to a sort of prison."

"Yes. That was during the evacuation. Japan had bombed Pearl Harbor in Hawaii in December 1941. William Lyon Mackenzie King was Prime Minister of Canada at that time, and he decided we were a threat, so he ordered us out. Our Uncle Kenji's fishing boat was impounded, taken away from him and sold to strangers, at Annieville Dyke on the Fraser River. We were Vancouver-born children of a landscape gardener; we were Canadians, but to the government, we were 'enemies.' I still have your great-grandmother's picture ID labelled *enemy alien.*"

"That's no thanks for all those sweaters you knit for the war effort!" said Allison. Her grandmother's face clouded over and her jaw tightened slightly.

Allison looked over the collection and pointed to another yellowed photo of a family wearing overalls and sitting on a wagon. "We were sent to a sugar beet farm in southern Alberta. Harvesting was back-breaking work, but no Caucasians wanted that kind of work. We had no electricity or running water. We did our homework by the light of a coal-oil lamp. My sisters used a bucket to draw water out of a cistern. When we cooked rice, the water turned the rice yellowish-green," Allison's grandmother continued.

Allison pointed to a photo of a woman with a cow and a bucket. "Your Great-Aunt Miyoko always milked Bossy the cow. After the war, our family moved to a big city in Ontario and never lived in the country again," said Mrs. Tanaka.

The last photo in the pile was a parade float with a row of Japanese Canadian girls, all clad in kimonos, aboard its long platform.

"I took that photo in 1956, during the Dominion Day parade in Toronto. Do you see my friend, Keiko, second to the left? The

Japanese Canadian Citizens' Association organized that float. Everyone in the crowd applauded," she said nostalgically.

"I don't think I could stand being in a kimono or having my hair pulled up like that," said Allison.

Her grandmother chuckled and said gently, "You shouldn't feel embarrassed about the way you look, especially if you're wearing our ancestors' clothing. Try a kimono sometime. You might like it."

"Maybe," said Allison doubtfully. "Thank you for telling your stories, Grandma." As Allison Kiku headed for the door, she winked at the white cat.

◆ ◆ ◆

"Think of a museum as a gathering place where yesterday meets today," said Mrs. Epstein to her class. Allison and her classmates stood near the giant stainless steel crab outside the Vancouver Museum and Pacific Space Centre. Inside the gift shop, Allison saw a tourist pull out a crisp fifty-dollar bill with the reddish-orange image of Mackenzie King on one side, and a snowy owl on the other. She remembered her grandmother's story and felt haunted by the late Prime Minister's gaze as the class walked to the exhibit.

Under the red and white banners hanging from the ceiling, the class wandered around the display of Japanese samurai sword guards in the Soul of the Samurai exhibit. Allison peered closely at the small, round guards she thought looked like large iron coins with holes. When attached to a sword, the sword guard or *tsuba*, prevented the warrior's hand from slipping onto the sharp blade.

Most of the sword guards showed flowers, birds, and insects carved in low relief. Allison saw dark dragons lurking in clouds or waves. Although dragons are popular in the supernatural world, Allison felt uneasy when the display's description said seeing an entire dragon's body meant death.

Another display case showed the work of eighteenth-century artisan, Nagatsune, who applied an inlay of brass, as well as silver and gold, or an overlay of high-relief carvings to create a colourful picture. Allison really liked the scene of three graceful silver herons and golden plants highlighted against the dark ironwork background of the sword guard.

Mrs. Epstein turned to her and said, "I know you were born here,

Allison, but have you been to Japan?"

"No," replied Allison. She remembered her Aunt Grace saying at the family reunion in Ontario last year, "Japan's the last place I'd want to visit."

Allison pulled herself out of her recollections and focussed on what was in front of her. The large mural of a fierce samurai warrior looked very foreign to Allison.

"Do you speak Japanese at home, Allison" asked Mrs. Epstein.

"No," Allison replied again. She remembered her Great-Uncle Tosh and his memories of the Japanese Language School on Alexander Street: "Every day after school I took the streetcar to Japanese School. That made for a really long day. When the Japanese School closed after Pearl Harbor, I was so glad. No more lessons in Japanese!"

"Do you eat Japanese food at home, Allison?" asked her class-mate, Tasha.

"No," replied Allison. She was getting tired of all these questions. She remembered sitting on her bed, unwrapping a small parcel of fruitcake Grandma Tanaka sent, not from Japan, but from Marks & Spencer!

"Hey, Allison," whispered her classmate, Vladimir. "Did you know you're part Japanese?"

"Stop bugging her," said Yvonne. "Allison is just like us. She always gets the top marks in English."

I wonder what was really on exhibit, the samurai sword guards or me? Allison wondered as they headed for the exit.

Later that spring Grandma Tanaka died. Allison returned to her house for the last time.

"I'm surprised Grandma told you as much as she did about those photos," said Allison's mother.

"Maybe she knew she had to tell somebody," said Allison.

"Your grandparents and great-grandparents didn't like to talk about the evacuation. I remember your Great-Uncle Tosh shrugging and saying, 'It can't be helped.'"

Allison looked sadly around the living room full of old albums.

Her mother was looking through Grandma Tanaka's papers when she found a heavy, cream-coloured paper with Canada's coat of arms.

In both English and French, the words of the then Prime Minister Brian Mulroney acknowledged:

> ...the Government of Canada, on behalf of all Canadians, does hereby:
> 1) acknowledge that the treatment of Japanese Canadians during and after World War II was unjust and violated principles of human rights as they are understood today; 2) pledge to ensure, to the full extent that its powers allow, that such events will not happen again; and 3) recognize, with great respect, the fortitude and determination of Japanese Canadians who, despite great stress and hardship, retain their commitment and loyalty to Canada and contribute so richly to the development of the Canadian nation."

Allison's father arranged for Grandma Tanaka's furniture to be donated to a senior citizens' lodge. Allison was told to choose a small memento of her grandmother for herself.

Allison pulled out the handle of the black case with latches. She filed through the aged photographs looking for the five photos she knew. She looked up, half expecting to see her grandmother sitting at her side.

Allison carefully placed the photos in an old envelope she found postmarked 1942. She took off her square neck scarf and wrapped the envelope in a neat bundle inside her knapsack. Allison also packed away the white ceramic cat.

As she turned her back to leave for the last time you could just see two eyes peeking out under the canvas flap, and one slender paw beckoning good luck.

1. RESPONDING TO THE STORY

a. How did Allison find out about the evacuation of Japanese Canadians during World War II? Have you ever learned interesting or important historical information in a similar way? If so, share the information with a partner.

b. What motives do you think lay behind the evacuation and internment of Japanese Canadians?

c. Why do you think Allison dislikes being questioned about her knowledge and experience of Japanese culture?

d. How does Allison feel about her Japanese heritage by the end of the story? Support your opinion.

2. LANGUAGE CONVENTIONS APPOSITIVES

Commas are often used to set off words or phrases that provide additional information about a noun or pronoun. The word or phrase that has been set off is called an *appositive*. Here's an example from "Remember, Chrysanthemum":

"During the war, *World War II I mean,* our whole class knitted sweaters..."

APPOSITIVE

In the example, Mrs. Tanaka uses an appositive to specify which war she is talking about. Notice that there is a comma before and after the appositive. If you read the sentence aloud without the appositive, the sentence still makes sense.

Reread "Remember, Chrysanthemum" to find one other sentence that contains an appositive. Write it in your notebook and then check with a partner to see whether you found the same example. Together, write two new sentences with appositives.

3. VISUAL COMMUNICATION PHOTO ESSAY

Perhaps you, like Allison, have access to family photos. If so, you can use them to create a photo essay about your heritage. First, select about five photos that show what life was like for your parents, guardians, grandparents, or other family members. Look especially for old photos that convey what life was like at a particular place or time. For each photo, write a caption that fills in the story behind the picture. Draft an introduction to your photo essay that briefly states what you know about your family history. Form small groups and share your photo essays. What else would you like to learn about your heritage?

Grandmother

Poem by Douglas Nepinak
Painting by Frank Howell

in her dreams there is no television
speaking incessantly in a foreign language
of grand magnificent things
beyond her means

in her dreams everyone speaks Anishinabe
there is no confusion
no lapses into english
her grandchildren are not silent to her

the world is whole to her again
she walks through the bush collecting berries   roots
and stories off the great tree with a firm shake
the wind smells of seasons to come
they are good   full

GOALS AT A GLANCE

■ Write a poem.
■ Interpret the significance of a painting's title.

336

Grandmother's Gift of Fire by Frank Howell (1937-1997). Frank Howell was an American artist and writer. Though he painted both landscapes and people, he is best known for works that portray Native Americans in a dramatic, mythical style.

1. RESPONDING TO THE POEM AND PAINTING

a. In the poem, what is the grandmother's idea of a better world? What aspects of life seem to be most important to her?

b. What kinds of changes might have happened during her lifetime to make her feel alienated?

c. What words would you use to describe the grandmother in the painting? What features of the painting prompted you to choose those words?

2. WRITING POETRY

Write a poem about the world you dream about. Begin by brainstorming, perhaps with a partner, about your dreams, daydreams, and wishes. What words and phrases could help you describe the world you've imagined? Now use a few sentences, as Douglas Nepinak has done, to create a poem that communicates your dream.

SELF-ASSESSMENT: Did you choose your words carefully? Do they help the reader to "see" your meaning? Did you learn something about yourself by writing this poem?

3. VISUAL COMMUNICATION PAINTING'S TITLES

Does the title *Grandmother's Gift of Fire* help you to understand the painting? Why or why not? List some ideas the word *fire* suggests to you. Are any of those meanings appropriate to the painting? Explain.

With a partner, look through one or two books of paintings. You could find other examples of Native art by checking the internet. Choose one painting that has either a title that helps to explain a confusing painting, or a title that is mysterious. Present your painting to the class and discuss it together.

*The Inuit sculptor knew
what his carving was worth.
Now he had to find the strength
to stand up for what was right.*

Nipikti the Old Man Carver

SHORT STORY BY ALOOTOOK IPELLIE

Nipikti was now an old man and took three times as long as any young Inuk to get from one point to another. Almost every week, he would get up from his small carving studio at home and start walking out to the Co-op where he sold at least a half a dozen carvings he had finished during the week. He hung the bag of carvings over his shoulder and started out the door, his walking stick leading the way for him.

"This is the day I will get the upper hand of the deal with the Co-op manager. I have no doubt he will fall in love with the carving I finished today," he said, as he closed the door behind himself.

On the way to the Co-op, Nipikti would stop several times to rest his tired old legs by sitting on the same rocks he had sat on for the last twenty years or so.

"Ahhh! Hi, Ojagajaak, it feels good to rest on you," he would say to the first rock, as if the rock was an old friend of his.

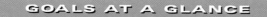

"These legs of mine are a little weaker than last week, so I will have to sit on you for an extra five minutes if you do not mind."

There he sat to rest on Ojagajaak and looked across the land where he had lived as a young man. That is the place where he had hunted the good animals of the land. That is where he had taken care of his wife and family when they were growing up. "Those were good times of the past," he thought, "times when carvings like these were toys and tokens to us Inuit."

He got up slowly and continued on to the Co-op where he would get the money to support his family. The Co-op was still quite far away.

"If I had my way, I would prefer to carve the stones and ivory to make toys for my children, and hunt the animals like I used to. I wasn't such a bad hunter in those days," Nipikti said to himself.

"I never thought I would be living off the very carvings I used to make only to keep my children happy."

Nipikti finally came to the rock where he sat to rest the second time along the way to the Co-op and said, "How are you today Ojagakaluk? I have come again to rest on you. I am an old man now, you know."

He sat on Ojagakaluk and took enough rest there to make it to the next rock. "I shall see you again on my way back. Just make sure the bulldozer doesn't push you under before then," Nipikti shouted back to the second rock as he slowly started walking on.

When he came to the third rock, he sat down and said, "You know, Ojagakutaaq, you are probably the most comfortable rock I have ever sat on in my life. I must say I will certainly miss you the day they remove you from this spot to make room for the new road. You have been a good rock to me and I must thank you in case they start building the road while I am at the Co-op."

He then got up to walk the last leg of the trip to the local Co-op and said to himself that it was time to think about how much he would persuade the Co-op manager to pay him for his carvings. Especially for the good one he finished earlier that day.

"I should be able to sell the good carving for $150 easily," he said. "I'm sure there isn't any other carving this week that was done any better than this one."

When he got to the Co-op, Nipikti took the six carvings out of the bag and laid them on the desk for the manager to look at.

The manager picked up the carvings one by one and looked them over carefully. When he came to the carving Nipikti had done that day, he immediately offered Nipikti $120 for it.

Nipikti stood leaning on his walking stick and counted on $150 as planned. Nipikti knew by experience that the carving was worth that much or even more. "$150," he said.

The manager looked up at Nipikti's face, then picked up the carving in question and mused over the fine detail of the work Nipikti had done. "OK," he finally said. "I'll give you $130 for it."

Nipikti looked at the manager's face and thought about the last offer for $130. "If you think you are going to play games with me, you might as well be prepared to do it for the rest of the day. I am not going to play that long," he said in Inuktitut.

The manager clearly understood that Nipikti was not about to change his original asking price of $150. He knew that the price was right for the carving. But he decided to try once more to buy the carving for less than that. "140," he said.

Nipikti just stood there and cleared his throat, then said for the last time, "150." And with that, he tapped the top of the desk with his right hand. It was a sign that he meant business.

At that moment, the manager decided to give up trying to persuade the old carver to say yes to what he wanted and agreed to pay the $150 he was asking for.

Nipikti had won the battle this time around. He took the money for the carvings he'd brought in, and went out the door to begin his journey back home with his walking stick in hand and money in his pocket to support the family for the next few weeks. He looked across the land and saw that the three rocks where he sat to rest each week were still there. No one had started to build the road yet. And he just smiled and said to himself that it was good.

"I had better make sure that they do not bulldoze my rock away. The way I see it, I am sure to win my case over that too," he said for the last time, and he slowly moved on toward home where he would start the next carving.

Nipikti the old man carver lives on.

1. Responding to the Story

a. All the way to the Co-op store, Nipikti talks to himself and the rocks. In what way are these conversations helpful to the reader?

b. Over the years, how has Nipikti's life changed? Which way of life does he prefer?

c. Why do you think the manager finally agreed to Nipikti's price?

d. What upcoming change to his community worries Nipikti the most? Do you think Nipikti will be successful in opposing that change? Why or why not?

2. Researching Review a Web Site

In a small group, locate and visit five Web sites relating to Inuit culture in Canada's North. Record the address of each home page, then quickly browse through each of the five sites. Select the one your group likes the best and explore it more thoroughly, taking notes about the information and different features you encounter. Organize your notes to create a review of the site that your group can present to the class. Your review should summarize the information you found and evaluate its quality. You should also comment on how easy it was to navigate the site, how good the graphics are, and whether the links are useful. You might print out some of the Web pages to accompany your presentation.

3. Visual Communication Inuit Carvings

The photo on page 343 shows one example of an Inuit carving. If you can, bring in books with photos of other Inuit sculptures. What materials do the artists use for their carvings? What are some typical subjects? As a class, discuss why Inuit sculpture appeals to so many people.

An Inuit sculpture.

Anywhere

Poem by Janet Wong

If you could live anywhere
in the world,
where would you live?

Know what I heard?

I heard there's a place
in the mountains
somewhere
where fun is free
and people play fair.
If you feel bad,
neighbours care.

The air smells green,
crisp and clean.
Water's fresh
from the spring.
You can pick berries
to picnic on
near waterfalls
and streams.

When school's out
I'm going there.
Want to come?

Come.

There's plenty
to share.

REFLECTING ON THE UNIT

SELF-ASSESSMENT: ORAL COMMUNICATION

As you worked on this unit, what did you learn about
- voicing your ideas in a group?
- exploring issues and solving problems through discussion?
- presenting information to your classmates?
- conducting a debate?
- delivering a speech?

Select and reread one draft piece of writing you worked on during this unit. Write notes on your draft, showing how you could improve it by using stronger verbs. You might wish to produce a good copy of your revised draft, asking a partner to compare it with the original and comment on the changes.

ORAL COMMUNICATION PROBLEM SOLVING

In a group of four or five, discuss the question "What changes are most needed to make the world a better place?" Make sure that everyone has a chance to speak, and that all ideas are considered. One group member should take notes on what everyone says. As a group, select the two or three ideas that you think are most realistic. Another group member will be the spokesperson who presents your ideas to the class.

MEDIA DESIGN POSTERS

Plan a poster campaign to fight discrimination in your school and/or community. Your posters might contain anti-discrimination messages or encourage respect toward others. Remember that a poster blends strong visuals with text that is punchy and easy to understand. Display the posters in your classroom or school.

WRITING CREATE A PROFILE

Do you have a class newsletter or school newspaper? If so, write a profile of someone who has made a positive contribution to your school or community. Ask your peers, teachers, family members, or community volunteers for names of people who deserve recognition for their efforts. Your profile should give background information about one person, and explain his or her contribution. Interview the person, if possible, so you can incorporate quotations into your profile. Include a photo of the person as well.

Adjective An adjective is a word that describes a noun or pronoun: *Her icy green eyes stared at the stars.* Adjectives, as well as describing, can also limit a noun: *I saw two movies on the weekend.*

Adverb An adverb is a word that modifies a verb, an adjective, or another adverb. *The rain fell steadily.*

Alliteration Alliteration involves the repetition of the same first sounds in a group of words or line of poetry: *The sun sank slowly.*

Appositive An appositive is a word or phrase that provides additional information about the noun or pronoun it follows. There is a comma before and after the appositive. *This book, a novel set in Newfoundland, is one of the best I've read.*

Ballad A ballad is a narrative poem that tells an exciting story in a series of vivid pictures. The stanzas are usually four lines each with a regular pattern of rhythm and rhyme.

Bias Bias is an opinion that may interfere with a fair judgment on an event or situation.

Caption A caption is an explanation or title accompanying a picture. Captions are most often used in newspaper and magazine articles.

Clause A clause is a group of words that has a subject (a noun) and a predicate (a verb and sometimes adjectives, adverbs, and phrases).

An **independent** or **main clause** is complete thought and stands alone as a sentence: *I shut the door. The cat ran into the street.*

A **dependent** or **subordinate clause** is not a complete sentence and doesn't stand alone as a sentence: *Although she missed the bus. Whenever Jack got the chance.*

Comedy Sketch A comedy sketch is a short scene or routine performed by stand-up comics.

Conflict Conflict is a problem or struggle in a story that the main character has to solve or face. Conflict is created in four classic way: human against self, human against human, human against nature, human against society. Writers may choose to use more than one conflict in a story, which can create an exciting plot.

Conjunction A conjunction is a word that connects other words, phrases, clauses, or sentences, such as *and, or, nor, because, since, for, yet, so.*

Dash [—] The dash is a mark of punctuation used to set off words that interrupt the main thought of a sentence, or to show a sudden change of thought.

Dialogue Dialogue is a conversation between characters. In narrative, every time a new character speaks a new paragraph is used. Quotation marks are used to indicate that dialogue is beginning and ending.

Ellipsis Points [...] Ellipsis points are a series of dots used to show that something has been left out. Use ellipsis points as follows.

- to show that one or more words have been left out of a quotation.
- to indicate that a sentence or thought has been left unfinished.

Five Ws The five Ws of journalism are the five questions that every newspaper or magazine article should answer: *who, what, where, when, why* (and sometimes *how*). By the end of the article, the reader should know who was involved in the story or event, what happened, where it happened, when it happened, why it happened, and how it happened.

Flashback A flashback is an event or scene that took place at an earlier point in a story. Writers use flashbacks to explain something that is presently occurring in the story. Flashbacks can also explain a character's motivation and help to clear up any unanswered questions in the plot.

Folk Tale A folk tale is a story or legend that originated a long time and has been handed down from generation to generation. A folk tale often contains one-dimensional characters and exaggerated events.

Foreshadowing Foreshadowing is a writing device used to give a hint about what is to come in a story. The hint, however, should not be too obvious to the reader because it will give the plot away and affect the suspense. Foreshadowing is used mainly in mysteries and suspense stories, but can be used in other genres as well.

Imagery Imagery is a technique poets and writers use to describe and appeal to the senses. There are many types of imagery including simile, metaphor, alliteration, and personification.

Informal Language Informal language is the kind of language most people use in a casual conversation with a friend. It is characterized by slang expressions, sentence fragments, and exclamations.

Lead A lead is the opening paragraph of a newspaper or magazine article. The lead should contain as many of the answers as possible to the five Ws of journalism: w*ho, what, when, where,* and *why.*

Legend A legend is a story from the past that has been widely accepted as true. For example, the story of King Arthur and his Knights of the Round Table is a legend. Such stories are not necessarily based on historical fact. Sometimes legends explain natural facts such as how mountains were formed.

Memoir A memoir is the recording of a person's own experiences, and involves the retelling of memorable experiences from that person's life. Each experience is told like a story, and is written from the first person point of view (*I, me, we, us*).

Metaphor A metaphor is a writing device in which a word or phrase that ordinarily means one thing is used to describe something else, suggesting that some common quality is shared by the two: *a heart of stone, copper sky.* As well as painting vivid pictures for the reader, metaphors help to make abstract ideas more concrete, add emotion, and show the writer's feelings.

Monologue A monologue is a long speech or a part of a play in which one person speaks alone. "The Winner" is an example of a story written as a monologue.

Mood The mood or atmosphere is the feeling that pervades a piece of writing or work of art. *The mood of* Frankenstein *is sombre and dark.* Mood is created through description and through the plot and the setting.

Myth A myth is a traditional story about superhuman beings, such as gods, goddesses, heroes, and monsters, usually explaining the origin of natural events and forces, and cultural practices. Some myths teach values, such as humility.

Narration Narration is the telling of an event or series of events. Narration is used in all types of writing including narrative, plays, and poetry.

Narrator The narrator is the person or character telling a story. See point of view.

Noun A noun is a word that names a person, place, thing, or quality. *An avalanche buried the skier.* A **proper noun** identifies one particular person, place, organization, or period of time, and begins with a capital letter. *Sandy was skiing in the Rockies.*

Paragraph A paragraph is a group of sentences that develop one aspect of a topic, or one phase of a narrative. The sentences in a paragraph should be clearly related to each other. Sometimes, especially in essays, the aspect or point being developed is expressed in a topic sentence, and the other sentences in the paragraph expand on this statement.

Parentheses ( ) Parentheses are used to set off comments or asides in a sentence. They are also used within scripts to frame stage directions.

Parody Parody is a humorous imitation of serious writing. It follows the form of the original, but changes its sense. "Every Day Is Earth Day" is a parody of *A Christmas Carol* by Charles Dickens.

Personal Essay A personal essay is a non-fiction format that offers a personal point of view on a subject.

Personification Personification is a literary device that gives human traits to non-humans: *The stream gurgled.* Personification is used most often in poetry and narrative writing but can be used as a technique in print ads.

Phrase A phrase is a group of words, used together in a sentence, that does not have a subject and a verb: Marcella spoke *for the first time.*

Plot The plot is the events in a story that make up the action. The plot in a story usually has four elements: the introduction, rising action, climax, and resolution.

- The **introduction** sets up the story by describing the main characters, the setting, and the problem to be solved.
- The **rising action** is the main part of the story where the full problem develops. A number of events is involved that will lead to the climax.
- The **climax** is the highest point of the story where the most exciting events occur.

- The **resolution** is the end of the story when all the problems are solved.

Point of View Point of view refers to the position from which the events of a story are presented to us. There are two main points of view: first person and third person narrative.

- **First person** means the story is told through one character's eyes and the events are coloured through that character's experience.
- The **third person** point of view means the story is told by an onlooker or narrator.

Profile A profile is a concise description of a peson's abilities, character, or career.

Pronoun A pronoun takes the place of one or more nouns or a group of words in a sentence. Some common pronouns include *I, it, me, he, she, we,* and *them.*

Reflections Reflections are personal observations or thoughts on a subject or situation. In "Laughter and Tears," for example, students reflect on the experience of being in a new country.

Rhyme Rhyme is the repetition of sound in different words, especially at the ends of words. For example, *see* rhymes with *bee.* Rhyme is one of the main techniques used in poetry.

Rhyme Scheme A rhyme scheme is the pattern of end rhymes used in a poem. The rhyme scheme is usually indicated by letters, for example, *abba abba cde cde* and *abab cdcd efef gg* are both rhyme schemes for a type of poetry called a sonnet.

Rhythm Rhythm is the arrangement of beats in a line of poetry. The beat is created by the accented and unaccented syllables in the words used in the line.

Run-on Sentence A run-on sentence is formed when two sentences run into one another. To fix a run-on sentence, add the proper punctuation, or change the wording to make it a single sentence.
Run-on: *The sky is clear it is spring at last.*

Better: *The sky is clear; it is spring at last.*
OR
The sky is clear, and it is spring at last.
OR
The sky is clear because it is spring at last.
You call two sentences separated by a comma a comma splice. Fix the comma splice the same way you would fix a run-on sentence.

Science Fiction A science fiction story takes readers to other worlds or to other times. Science fiction writers sometimes base their stories on scientific facts or scientific possibilities that haven't been proven yet. Plots often deal with the impact of science and technology on humans and the world. Popular science fiction themes include space travel, time travel, advanced technology, and life in the future.

Script A script is a story written to be performed as a play or developed into a movie or TV show. The script tells a story with setting, plot, and characters. The story is told through dialogue between characters and through narration as well. Characters are usually listed on the left side of a script and their "lines" are included beside the character name. Scripts also contain stage directions that give instructions for setting up the stage and for the actors.

Semicolon [;] Use a semicolon to separate two related sentences: *I love watching television after school; it relaxes me.*

Sentence A sentence is a group of words that expresses a complete thought. Every sentence needs a subject and an action.

A **simple sentence** has one subject and one verb: *Yukio's house has five bedrooms.*

A **compound sentence** has two or more main clauses (that is smaller sentences that can stand alone). The sentences are usually joined together by a semicolon, or by a comma or semicolon followed by *and, or, nor, for, but, so,* or *yet*: *Yukio's house has five bedrooms, and the yard is huge.*

A **complex sentence** has a main clause that can stand alone as a sentence, and one or more subordinate clauses that cannot stand on their own as sentences. In the following example of a complex sentence, the main clause is underlined, and the subordinate clause is in italics:
<u>Yukio's house</u>, *which he built himself,* <u>has five bedrooms.</u>

Sentence Fragment A sentence fragment is a group of words that is set off like a sentence, but lacks either a verb or a subject. Sentence fragments are acceptable in informal writing, dialogue, and spoken English, but are not appropriate in formal writing:
Fragment: *We went to the game. Josh and I.* (lacks a verb)
Revised: *Josh and I went to the game.*

Sentence Types There are four basic types of sentences.
- A statement makes an assertion and ends with a period: *He ordered a hockey sweater.*
- A question asks for information and ends with a question mark: *When are we leaving?*
- A command gives an order or makes a request and ends with a period: *Please let me come in.*
- An exclamation expresses expresses surprise a strong feeling and ends with an exclamation mark to show emphasis: *Look at that accident!*

Setting The setting is the place and time where a story takes place. Setting plays an important role in many types of stories: science fiction, historical fiction, fantasy, and adventure stories.

Simile A simile is a comparison of two different things using the words *like* or *as*: *My ears buzzed like a mosquito.* Similes are used in both prose and poetry.

Stanza A stanza is a group of lines of poetry arranged according to a fixed plan. Stanzas usually contain the same number of lines, metre, and rhyme scheme.

Stereotype A stereotype is an oversimplified picture, usually of a group of people, giving them all a set of characteristics, without consideration for individual differences. Avoid stereotypes in your writing. Try to create fresh, real characters.

Suspense Suspense is a feeling of tension, anxiety, or excitement resulting from uncertainty. An author creates suspense to keep the reader interested

Symbol/Symbolism A symbol is a person, place, thing or event that is used to represent something else. For example, a rainbow is often used as a symbol of hope.

Tone Tone is the atmosphere or mood of a piece. It can also refer to the author's

attitude or feeling about the reader (formal, casual, intimate) and his subject (light, ironic, solemn, sarcastic, sentimental).

Transcript A transcript is a written copy of an oral format such as radio or TV. "Springhill Miner," for example, is a transcript of a Heritage Minute broadcast.

Verb A verb is a word that expresses an action or a state of being. Verbs that express a state of being are sometimes called linking verbs, because they link the subject to another word that describes the subject.
Action verb: *Sunil* <u>*ran*</u> *to school*.
Linking verb: *Mariko* <u>*seemed*</u> *tired*.
The verb *be* is the most common linking verb, but verbs like *seem*, *appear*, *feel*, *smell*, and *look* can act as linking verbs.

INDEX OF ACTIVITIES

Answers to Canadian Inventors Quiz, page 81 1. c   2. a   3. a   4. c   5. b   6. c   7. b   8. a

ACKNOWLEDGMENTS

Every reasonable effort has been made to trace ownership of copyrighted material. Information that would enable the publisher to correct any reference or credit in future editions would be appreciated.

10-11 "Cooks Brook" by Al Pittman from *Once When I Was Drowning* © by Al Pittman. Reprinted with permission from Breakwater Books./ **12-15** "An Olympic Moment" (originally entitled "Gaetan Boucher") from *Frozen In Time: The Greatest Moments at the Winter Olympics* by Bud Greenspan. Reprinted by permission of Cappy Productions Inc./ **17** "As Soon As I Find Out Who I Am You'll Be the First To Know" by Angela Shelf Medearis from *Skin Deep and Other Teenage Reflections*. Reprinted with the permission of Atheneum Books for Young Readers, an imprint of Simon & Schuster Children's Publishing Division. Text © 1995 Angela Shelf Medearis./ **19-28** "Some Days You're the Puppy" by Trudy Morgan-Cole. Reprinted with permission of the author./ **31-33** "Where I'm Coming From" (originally entitled "Sometimes Too Much Advice") from *33 Things Every Girl Should Know* by Barbara Brandon, Crown Publishers Inc., a division of Random House./ **35-39** "South African Adventure" is a collection of excerpts from "Discovering Wild Africa" from *South African Passages*. Reprinted with permission from *South African Passages: Diaries of the Wilderness Leadership School*, Introduction by Dr. Ian Player, edited by Elizabeth Darby Junkin, © 1987, Fulcrum Publishing, Inc., Golden, Colorado USA. All rights reserved./ **41-51** "A Mountain Legend" by Jordan Wheeler from *Voice Under One Sky*. Reprinted by permission of the author./ **56-59** "Courage in Orbit" from *Roberta Bondar: True Courage* by Barbara Bondar, Nelson Canada Publishing Co./ **64** "To You" from *Collected Poems* by Langston Hughes. © 1994 by the Estate of Langston Hughes. Reprinted by permission of Alfred A. Knopf Inc./ **65-68** "A Spider For The Bones" text by Sheree Haughian. Illustration by Patricia Lau, Olivia Maginley, Robyn Massel, and Katie Mogan./ **70-75** "Photographer At Play" (originally entitled "Jacques-Henri Lartigue: Photographer at Play") by John Cech from *Muse Magazine* (Vol. 2, No. 1). Reprinted by permission of the author./ **78-83** "Eureka! We've Done It!" by Winston Collins from *Bright Ideas* (Fall 1992). Reprinted by permission of *The Royal Bank Reporter*./ **90** "Bananas" by Donna Wasiczko from *Peeling the Onion: An Anthology of Poems Selected by Ruth Gordon*./ **91** "Empty Head" by Malick Fall, translated from the French by John Reed and Clive Wake, from *Peeling the Onion: An Anthology of Poems Selected by Ruth Gordon*./ **92-97** "Cyberspace Sam" by W.D. Valgardson from *Garbage Creek and Other Stories*. Text © 1997 by W.D. Valgardson. First published in Canada by Groundwood Books/ Douglas & McIntyre./ **100-103** "Inventively Female" adapted from "Patently Female,"

an article from *Newscience* (Spring 1989, Vol. 14, No. 2). Reprinted with permission of the Ontario Science Centre./ **105-107** "A Collaboration With Nature" by Agnieszka Biskup. Reprinted by permission of *Muse* magazine, July/August 1998, Vol. 2, No. 4, © 1998 by Carus Publishing Company./ **109-113** "Daedalus and Icarus" from *Heroes and Monsters: Legends of Ancient Greece retold by James Reeves*, published by Blackie & Sons Ltd,. © 1969, 1987 by the Estate of James Reeves./ **118-122** "The Hockey Sweater" by Roch Carrier, translated by Sheila Fischman. © 1979 by Roch Carrier. Reprinted by permission of House of Anansi Press, 34 Lesmill Road, Toronto, Ontario, Canada, M3B 2T6./ **124-129** "Geraldine Moore the Poet" by Toni Cade Bambara./ **131-133** "Zoo" by Edward D. Hoch from *Short Stories: The Plot Thickens*. Reprinted by permission of the author./ **135-148** "For Pete's Snake" by Ellen Conford from *Short Circuits*, published by Delacorte Press. © 1992 by Ellen Conford. Reprinted by permission of McIntosh and Otis, Inc./ **152-159** "All Is Calm" by Ann Walsh from *The Blue Jean Collection* (Thistledown Press, 1992). This version is an abridgment of the original./ **162-170** "The Hope Bakery" from *Some of the Kinder Planets*. Text © 1993 by Tim Wynne-Jones. First published in Canada by Groundwood Books/Douglas & McIntyre. Reprinted by permission of the publisher./ **176-179** "Avalanche!" by Bill Corbett from *Explore Magazine* (November/December 1998). Reprinted by permission of the author./ **180-182** "Oh So Silent" by Wayne Grams and Sandy Wishart from *Explore Magazine* (November/December, 1998). Reprinted by permission of the authors./ **184-186** "Earthquakes Rock the World!" by Barbara Saffer from *YES Mag* (Autumn 1998). Reprinted by permission of the author./ **187-189** "Measuring Earthquakes" and "Where Canucks Feel Quakes" by Kathiann M. Kowalski from *YES Mag* (Autumn 1998). Reprinted by permission of the author./ **191-197** "Canned Catastrophes: Special Effects in Disaster Movies" (originally entitled "Having an Effect") by Jake Hamilton from *Special Effects in Film and Television* © 1998./ **204-205** "Ballad of Springhill" by Peggy Seeger and Ewan MacColl from *The Nova Scotia Song Collection*./ **206-207** "Springhill Miner" by Patrick Watson. Reprinted with permission of The CRB Foundation Heritage Project./ **209-210** "Tuning in to the News" is a newscast from CTV National News./ **212-215** "Photojournalist: In The Middle of Disaster" text by Keith Elliot Greenberg, photos by John Isaac./ **220** "Gwaii Haanas" by Jenny Nelson from *West Coast Rhymes*. Reprinted with permission of the author./ **222-232** "Every Day Is Earth Day" by Steven Pricone./ **238-240** "Just For a Laugh" (originally entitled "They Just Don't Get It") by Jane Wagner from *My Life, So Far: Edith Ann*, © 1994 Jane Wagner; "Fire and Bad Clothes" by Denny Dillon./ **242-246** "Frog" from *Tales from the Brothers Grimm and the*

Sisters Weird by Vivian Vande Velde. Text © 1995 by Vivian Vande Velde. Reprinted with permission of Harcourt Inc./ **248** "The Fly" from *Verses from 1929 On* by Ogden Nash. © 1942 by Ogden Nash; first appeared in *The Saturday Evening Post*. By permission of Little, Brown and Company (Inc.)./ **248** "The Mules" from *Verses from 1929 On* by Ogden Nash. © 1950 by Ogden Nash; © renewed 1977 by Frances Nash, Isabel Nash Eberstadt, and Linnedll Nash Smith; first appeared in *The New Yorker*. By permission of Little, Brown and Company (Inc.)./ **248** "The Jellyfish" from *Verses From 1929 On* by Ogden Nash. © 1942 by Ogden Nash. By permission Little, Brown and Company (Inc.)./ **248** "The Baby" from *Verses From 1929 On* by Ogden Nash. © 1931 by Ogden Nash. By permission of Little, Brown and Company (Inc.)./ **249-250** "And By That You Mean...?" and "Classified Goofs" (originally entitled "Unclassifiable Classifieds") from *Cyber Jokes: The Funniest Stuff on the Internet* by Doug Mayer. Published with permission © 1996 becker& mayer!, Ltd. All rights reserved./ **252-253** "For Better or for Worse" © by Lynn Johnston Productions Inc/Dist. by United Feature Syndicate, Inc./ **255-261** "Writing on the Funny Side of The Brain" from *Drawing on the Funny Side of the Brain* © 1998 by Christopher Hart, published by Watson-Guptill Publications (New York)./ **263-266** "The Friends Of Kwan Ming" by Paul Yee from *Tales From Gold Mountain*. © 1989 by Paul Yee. / **268-269** "Red's Mail Call" from *The Red Green Show*, S&S Productions, Inc./ **272-273** "Great Cows Of History" from *The Cow Book* by Marc Gallant. © 1983 by Marc Gallant and Periwinkle Publishing Jersey Ltd. Reprinted by permission of Alfred A. Knopf, a Division of Random House, Inc./ **275-277** "Thank You, Uncle Ben" (originally entitled "Thank You, Uncle Ben For The Nicest Whatever-It-Is That Ruined a House") by Maggie Grant./ **279-289** "Introducing Norbert" by Richard Scrimger from *Laughs*./ **294** "Plenty" by Jean Little from *Round Slice of Moon and Other Poems For Canadian Kids*. © 1960 by Jean Little. Reprinted with permission of the author./ **297-300** "Reaching Out to a Stranger" from *Kids with Courage* by Barbara A. Lewis © 1992. Used with permission from Free Spirit Publishing, Minneapolis, MN; 1-800-735-7323; *www. freespirit. com*; All Rights Reserved./ **302-305** "The Winner" by Peg Kehret from *Winning Monologs for Young Actors*. © 1986 Meriwether Publishing Ltd., Colorado Springs, CO 80907. Used by permission./ **307** "Calvin And Hobbes" from *The Essential Calvin and Hobbes: a Calvin and Hobbes Treasury* by Bill Watterson. © 1988 by Universal Press Syndicate./ **309-317** "Free the Children" (originally entitled "Thornhill") by Craig Keilburger with Kevin Major. Used by permission, McClelland and Stewart, Inc. *The Canadian Publishers*./ **322-327** "Laughter and Tears: Adjusting to Canada" are selections from *New Canadian Voices*, Jessie Porter, editor. © 1991 by Jessie Porter: **322-323** "Pronunciation Problem" by Sung Ja Hong, **323** "Afraid of Everything" by Amy Tam, **324-325** "A Letter Home" (originally entitled "I Lost Myself") by Su Wang, **326** "Should I Change My Name?" by Matheyalagan Nagaranthy, **326** "Valentine's Day" by Tong Ang, and **327** "Do You Want to Dance?" by Joseph Csermak./ **329-334** "Remember, Chrysanthemum" by Kathryn Hatashita-Lee. First published in *Winds Through Time: An Anthology of Canadian Historical Young Adult Fiction*, by Beach Holme Publishing Ltd., 1998./ **336** "Grand mother" by Douglas Nepinak, originally published in *Out of Peace* by Coteau Books. Reprinted with the permission of the author./ **339-342** "Nipikti the Old Man Carver" by Alootook Ipellie from *Inukshuk*, Vol. III, No. 50./ **344** "Anywhere" by Janet S. Wong from *Good Luck Gold and Other Poems*. © 1994 by Janet S. Wong. Margaret K. McElderry Books. Reprinted with permission of the The McGraw-Hill Companies.

Photo Credits

12-14 CP Photo; **17** First Light; **35** Wilderness Leadership School; **36-38** From *Safari* by Robert Bateman, © 1998 by Boshkung. Reprinted by permission of Penguin Books Canada Limited; **39** Gary Fiegehen Photography; **56-59** NASA; **62-63** Copyright The Netherlands by Meulenhoff International. Reprinted by permission; **65** Nick Didlick/*Vancouver Sun*; **70-72, 73** (**bottom**), **74-75** Photographie J.H. Lartigue, © Ministère de la Culture, France; **73** (**top**) Sheree Haughian; **82** (**bottom right**) The Granger Collection; **82** (**bottom left**) McGill Archives; **83** (**top**) Charles Weiss; **83** (**bottom**) The Royal Bank Reporter **89** Carol Weinberg/BMG Records; **100** CORBIS/ Bettmann; **101** The Granger Collection; **102-103** Women Inventors Project; **102, 297, 323, 327** Ian Crysler; **106-107** Copyright © Andy Goldsworthy and Cameron Books, 1990. Reprinted by permission of Harry N. Abrams, Inc., New York **119** Art Resource; **119-121** Taken from *The Hockey Sweater* © 1984 Sheldon Cohen, illustrations published by Tundra Books; **125, 129** "Virtual Reality" by Howard Lieberman, first published in *The Artist's Magazine*, Cincinatti Ohio; **177** Pat Morrow/First Light; **178** Bruce Jamieson; **184** Murad Sezer/AP/CP Photo; **187** Ontario Science Centre; **192** Ron Batzodorff/The Kobal Collection; **193** (**top**) from *Hard Rain*, 1998, Polygram; **193** (**bottom**) from *Volcano*, 1997, 20th Century Fox; **194-195** from *The Mosquito Coast*, 1996, Paramount; **195** (**top**) from *Ghostbusters*, 1984, Columbia/Delphi; **196** from *Speed 2—Cruise Control*, 1997, 20th Century Fox; **197** from *Goldeneye*, 1995, UIP/UA/EON/DANJAQ (courtesy of Moviestore); **200-202** R. Maisonneuve /Publiphoto; **212-214** John Isaac; **217** CP Archive; **219** CP Photo; **221** *Plumed Firs* by Emily Carr, reproduced by permission of the Art Gallery of Victoria; **268** S&S Productions; **295** Ivy Images; **299** Jack Orton/ *Milwaukee Journal Sentinel*; **309** Tom Hanson/CP Photo; **310-315** Free the Children; **337** Frank Howell; **343** The Bettmann Archive; **344** Bonderud/First Light.

Illustrations

Front Cover, **292-293** Robert James Potvin; **8-11** Gordon Sauvé; **19, 21, 25** John Mardon; **41, 43, 45, 48** Wesley Bates; **78-79** Clarence Porter; **93-97** Tadeusz Majewski; **116-117, 275-277** Bernadette Lau; **131-132** Peter Yundt; **135, 138, 143, 147** Scott Galley; **153, 155, 158** John Fraser; **163, 65, 168, 170** Sarah Jane English; **174-175** Chantal Rousseau; **204, 223-232** Peter Cook; **236-237** Keri Smith; **244** Audrey Smith; **248-249** Francis Blake; **279, 283, 287, 289** Boyan Stergulc; **302, 304** Russ Wilms; **329, 330** Masumi Suzuki; **338** Roy Schneider.